6/90

Jack the Ripper

Jack the Ripper

The Uncensored Facts

A documented history of the Whitechapel murders of 1888

by

Paul Begg

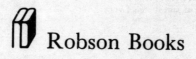 Robson Books

First published in Great Britain in 1988 by Robson Books Ltd,
Bolsover House, 5–6 Clipstone Street, London W1P 7EB.

Reprinted 1989, 1990

British Library Cataloguing in Publication Data

Begg, Paul
  Jack the Ripper : the facts.
  1. London. Murderers : Jack the Ripper
  I. Title
  364.1'523'0924

ISBN 0 86051 528 1 (cased)
      0 86051 583 4 (pbk)

Printed and bound in Great Britain by
Biddles Ltd, Guildford and King's Lynn

This is a book about murder
but it is given with the greatest love to
SIOBÁN RHIANNON BEGG

'I look upon this series of murders as unique
in the history of our country...'

Sir Charles Warren, Commissioner,
Metropolitan Police. Confidential
report to the Home Office dated
17th October, 1888 (A49301 B, sub. 12)

Contents

Acknowledgements

Although my name appears on the cover of this book, no history can ever be the work of a single person. A great many people gave of their time and expertise, or otherwise gave assistance, and I am grateful to them all.

I owe a great debt to my wife, Judy, for her support and assistance in so many ways. Also to my daughter, Sióban, simply for being everything she is.

I am grateful to Keith Skinner for generously undertaking research work for me in London when commitments elsewhere prevented me from doing the work myself. His determination, diligence and ability to ferret out the most obscure information was nothing less than remarkable. I must also thank Keith Skinner and Martin Howells for making available to me information which they did not use in their own book, *The Ripper Legacy*.

My thanks too to Martin Fido, who generously read through the MS and made some very valuable comments. I cannot agree with his theory, but I have greatly enjoyed our long and entertaining conversations on the subject. Both Martin and Keith have displayed true professionalism towards a fellow writer.

I am grateful to the following for their kindness and help: Richard Abberline, Joyce Abberline, David Abberline; Bath City Archivist; Bibliotheque Nationale; Bodleian Library, Department of Western Manuscripts; Stéphane Bourgoin; David Briggs; Library of the British Coal Corporation (Lesley Brown); British Music Hall Society (Dick Playle); British Library, Music Library; British Medical Association; Catholic Central Library (Brother Alan LeMay); *Church Times*; City of London Police Museum (Ray Hayter); Mr A W Cooper; Her Majesty's Coroner for Greater London; Corporation of London Records Office; Department of Health and Social Security; Dorset County Record Office; Gerald Duckworth (Gertrud Watson and William Fishman); London Borough of Ealing, Local History Library; Ealing Hospital; East Sussex

County Records Office and Brighton Library; Mr Edgington, Bournemouth Public Library (for considerable help); Mr Sven Evander; Mrs J. Gammon, Carmarthen Public Library; Greater London Record Office; Local History Library, Greenwich; County Records Office and Newport Central Library, Gwent; Jenny Golden, Hackney Archives Dept; Hammersmith and Fulham Libraries; Home Office; Honourable Society of the Inner Temple; Chiswick Public Library, Hounslow; House of Lords Record Office; J M Hamill, Library of the United Grand Lodge of Freemasons; Lewes Town Council and Mayor of Lewes; London Hospital Medical College; Leeds University Library (much appreciation to Helen Rainford for her help); O A Diakanova, The Lenin State University Library of the U.S.S.R., Department of International Library Relations; Local History Centre, Lewisham; Llanelli Public Library; Mid-West Archives (Mary O'Grady-Pyne & Chris O'Mahony); Marylebone Library; Metropolitan Police (many, many people, but especially Paul Williams, Metropolitan Police Museum and William Waddell); National Library of Wales; National Library of Ireland; National Army Museum; National Railway Museum; Prefecture de Police; Rear Admiral Ian Pirnie; Public Records Office (Anne Crawford and Martin Burtinshal for considerable assistance); Mr Neil Rhind; Royal Commission on Historical Manuscripts; Royal College of Psychiatrists; Royal College of Surgeons; Schweizerische Landesbibliothek; Services des Renseigncents et des Recherches Historiques; Staatskanzlei des Kantons Luzern; Sandra Stewart (Customs House, Dublin); Mr J D Swanson (especial thanks and appreciation); Taunton Public Library; Mrs E F Thomson; Tower Hamlets Library, Bancroft Road (Stephen Beckett and others); Superintendent Les Waters; Lt-Commander Malcolm Warr; Wellcome Institute for the History of Medicine; West Sussex County Records Office; Wolverhampton Public Library; Peter J Wood, Convalescent Police Seaside Home.

Introduction

Not another book about Jack the Ripper! Surely everything
there is to say has been said many times already?

Everything has not been said!

At the end of 1987 new information came to light which
seems to provide the answer to the mystery of Jack the Ripper's
identity. Indeed, evidence that the police knew his identity has
been in the public domain – and been pretty consistently
ignored or misunderstood – since at least 1908!

But even without this valuable new information one could
still confidently assert that much remains to be said about the
Whitechapel murders. Any comparison of the books about
Jack the Ripper will reveal contradictions and a wealth of
deceptive, unsupported, and in some cases utterly false detail.
The names of witnesses have been incorrectly given, some
important witness testimony has been omitted or given
insufficient attention, relevant documents have been
misunderstood or misinterpreted, sources have not been cross-
checked and errors have not been corrected.

In saying this it is not my intention to appear critical of other
writers on the subject. The documentation is so vast and
disparate that errors are easily and unintentionally made by
even the most diligent researcher. Also, the majority of books
on the subject have been largely devoted to the presentation or
discussion of the various theories. As the number of theories
has increased, so the space given to discussion of the crimes
and the police investigation has correspondingly diminished.
Much energy has been spent in learning more about the
various suspects, producing much valuable information, but
the crimes have been treated as if the facts were well-
established and well-known.

As I have said, the facts are not well-established. Moreover,
those books which discussed the crimes at length are now out of
date and out of print. Anyone unfamiliar with the crimes would
be hard-pressed to find a book which describes them.

This book is a simple, straightforward account of what

happened. Of who saw and said what, where and when.

But my object in writing it has not simply been to establish the facts for the sake of correcting the errors of others. As far back as 1959, when some private papers concerning the Whitechapel murders came to public attention, it became clear that at the very least the police may have had a shortlist of probable suspects and that the mystery of the Ripper's identity was not as insoluble as it seemed. Indeed, if Sir Robert Anderson, head of CID at the time of the murders, is to be believed, the identity of Jack the Ripper was an established fact.

My own view has been that even if it should prove impossible to establish the identity of the man referred to by Anderson – which is probably not the case – analysis of the abundant source material might at least indicate the direction in which the police were pursuing their inquiries and in which research should be concentrated. The smallest detail could therefore be of the greatest significance.

But the facts are important in other respects. Apart from the plethora of theories, the Whitechapel murders have been the inspiration for novels, short stories and films, in which the historical facts have either been ignored or manipulated to suit the structure of the fiction or the author's whims. When an historical event is used for fiction the fiction can rapidly enter the popular imagination as fact. When the reality becomes submerged under fiction, it can often prove impossible to raise the truth from the depths.

Fact can be as interesting as fiction. I hope that this book will prove interesting to confirmed 'Ripperologists', to those who are new to the subject and to anyone who may in the future apply their abilities to the investigation of these infamous murders of 100 years ago.

CHAPTER ONE

A Background to the Whitechapel Murders

WE CAN WALK down many of the same streets, shop in the same shops, drink beer in the same pubs and read newspapers with the same titles as Jack the Ripper might, and in some cases certainly did, know and use. But in many respects our world is as different from the world of Jack the Ripper as reality is from the imaginative creations of the science-fantasy writer.

Life could be very hard in the 1880s. Even being born was not easy. Infant mortality was high. Between 1880 and 1889 an average of 142 infants in every 1,000 live births died within their first year, as against a current average of about 18 in every 1,000. The chances of survival were nevertheless better than they had been in the eighteenth century and better than in Russia, Italy, France, Germany and Austria[1].

Having survived infancy, childhood was fraught with dangers. Between 1881 and 1890, 821 boys and 552 girls out of every million died through accidents[2]. And life expectancy was shorter, as is indicated by the fact that just under half the population of England and Wales, 46%, were under 20 years of age[3].

Elementary education was not provided by the State until the Education Act of 1870 and the Act was largely the result of improved educational standards among Britain's main commercial rivals. Locally-elected school boards were established by the Act and these could compel attendance to the age of 13, though fees had to be paid by those who could afford them.

Improved education led to increased literacy among the population – in 1886 only 2.7% of the British electorate was illiterate[4] – and improved literacy led to greater interest in newspapers.

In 1853 the tax on advertisements had been abolished. This was followed in 1885 by the abolition of the newspaper tax and in 1861 by the duty on paper. The removal of these 'taxes on knowledge', coupled with improvements in newspaper technology – which led to quicker reporting and a reduction in price – led to a dramatic increase in the number of newspapers. The number of daily newspapers in the United Kingdom in 1846 was 14. By 1880 the figure had risen to 158. During the 1880s a further 22 daily newspapers appeared. There was an equally impressive increase in the number of newsagents.

The most popular newspapers were the penny dailies – *Daily Telegraph, Daily News, Daily Chronicle,* and *Morning Post.* They were aimed at and almost exclusively read by the male upper and middle classes. It was in 1880 that the branch manager of a fancy goods business realised that nobody was catering for the newly literate. His name was George Newnes and in that year he launched *Tit-Bits,* a weekly specifically designed to cater for those for whom reading was a new and difficult skill. Alfred Harmsworth, a young man working for Newness, who in 1896 founded the *Daily Mail,* made his first publishing venture in 1888 when he launched *Answers to Correspondents.* In contrast to Harmsworth's venture, 1888 also saw the launch of the *Financial Times.*

Harmsworth changed the face of British newspapers. He said of his publications 'that whatever benefits them is justifiable, and that it was not his business to consider the effect of their contents on the public mind'[5]. He appreciated that newspapers brought money and power. 'He never appreciated that they brought responsibility'[6].

The 1880s saw a profound change in newspapers. Hitherto they had carried the news and left the reader to form his own opinions. The 'new' newspapers introduced spice and sensationalism, serving up ready-made opinions. They relied heavily upon death, crime and sensational law cases for their circulation. Chief among the newspapers of this type was the *Pall Mall Gazette,* edited from 1883 to 1889 by W T Stead, who published many sensational stories which, though in some cases aiding social reform, were written wholly to make money. The most notable of these was his 'Maiden Tribute of Modern

14

Babylon' series, an exposé of vice in London.

The boom in newspapers and the battles for circulation coincided with the Jack the Ripper murders and it was the newspaper coverage of the crimes which turned them into a national and ultimately an international sensation. A reporter for the *Bath and Cheltenham Gazette* very perceptively stated this basic truth to his readers:

> Up to the present time of writing no further murders have been committed, and no arrests of any importance have been made. This really summarises the whole of the voluminous 'reports' with which some of the London dailies have been edifying their readers during the past week. That the excitement has been great there is no denying, but it has been largely stimulated and fed by the great and unnecessary prominence given to the subject and by the many foolish rumours which have been published[7].

The journalist William Le Queux wrote of how he and two colleagues, Charles Hands of the *Pall Mall Gazette* and Lincoln Springfield of the *Star,* competed with one another to produce theories about the murderer: 'One evening Springfield of the *Star* would publish a theory as to how the murders had been done . . . Next night Charlie Hands would have a far better theory in the *Pall Mall,* and then I would weigh in with another story in the *Globe.*'[8]

When the murders took place the Metropolitan Police had only been in existence for 59 years and only existed at all because of a hard-fought battle by Sir Robert Peel, together with various champions of penal reform such as Sir Samuel Romilly, Sir James Mackintosh, Foxwell Buxton and William Wilberforce.

The normal reaction of Parliament to disorder was simply to increase the number of offences for which the death sentence could be imposed, of which there were about 220, among them the theft of 5 shillings or more from a shop, damaging Westminster Bridge, or impersonating out-pensioners from Chelsea Hospital. The laws and penalties were savage. In 1830 starving field labourers in the south of England rioted in

15

support of their demands for a wage of 2/6 a day. Three were hanged and 420 were deported to Australia.

There was considerable opposition to an organised police force. A report by a special commission created to examine the problem in 1822 contained the memorable statement:

> It is difficult to reconcile an effective system of police with that perfect freedom of action and exemption from interference which are the great privileges and blessings of society in this country; and Your Committee think that forfeiture or curtailment of such advantages are too great to sacrifice for improvements in police, or facilities in detection of crime, however desirable in themselves if abstractly considered.

Such objections lingered into and beyond the 1880s. There was considerable fear of a political police, spying and reporting on overheard conversations. When, in 1829, Parliament passed the Metropolitan Police Act, the police were uniformed and not even allowed to dress in civilian clothes when off duty.

The headquarters of the Metropolitan Police – who have never had jurisdiction within the boundaries of the City of London, the commercial heart of the capital – were established at 4 Whitehall Place. There was a police station at the back of this building in what was known as Scotland Yard. The name Scotland Yard was soon applied to the Whitehall Place HQ and it stuck, even when the HQ was changed to a new building on the banks of the Thames in 1890.

Originally the senior level of the Metropolitan Police consisted of two commissioners (then called justices) and a Receiver, who handled the finances of the force, but from 1855 there has only been one Commissioner, directly responsible to the Home Secretary.

In 1842 the Home Secretary, Sir James Graham, sanctioned the creation of a small detective force – two inspectors and six sergeants – in an office at Scotland Yard. These were the men on whom Charles Dickens based the characters of Inspector Bucket in *Bleak House* and Wilkie Collins drew the character of Sergeant Cuff in *The Moonstone*. They were not popular, even within the force as a whole. Almost thirty years later, in 1868, the total number of detectives numbered 15 men in a force of almost 8,000.

The world-famous Criminal Investigation Department, the CID, was conceived at 3.45 pm on Friday 13 December 1867. A barrel of gunpowder was exploded against the wall of the exercise yard of the Clerkenwell House of Detention, killing and injuring a number of men, women and children, and wrecking a street of houses. The 'bomb' had been intended to do no more than blow a hole in the wall through which a prisoner could escape, but it was thought to be the start of a terrorist campaign by the Fenians (The Irish Republican Brotherhood) and the public outcry, to which Queen Victoria added her own voice, led to an increase in the personnel of the detective force and the Metropolitan Police in general. It also resulted in the creation of what was to be a temporary Secret Service Department which was placed by the Home Secretary in the hands of Colonel the Hon William Fielding of the Guards. Chosen to assist was an Anglo-Irish lawyer named Robert Anderson, who arrived in London from Dublin on 19 December 1867. His task, he later wrote, was 'chiefly aimed at preventing or exploding scares', an ill-chosen turn of phrase for a man whose work involved a supposed bombing campaign[9].

Robert Anderson was the head of the CID at the time of the Ripper murders. The son of Matthew Anderson, a lawyer who was the Crown Solicitor for the County and City of Dublin, Robert married the daughter of the Earl of Drogheda in 1873.

The Secret Service Department was closed down three months later, but the Home Secretary, Gathorne Hardy, encouraged Anderson to remain in London and take charge of Irish business at the Home Office. In April 1868 he was appointed Advisor at the Home Office in matters relating to political crime and he moved from the Irish Office to Whitehall.

The Metropolitan Police received a new Commissioner on 13 February 1869, Colonel Sir Edmund Walcot Henderson. He made a number of changes to the force, including the Detective Department, which he reorganized. He also allowed policemen to dress in mufti when off duty.

Although the CID was conceived in 1867, it was not born

until 1878, the birth being accompanied by considerable pain. In 1877 the reputation of the Detective Department was severely damaged in what became known as the 'Great Scotland Yard Scandal', a corruption scandal in which senior detectives were found guilty of conspiring with a gang of swindlers to carry on fraudulent betting agencies. Two chief inspectors and one inspector were sent to prison for two years and another chief inspector, though aquitted, retired.

The scandal led to the appointment of a departmental committee to inquire into the detective service. The Chairman, Sir Henry Selwyn Ibbetson, the Parliamentary Under-Secretary of State, was particularly impressed by a report submitted by a young barrister named Howard Vincent. The Committee recommended that the Metropolitan Police should have a separate detective force headed by 'An Assistant Commissioner . . . ranking next to the Commissioner, and having charge of the whole force in his absence'. The new department, which came into being in March 1878, was called the Criminal Investigation Department (CID), but its first 'Director', Howard Vincent, had neither a statutory position nor disciplinary powers. The full recommendations of the Committee were not implemented until the Metropolitan Police Act of 1884. During Vincent's tenure of office, the Detective Department's personnel was increased to nearly 800 men.

In January 1881 the Fenians planted a bomb at Salford barracks which killed a 7-year-old boy and injured three other people. Sir William Vernon Harcourt, the Home Secretary, who correctly judged it to be the start of a major bombing campaign, was considerably alarmed and concerned at 'the absolute want of information in which we seem to be with regard to Fenian organisation in London. All other objects should be postponed in our efforts to get some light into these dark places.'[10]

In March 1881 a bomb was found at the Mansion House shortly before the Lord Mayor of London's banquet was due to be held. On 22 April 1882 assassins were waiting for the Irish Secretary, who had fortunately and unexpectedly taken an earlier train to a cabinet meeting in London. In May 1882 another bomb at the Mansion House failed to go off, but this event was overshadowed by the assassination on 6 May of the new Irish Secretary, Lord Frederick Cavendish, and his Under-Secretary, Thomas Burke, in Dublin's Phoenix Park by a band of assassins called 'the Invincibles'. In January 1883 a gasometer in Glasgow was blown up; a bomb at the offices of *The Times* failed to explode in March, but another bomb did go off in government offices in Whitehall. On 30 October an explosion at Praed Street Station, one of two explosions on the London Underground, caused 72 casualties. In February 1884 bombs were found at four London main-line stations. In May three bombs went off in the West End of London, one of them at Scotland Yard, and in December three conspirators were killed when their device exploded on London Bridge. The year 1885 was ushered in by an explosion on the Underground and on 24 January bombs were simultaneously exploded at the Tower of London, Westminster Hall and the House of Commons.

In February 1887 Edward Jenkinson resigned. He had been the head of an intelligence section separate from the Metropolitan Police and distinct from the Irish branch of the CID, which was known as Section D and headed by Superintendent Frederick Adolphus 'Dolly' Williamson. Jenkinson was not replaced. His Section was handed over to Vincent's successor, the first Assistant Commissioner CID, James Monro.

The son of an Edinburgh solicitor named George Monro, James Monro had received his education in Edinburgh and Berlin, then entered the Indian Civil Service in 1857. Twenty years later, in 1877, he was selected by Sir Ashley Eden to be Inspector General of Police in Bengal. He held this post until 1883, when he was appointed Commissioner of the Presidency Division, which he left to take up his appointment with the CID in June 1884.

For assistance in his additional duties regarding undercover work against the Fenians, Monro, according to Robert Anderson, 'stipulated upon having my assistance'[11]. This was in spite of objections from Godfrey Lushington, the Permanent Under-Secretary of State[12]. The new section was staffed by Chief Inspector John Littlechild and three second-class inspectors, all of whom were financed out of Imperial, not Metropolitan Police, funds, and it was called Section D. It was

19

also known by other titles: Special (Secret) Branch and Home Office Crime Department, Special Branch.

Meanwhile, the ordinary uniformed branch had been faced with outbreaks of unrest caused by growing unemployment. 'Unemployed' as a noun first occured in 1882 and the term 'unemployment' was first used by the economist Alfred Marshall in a study of economics published in 1888. The winter of 1886-7 was a particularly severe one for the London working class and public concern resulted in a survey carried out in four areas of London on 19 March 1887.[13] For years the report of this survey lay buried among parliamentary papers, ignored by many historians because William Ogle, Superintendent of Statistics at the General Register Office, dismissed the returns as 'of very small statistical value'. They are in fact of considerable value, as some historians in recent years have begun to appreciate. The survey showed that of the 29,451 men interviewed on that day, 27% claimed to be unemployed and 30% to have been out of work for more than 12 weeks out of the previous 20.[14]

In 1881 an ex-Conservative journalist and stockbroker named Henry M Hyndman founded the Democratic Federation – later named the Social Democratic Federation (SDF). The years 1885-6 saw another slump in trade and a consequent rise in unemployment. The leaders of the SDF organized marches and meetings of the unemployed. On Monday 8 February 1886, one such meeting in Trafalgar Square led to an outbreak of violence when a small mob, said to be from the East End, rioted through the streets, breaking windows in Pall Mall and St James's, and attacking shops in and around Oxford Street. Queen Victoria was consumed with indignation 'at the monstrous riot'[15] and Gladstone thought that it had 'stained the reputation of the country in the eyes of the civilized world'.

On the following Wednesday there was a dense fog. A rumour spread that it was providing cover for a large mob. Scotland Yard ordered that shops in the West End should be closed and this order led to widespread panic which turned to indignation when it was learned that the mob was imaginary and that the police had reacted without the least evidence. The Home Secretary, Hugh C E Childers, blamed the Commissioner of Police, Sir Edmund Henderson, who felt that he had no alternative but to resign. He was replaced by Major-General Sir Charles Warren.

At the time of Henderson's resignation public confidence in the police seemed to be shattered and there were widespread demands for a reorganization of Scotland Yard at a senior level. Childers rejected over 400 candidates for the post of Commissioner and on 13 March 1886 sent a telegram to Suakin – a port on the Red Sea in Sudan – offering the Commissionership to Warren. Warren, who had only joined the staff commanding the troops in Suakin in January of that year, immediately accepted and returned to London, where he took up his new duties on 29 March 1886.

Charles Warren was the fifth of six children born to Major-General Charles Warren and Mary Anne Hughes. He was born on 7 February 1840 at a house called 'Fairview' in Bangor, North Wales, and received his education in Shropshire and then at the Royal Military Academy at Woolwich. On 27 December 1857 he received a Commission in the Royal Engineers. In the year before accepting the Commissionership of the Metropolitan Police, Warren stood as a Liberal representing the Hallam Division of Sheffield in the election of 25 November. He was narrowly beaten by the Conservative candidate, C B Stuart-Wortley, by 609 votes.

Warren's appointment was received with general enthusiasm from the press. *The Times* reported:

> In many essential respects, Sir Charles Warren is precisely the man whom sensible Londoners would have chosen to preside over the Police Force of the Metropolis. Though he is in the prime of life (he is only forty-six), there are few officials in Her Majesty's service who have had more varied experience. He is at once a man of science and a man of action; and for nearly twenty years he has been engaged in the work of the kind most likely to develop the administrative faculties.[16]

The *Pall Mall Gazette* warned that Warren 'is most like General Gordon in conviction, in temper, and in impatience of being meddled with', and it urged Hugh Childers to allow

21

Warren 'a free hand, and to back him up like a man'.[17]

Whether Childers and Warren would have enjoyed a harmonious working relationship was never put to the test. Six months later there was a general election and the Liberal Government was defeated by the Conservatives. In August 1886, Henry Matthews was appointed Home Secretary. He did not get on with Warren and over the next two years relations between the two men deteriorated alarmingly.

Those two years also saw Warren's support in the press turn sour and hostile and he has received an almost uniformly bad press ever since, even from those writers who really ought to have known better. Belton Cobb, for example, was clearly biased against him when he wrote that Warren was 'an autocratic, elderly soldier who wanted to run everything his own way – the military way'.[18] To describe him as 'elderly' at the age of 46 is both erroneous and insulting.

It is difficult to assess Sir Charles Warren properly because he was effectively embroiled in clashes of personality with Monro and Matthews, neither of whom have left many documents of a personal nature from which to judge their character. Both Monro and Matthews were involved in bitter rows with others as well as Warren, and with each other.

It would be tedious to examine each of the allegations against Warren in detail. It is sufficient to say that he was a military man by upbringing, education and inclination. That he should have seen a solution to a problem from a military point of view was therefore only to be expected. If this made him unsuitable for the job, the fault lay with Childers for making the offer, not with Warren for accepting it. In fact Warren *was* suited to the job, as *The Times* article makes clear. He was chosen because he could exercise authority over and organize what many people regarded as a disorganized and undisciplined force and because he could employ tactics and strategy when faced with the kind of unrest and rioting which had contributed to the downfall of Sir Edmund Henderson.

Warren was not a thief-taker but an administrator. There were people who recognized this. A correspondent who signed himself 'A Retired Chief of Police' wrote to the *Morning Post:*

It has been suggested that Sir Charles might with greater

22

advantage have been deputed simply to inquire into the workings of the Force, with a view to its reorganization, and if necessary, given temporary supreme command without the title or permanent rank of Commissioner, and, no doubt, had this been done, perhaps he might have escaped the cavils of his ignorant and self-sufficient commentators. But the final result in that case would have been much the same as at present, and equally satisfactory from the public point of view – namely, that the department would have been, as it now has been, overhauled and remoulded by a strong hand.[19]

Apart from disagreements with Matthews and Monro, Warren also fell out with the Receiver of the Police, Richard Pennefather. According to Warren's biographer, Watkyn Williams, Warren 'was dissatisfied with the way in which police pensions were administered, and considered that in other respects many items of expense were unnecessary and excessive. Matthews, however, completely ignored Warren's views'. There is ample evidence to support Watkyn Williams. Decisions affecting the force were indeed taken without consultation with Warren and even without his knowledge.

Sir Evelyn Ruggles-Brise, who was Matthews's Private Secretary, summed up Matthews, Warren and Pennefather as follows:

> Pennefather was a very able man, but disagreeable to deal with; he rubbed everybody up the wrong way. Warren was the finest man we had in Whitehall, but probably the worst appointment, because he *must* be independent, and the Commissioner of Police is held in very tight bonds by the Home Office. Matthews was an exceedingly able lawyer, but quite incapable of dealing with men: he was a regular Gallio in his attitude towards Warren's complaints. Later on he quarrelled with Bradford [a subsequent Commissioner], and if you couldn't get on with Bradford you could get on with nobody.[20]

According to Sir Robert Anderson, the rank and file did

not take to Warren at first. 'There is no doubt that sedition was smouldering throughout the Force and serious trouble might have resulted . . .'[21] But Warren put an end to it through his defence of his men in times of crisis and that he left the Metropolitan Police to their genuine regret is surely a tribute to the man, for he had not been given their respect as a token of his rank – he had earned it.

Sir Charles Warren eventually resigned. When news of his resignation became known a deputation of officers from the force visited Warren at his home, where their spokesman, Superintendent Draper, stated that 'in his retirement Sir Charles carried with him the respect and admiration of every man in the Force'.[22]

A particular thorn in Warren's side was James Monro (and vice versa), the cause of the friction, apparently, being Monro's Secret Service work, which gave him direct access to the Home Secretary. Relations between the two men hit bedrock when Warren objected to the appointment, agreed by the Home Office[23], of Sir Melville Macnaghten to the post of Assistant Chief Constable, CID.

Monro and Macnaghten had met each other in India when Monro was Inspector General of the Bengal Police. In 1881 Macnaghten had tried to settle some trouble with the natives, but they had turned on him 'and assaulted me so badly that I was left senseless on the plain'.[24] Through this incident Macnaghten and Monro met. 'Four years later,' wrote Macnaghten in his autobiography, 'on my return from India, he asked me if I was prepared to take up work as his Assistant Chief Constable at Scotland Yard. Flattering though the proposal was, I was not in a position to accept it at the moment, as family work and private interests claimed my whole attention, but, when the offer was made again a year later, I gladly answered in the affirmative.'[25]

Monro had in fact told Macnaghten that the job was his if he wanted it.[26] Whether or not Macnaghten in truth refused because of other commitments, he did not get the job because Warren had opposed the appointment, among his reasons being that Macnaghten was 'the one man in India who had been beaten by Hindoos', and the appointment was rescinded.[26]

James Monro finally resigned as head of the CID, but

moved to the Home Office, where he continued with his Secret Service work. In writing of his resignation Monro placed the responsibility wholly on Warren. 'Sir Charles Warren made life so intolerable that I resigned. What the Home Secretary thought of the merits of the matters at issue between us may be gathered from the fact that he retained me as Chief of the Secret Department.'[27]

Monro was replaced by Robert Anderson.

> Mr Monro was not 'an easy man to follow', and my difficulties in succeeding to the post were increased by the foolish ways of the Home Office, as well as by the circumstances of the times. As I have already said, Sir Charles Warren had then secured the loyal support of the Force generally. But the officers of the Criminal Investigation Department were demoralized by the treatment accorded to their late chief; and during the interval since his practical retirement sinister rumours were in circulation as to the appointment of his successor. If the announcement had been made that, on his official retirement on the 31st of August, I should succeed to the office, things might have settled down. For all the principal officers knew and trusted me. But for some occult reason the matter was kept secret, and I was enjoined not to make my appointment known . . . I had some difficulty in preventing Chief Superintendent Williamson from sending in his resignation.
>
> Then again, I was at that time physically unfit to enter on the duties of my new post . . . And so, after one week at Scotland Yard, I crossed the Channel.[28]

Anderson took office the day after the murder of Mary Ann Nichols, the Ripper's first victim, and he did not return to London until after the murders of Elizabeth Stride and Catharine Eddowes, the third and fourth victims.

When Jack the Ripper struck, the CID consisted of 'Indians' with no 'Chiefs'. Fortunately the 'Indians' were capable men. Sir Charles Warren was on holiday in the South of France; Assistant Commissioner Anderson was on holiday in Switzerland; Chief Constable Williamson was too ill with heart trouble to take any active interest; Superintendent John Shore was preoccupied with other matters.

Overall supervision of the murder investigations was put in the hands of Detective Chief Inspector Swanson, who has largely been forgotten and is not even mentioned by several Ripper authors[29]. Swanson, who did not court publicity, would probably have been pleased by this. Instead the fame has fallen on Detective Inspector Abberline, who headed the investigation on the ground. Abberline has remained a shadowy figure, almost as shadowy as his 'Moriarty', Jack the Ripper.

Frederick George Abberline was born on 8 January 1843, the third child of Edward Abberline, a saddler, and his wife Hannah (née Chinn). He was born in Blandford, Dorset. His sister, four years his senior, was named Harriett, and his brother, his senior by three years, was Edward, who served in the army and died on 29 February 1916, leaving a widow, Helen.

Edward Abberline (father) died before Frederick George was eight. The 1851 census for Blandford shows that the family were living at 11 East Street. Hannah's age is given as 49 and her occupation as shopkeeper.

Frederick Abberline joined the Metropolitan Police on 5 January 1863 (Warrant No. 43519) and was posted to N Division (Islington). His promotion through the ranks was steady. He was promoted to Sergeant on 19 August 1865 and on 30 October of that year was transferred to Y Division (Highgate).

In March 1868 he married Martha Mackness, the daughter of a labourer named Tobias Mackness, at St James's Church in the parish of Islington. Both gave their residence at the time of the marriage as St James's, Holloway, and the marriage was witnessed by Tobias Mackness and Elizabeth Patchell. By May that same year, 1868, Martha was dead. She died of consumption on 23 May at Elton, Northamptonshire, aged 25.

On 10 March 1873 Abberline was promoted to Inspector and three days later transferred to H Division (Whitechapel).

On 17 December 1876 he married his second wife, 28 year old Emma Beament, the daughter of a merchant of Wembley named Henry Beament, the marriage being witnessed by Henry and Annie Beament.

On 26 February 1887 he was transferred to A Division (Whitehall), promoted to Second-Class CID Inspector on 25 July, and transferred to Central Office, Scotland Yard, on 19 November. He was promoted to First-Class Inspector on 8 February 1888 and to Chief Inspector on 22 December 1890.

Abberline resigned from the Metropolitan Police on 7 February 1892. He was at that time living at 41 Mayflower Road, Clapham, and he received a pension of £206 13s. 4d. per annum.

After a career spent in London, he decided to spend his retirement in Bournemouth. He moved with Emma to 195 Holdenhurst Road. Writing in 1914, Sir Melville Macnaghten said that Abberline 'knew the East End of London as few men have since known it. He is still hale and hearty and as successful in his gardening operations in Bournemouth as he was in turning the crooks out of the rooms at Monte Carlo when he was given a free hand by the authorities in Monaco some sixteen years ago'.[30] This would have been after his retirement from the Metropolitan Police and suggests that Abberline, like other detectives, took on private inquiry work.

He died aged 86 on 10 December 1929 of bronchitis and mitral valvular disease of the heart at his home in Bournemouth. His death was reported to the Registrar by a lady named Bella Huslling[31]. Emma Abberline died on 15 March 1930 of myocardial degeneration at home in Bournemouth aged 85.

When Frederick George Abberline died he did not even receive a few lines of remembrance in the obituary columns of the local Bournemouth newspaper. Today the internationally-known actor Michael Caine is portraying him in a major television drama.

The East End of London which Abberline knew 'as few men have since known it' was Whitechapel, the 'Skid Row' of the metropolis, the final resting place of people who had fallen so low that they had no further to go – except beneath the ground.

Death through violence was more visible than it is today. Funerals were occasions of great pomp and ceremony for those who could afford it and many people were consumed with an interest in and fear of the judgements of the after-life. Even among the poor death assumed an importance which seems strange today. 'People who couldn't afford a funeral had a "pauper's burial", paid for by the local workhouse, without a hired car or an individually marked grave. This was regarded as the worst possible humiliation, and many families saved all their lives with a burial club . . . to ensure a modest but respectable funeral.'[32] Some of the victims of Jack the Ripper had far grander funerals than they would have been able to afford and are today remembered, their wealthier contemporaries being forgotten. It is little consolation that Jack the Ripper bestowed upon them a sort of immortality, but it is a consolation nevertheless.

It has been said that 'the proportion of the annual average contributed by deaths from violence has not altered greatly – 3.5 per cent in the four-year period 1881-4 and 3.8 per cent in 1971-4'[33], but the causes have changed. Drowning accounted for 15% of the total, for example, and this is not the case today. The number of murders in England and Wales seems to have increased slightly, but the rate of manslaughter, assault and infanticide has shown a marked decline during the present century.

Whitechapel had once been fields and gardens. In Elizabethan times over 100,000 Huguenots arrived in Britain following the revocation of the Edict of Nantes in 1685. Although they entered many trades, they were principally silk-weavers and they concentrated in the area known as Spitalfields, which took its name from the priory and hospital ('spital') of St Mary, founded in 1197. By 1775 the fields and gardens had almost completely vanished beneath streets and alleys.

The building continued as more and more of Europe's refugees poured into the area. It was the first resting place of the Jews who came to Britain in consequence of the anti-Jewish pogroms in Europe which followed the assassination of Tsar Alexander II on 13 March 1881. For the most part they were starving and desperate. As many as 88% of all the immigrants during this period came from Europe, most of them Jews. Prejudice was widespread. Whether or not feelings had reached a point where there was a real threat of anti-Jewish riots is uncertain in the face of conflicting evidence, but it was believed to be a very real and serious possibility.

The East End was an area of the most extreme poverty. 'Those who have never seen the inhabitants of a nineteenth-century slum can have no idea of the state to which dirt, drink and economics can reduce human beings.'[34] So wrote Leonard Woolf in 1960.

The poorest people lived in grim slums, in a furnished room – a bed, table and chair – if they could afford one, or in a common lodging house, often sharing a bed. It was estimated that in 1888 there were 233 common lodging houses, accommodating 8,530 people, in Whitechapel alone.[35] The slums were the ultimate degradation. Sanitation was inadequate, unavailable, or unused through ignorance. Samuel Smith, writing of Liverpool in the 1870s, recalled teaching Sunday School classes: 'The filth and stench of the audience was indescribable. One could hardly walk through to the platform without feeling sick'.[36] In 1885 Arthur Brinckman advised ladies who reclaimed prostitutes to wear plain dresses of a single colour 'so that any representative of an unwelcome department of animal life can be readily observed'.[37]

Prostitution was a problem of great concern. It was estimated that in the Whitechapel area there were 62 houses known to be brothels 'and probably a great number of other houses which are more or less intermittently used for such purposes'. The number of prostitutes in the district was estimated at 1,200[38], but the figure was probably far higher than this because in such areas of extreme poverty many women resorted to casual prostitution from time to time. Indeed, a woman was lucky if she managed to avoid prostitution at all.

In 1885 W T Stead published a series of articles in the *Pall Mall Gazette* exposing prostitution and the trade in young girls. The articles were a sensational stunt to increase the circulation of his newspaper and a spectacular coup was when he bought a virginal child from its mother for a few pounds and took her to France. He thus demonstrated that there were mothers willing to sell their children, but not, as he claimed, that the purchase and exportation of children for European brothels was a regular and common event. Debauching minors in fact carried much stricter penalties in France than it did in Britain.

However, there is no doubt that the cross-channel traffic in English girls for the brothels of France and Belgium did take place. One of the victims of Jack the Ripper, Mary Kelly, claimed that on her arrival in London she had been befriended by a French woman who put her to work in a West End bordello. Kelly said that later she had been taken to France, but had not liked it there and had returned to England. Since it is possible that she may have fallen into the hands of a *placeur* operating in London, it might be profitable to understand a little more about this aspect of the vice trade in London in the 1880s.

In countries such as France, Belgium and Holland, prostitution was controlled by the police and the brothels were licensed. Prostitutes had to make a statutory declaration and have their papers endorsed as working in a specific brothel. On so doing the woman virtually became the property of the brothel-keeper. There was a demand for young, undiseased and 'virginal' girls from England who, unaware of the conditions in which they were to work, would sign the papers and commit themselves to a life of virtual slavery. The traffic was investigated by a Lords committee of 1881-2 and the inquiry revealed it to be a well-established trade.

CHAPTER TWO

The Beginning

THE MURDERS committed by the creature known to posterity by the chilling soubriquet 'Jack the Ripper' were characterized by extensive mutilation of the victim, the womb being the target of his attacks. It is generally accepted that he only killed five women, the characteristic mutilations being absent in one instance because the murderer was probably disturbed. However, it is doubtful the murderer began his career with a full-blown murder and mutilation. He may have begun with acts of lesser violence, acts which bore none of his hallmarks. In any event, a series of violent attacks on and murders of women in Whitechapel prior to the first accepted Jack the Ripper murder, whether or not any of them were committed by Jack himself, primed both the press and the public to react with outrage and horror when the first Ripper murder took place.

The earliest of these attacks, according to Tom Cullen, was that on 'Fairy Fay',

> which was the rather whimsical name which the press gave to the unidentified woman whose mutilated body was discovered near Commercial Road on Boxing Night 1887. 'Fairy Fay' lost her life as a result of a wrong decision: she decided to take a short cut home when the pub in Mitre Square where she had been drinking all evening closed after midnight, and in the dim warrens behind Commercial Road she was struck down and carved up by an unknown assassin.[1]

Cullen says that the nickname of the murdered woman was bestowed upon her by the press, from which we may infer that her murder was reported in one or more newspapers.

31

However, nobody has as yet found any such account of 'Fairy Fay'. Martin Fido, who seems to have made the most determined attempt to learn more about her murder, and has even searched the death registers without success, has concluded that she is mythical, the mode of her death being derived from Emma Smith, murdered on 3 April 1888, and the date from Rose Mylett, killed in Christmas week 1888.

In fact Fido's conclusions cannot be correct. In the first place, though Fido states that 'Fairy Fay' died when 'a stake had been thrust through her abdomen', which was a similar mode of death to that of Emma Smith, Cullen does not say that this was how 'Fairy Fay' was murdered. I can only assume that the stake as a murder weapon is derived from a later source. Be this as it may, there are several newspaper reports which pre-date the murder of Rose Mylett and refer to a woman having been murdered in Christmas week 1887 near Osborne and Wentworth Streets in Whitechapel. These references, such as the one in the *Western Mail* (Cardiff) on 10 November 1888, show that Mylett's killing cannot have contributed to the myth – if myth it be – of 'Fairy Fay'. At present, therefore, the murder of 'Fairy Fay' cannot be wholly dismissed.[2]

A woman named Ada Wilson was attacked and stabbed twice in the throat in her room at 19 Maidman Street, Mile End, in March 1888, by a man who had forced entry and demanded money. She survived the attack and described the man as about 30, with a sunburnt face, fair moustache, about 5ft 6ins tall, and wearing a dark coat, light trousers and wideawake hat.[3]

On Monday 3 April 1888 a 45 year old prostitute named Emma Elizabeth Smith was followed by a gang from Whitechapel High Street to Wentworth Street, where she was stopped, beaten and raped by three or four young men. One of them rammed a blunt instrument into her vagina, tearing the perineum. Somehow she managed to reach her home, from where she was rushed to the London Hospital, there remaining conscious for long enough to give a description of her assailants. She died four days later.[4]

Martha Tabram, who was also known as 'Emma' was long believed to have been a victim of Jack the Ripper. At 10.00 p.m. on Monday 6 August 1888, in company with a tall,

32

masculine-looking woman named Mary Ann Connelly, known as 'Pearly Poll', she entered a pub with two soldiers, a corporal and a private. The two women had known each other for four or five months. For the previous two months Connelly had been living in Crossingham's lodging house in Dorset Street. Martha Tabram, who was said to have been aged about 37, 5ft 3ins. in height, with dark hair and dark complexion, was a married woman. Some time before 1870 she had married Henry Samuel Tabram, who at the time of his wife's death was living at 6 River Terrace, East Greenwich, and was employed as a foreman packer in a furniture warehouse. They had two children, both sons, the eldest being 18 and the youngest 15. In 1875 Henry Tabram finally refused to live with Martha because of her drinking habits and the couple separated. By 1878 she had taken up with William Turner, a carpenter by trade but at the time of the murder a hawker. He had lived with her on and off since that time, but had frequently been forced to leave her because of her drunken fits. He had left her for this reason some three weeks before her death and had last seen her alive on 4 August in Leadenhall Street, near Aldgate Pump. The couple had been living at 4 Star Street, a common lodging house run by Mary Bousfield, the wife of a woodcutter named William Bousfield, but when Turner left her, Tabram absconded owing her rent.[5] Since then she had been living in a common lodging house at 19 George Street, using the name 'Emma'.[6] Martha Tabram was known to the police, having once been sentenced to seven days' hard labour for having consistently annoyed Ann Morris of 23 Lisbon Street, Cambridge Heath Road, the widowed sister of Henry Tabram.

At 11.00 p.m. Ann Morris saw Tabram outside the White Swan public house in Whitechapel Road. At 11.45 p.m. Martha Tabram and Mary Connelly separated with their respective soldier clients. Connelly took her customer, the corporal, up Angel Alley. Martha and the private appeared to go off towards Whitechapel. Connelly's business soon concluded, she left the corporal at the corner of George Yard at 12.15 a.m. and went off towards Aldgate.

At 1.40 a.m. Joseph Mahoney, a carman, and his wife Elizabeth, who worked at a match factory in Stratford, returned to their home at 47 George Yard Buildings. Mrs Mahoney, a young woman aged 25 or 26, returned down the stairs some five minutes later to get some supper from the chandler's shop in Thrawl Street. She returned within ten minutes. The staircase was unlit and she did not notice anything suspicious on the stairs, nor did she hear any unusual sounds during the rest of the night.

At 2.00 a.m. PC Thomas Barrett, 226 H, saw a soldier, a Grenadier, in Wentworth Street. He described the man as aged between 22 and 26, 5ft 9ins. in height, of fair complexion with dark hair and a small brown moustache turned up at the ends. PC Barrett asked the man why he was loitering in the street and the soldier replied that 'he was waiting for a mate who had gone with a girl'.[7]

At 3.30 a.m. Alfred George Crow[8], 35 George Yard Buildings, a cab driver (cab no. 6.600), went up the same steps as Mahoney and noticed a body lying on the first floor landing. Since it was not uncommon for him to see people asleep or drunk on the landing he did not pay any attention.

At 4.45 a.m. John Saunders Reeves, a young man of 23 or 24, a waterside labourer, left his room at 37 George Yard Buildings. On the first floor landing he saw the body of Martha Tabram lying in a pool of blood. Without bothering to examine the body, Reeves ran for a policeman and returned with PC Barrett. Barrett immediately summoned another constable and sent him for Dr Timothy Robert Keleene of Brick Lane. It was 5.30 a.m. when Keleene examined the body and estimated that death had occurred about two hours earlier (about 3.30 a.m. – about the time when Alfred Crow had returned home).

Martha Tabram had been stabbed 39 times. Among the wounds there were 5 in the left lung, 2 in the right lung, one in the heart, 5 in the liver, 2 in the spleen and 6 in the stomach. The breasts, stomach, abdomen and vagina had been the target of the murderer. With one possible exception, all the wounds had been made by a right-handed man, and all but one of the wounds could have been inflicted with an ordinary penknife. The exception was a wound on the chestbone which appeared to have been made with a dagger or sword bayonet. A photograph of the corpse was taken on 8 August 1888.

The only real clue was that 'Pearly Poll' had claimed that she and Martha Tabram had spent some time with a couple of soldiers, that Martha Tabram had gone off with one of them, a private, and that so far as was known nobody had subsequently seen her alive. This had been at 11.45 p.m. Some 2¼ hours later P.C. Barrett had spoken to a Grenadier guardsman who was loitering in Winthrop Street, waiting for a 'mate' who had 'gone with a girl'.

Over the next few days Detective Inspector Edmund Reid personally supervised several line-ups of soldiers. The first, on 7 August, was at the Tower of London where several Grenadier guards were brought before PC Barrett in the guardroom, but he failed to recognise any as the man he had seen in Wentworth Street. At 11.00 a.m. the following day those Grenadier guards who had been on leave on the night of the murder were again paraded before PC Barrett, who picked out two men. Both were taken to the orderly room, where PC Barrett immediately said that he was mistaken about the first man, who was allowed to leave without his name being taken. The second man, whose name was John Leary, proved able to give an account of himself on the night of the murder. His alibi was independently confirmed by a private named Law and satisfied the police.

A Corporal Benjamin, who had been absent without leave since 6 August returned to barracks during the time that the police were there. His clothing and bayonet were examined, but no marks of blood were found on them and he was able to satisfy the police that he had been staying with his father, the landlord of the Canbury Hotel, Kingston-on-Thames, at the time of the murder.

The Metropolitan Police (MEPO) files held at the Public Record Office, commonly known as the PRO, also refer to a 'Mrs Jane Gilbank and her daughter residing at 23 Catherine Wheel Alley, Aldgate', who claimed to have seen Tabram with a private of the Guards on the night of her murder. They were brought to the Tower by Sergeants Leach and Caunter, and were sent one at a time along the rank, but failed to pick out anyone. It was subsequently realised that the women they thought had been murdered and had seen was a Mrs Withers, who was afterwards found alive.[9]

At 11.00 a.m. on 10 August a parade at the Tower was arranged for 'Pearly Poll', but it had to be postponed because she could not be found. She was eventually located by Sergeant Caunter and the identity parade took place on 13 August. She looked at the men and said, 'They are not here, they had white bands around their caps.' This indicated that the men belonged to the Coldstream Guards and those who had been on leave on the night of the murder were paraded before Connelly at Wellington Barracks on 15 August. She unhesitatingly identified two men. Both were privates, though one had two good conduct stripes and could have been mistaken for a corporal. One was named Private George and the other was Private Skipper. Both had alibis. One was at home, 120 Hammersmith Road, with his wife or a woman 'supposed to be his wife'[10], and the other was in barracks.

As for the murder weapon being a bayonet, it was learned that old bayonets could be bought at any time in Petticoat Lane and elsewhere for about 1d. each and were frequently to be seen as playthings in the hands of children.

The inquest was opened on the afternoon of 9 August 1888 in the large Alexandra Room, a lecture room and library at the Working Lads' Institute in Whitechapel Road. On the walls around the room were portraits of the Royal Family and landscape pictures. One particularly magnificent portrait was of the Princess of Wales painted by Herr Louis Fleischmann. This hung above the seat occupied by the coroner, who on this occasion was George Collier, the deputy coroner of the South-Eastern Division of Middlesex. Public interest in the case was minimal, hardly anyone but the authorities and witnesses being present. The *East London Advertiser*[11] noted that the police – the case having been placed by Inspector Ellisdon of the Commercial Street Police Station in the hands of Inspector Reid of the CID – 'are very reticent upon the matter generally, and are not disposed to assist in the publication of details'. After several adjournments the coroners' jury concluded that Martha Tabram had died as a result of 'murder by some person or persons unknown'.

CHAPTER THREE

Mary Ann Nichols

(aka Polly Nichols)
(found murdered on Friday 31 August 1888)

SHE WAS christened Mary Ann Walker in or some years before August 1851[1], the daughter of a blacksmith named Edward Walker.[2] On 16 January 1864, she married William Nichols[3], a printer, the marriage being performed by Charles Marshall, the Vicar of St Bride's Parish Church, in the presence of Seth George Havelly and Sarah Good.[4] They had two children, one being born about 1867 and the other about 1879.

The marriage was marked by a series of separations caused by Mary Ann Nichols's drinking. William Nichols took Mary Ann back time after time, but always she returned to the alcohol and eventually there was no reconciliation. In 1880 or 1881 they separated for good. Edward Walker, Mary Ann's father, claimed that William Nichols had in fact gone off with the woman who had nursed Mary Ann through her last confinement. Nichols denied the allegation. 'I have a certificate of my boy's birth two years after that,' he told the inquest.[5]

Mary Ann Nichols's whereabouts are suprisingly well documented, possibly the best-documented of all the victims of the Whitechapel murderer.

24th April 1882 – 18th January 1883: Lambeth Workhouse.

18th January 1883 – 20th January 1883: Lambeth Infirmary.

20th January 1883 – 24th March 1883: Lambeth Workhouse.

24th March 1883 – 21st May 1883: No Record. This would most probably be the time when her father said that she was living with him. He said that he had not found her to be a sober woman, though she was not in the habit of staying out late at night. Her drinking had nevertheless caused friction and they had had words. He had not thrown her out, but she had left the following morning.

21st May 1883 – 2nd June 1883: Lambeth Workhouse.

2nd June 1883 – 26th October 1887: No Record. This would correspond with the time when she was said to have been living with a man named Drew, a blacksmith with a shop in York Street, Walworth. In June 1886, respectably dressed, Mary Ann Nichols had attended the funeral of her brother who had been burnt to death when a paraffin lamp exploded.

26th October 1887 – 2nd December 1887: Strand Workhouse, Edmonton.

2nd December 1887 – 19th December 1887: No Record. It was revealed that at this time she was in the habit of sleeping in Trafalgar Square. When a clearance of the area was made, it was discovered that she was destitute and had no means of subsistance, and she was admitted as an inmate of Lambeth Workhouse.

19th December 1887 – 29th December 1887: Lambeth Workhouse.

29th December 1887 – 4th January 1888: No Record.

4th January 1888 – 16th April 1888: Mitcham Workhouse (Holborn) and Holborn Infirmary (Archway Hospital).

16th April 1888 – 12th May 1888: Lambeth Workhouse.

12th May 1888 – 1st August 1888; No Record. During this time Mary Ann Nichols had obtained a position as a servant in the household of Mr and Mrs Cowdry at 'Ingleside', Rose Hill Road, Wandsworth. She wrote to her father:

> I just write to say you will be glad to know that I am settled in my new place, and going all right up to now. My people went out yesterday, and have not returned, so I am left in charge. It is a grand place inside, with trees and gardens back and front. All has been newly done up. They are teetotallers, and religious, so I ought to get on. They are very nice people, and I have not too much to do. I hope you are all right and the boy has work. So goodbye for the present. – From yours truly, 'Polly'. Answer soon, please, and let me know how you are.[6]

Mr Walker had replied to this letter, but did not hear from his daughter again. In fact, on 12th July 1888, she had stolen clothing worth in excess of £3. 10s. 0d. from her employers and had absconded.

1st August 1888 – 2nd August 1888: Grays Inn Temporary Workhouse[7].

In August 1888 Mary Ann Nichols lived in a lodging house at 18 Thrawl Street, where she shared a room with four women and paid 4d. a night for a bed. On 24th August she was sleeping at a lodging house known as the White House, 56 Flower and Dean Street, where men and women were allowed to doss together.

Mary Ann Nichols was described as dark haired, with small and delicate features, high cheekbones and grey eyes. Her teeth were a little discoloured[8], with five missing. She was about 5 ft 2 ins. in height. Her friend Emily Holland described her as 'a very clean woman' who always seemed to keep herself to herself'[9]. Nichols was almost certainly an alcoholic, two men having left her because of her drinking habits.

Whereas the films always seem to portay the victims of the Whitechapel murderer as buxom, attractive and jolly sorts of women, the books almost universally present them as the dregs of humanity, looking at least twenty years older then their actual age. Mary Ann Nichols did not fit the film-makers' image, but neither was she a piece of human chaff. She had been an attractive woman with her high cheekbones and grey eyes. She also had a youthful appearance. The reporter for the *East London Observer*[8] guessed her age as between 30 and 35, but at the inquest her father stated that 'she was nearly 44 years of age, but it must be owned that she looked ten years younger'[9].

Mary Ann Nichols was found dead in Buck's Row, later renamed Durward Street and now obliterated in a massive clearance and rebuilding scheme. Writing in 1929, Leonard Matters described the street as it was at that time:

> . . . Buck's Row cannot have changed much in character since its name was altered. It is a narrow, cobbled, mean street, having on one side the same houses – possibly tenanted by the same people – which stood there in 1888. They are shabby, dirty little houses of two storeys, and only a three-feet pavement separates them from the road, which is no more than twenty feet from wall to wall.

On the opposite sides are the high walls of warehouses which at night would shadow the dirty street in a far deeper gloom than its own character in broad daylight suggests.

All Durward Street is not so drab and mean, for by some accident in the planning of the locality – if ever it was planned – quite two-thirds of the thoroughfare is very wide and open.

The street lies east and west along the London and North Eastern Railway line. It is approached from the west from Vallance Street, formerly Baker's Row. On the left are fine modern tall warehouses. I was interested to note that one of them belongs to Messrs Kearley and Tonge, Ltd, in front of whose other premises in Mitre Square a murder was committed on September 30th. On the left side of the street is a small wall guarding the railway line, which lies at a depth of some twenty feet below the ground level. Two narrow bridge roads lead across the railway into Whitechapel Road. The first was called Thomas Street in 1888, but is now Fulbourne Street. The other is Court Street. By either of these little lanes, no more than two hundred and fifty yards long, the busy main artery of the Whitechapel area can be reached from the relatively secluded Buck's Row.

Going still further east, an abandoned London County Council school building breaks the wide and open Durward Street into two narrow lanes or alleys. The left hand land retains the name of Durward Street, 'late Buck's Row', and the other is Winthrop Street. Both are equally dirty and seemingly disreputable . . .[10]

Heading down Buck's Row from the direction of the grim structure of the board school were some gates, about nine to ten feet in height, leading to some stables belonging to a Mr Brown. Next to the gates was a row of simple houses which, despite their appearance when Matters wrote in 1929, were described in *The Times*[11] as being tenanted by a 'respectable class of people superior in many ways to many of the surrounding streets.' The first house next to the stable gates was called New Cottage. It was occupied by a widow, Mrs

Emma Green, and her two sons and daughter. That night, 31 August, one of the sons went to bed at 9.00 p.m., the other son followed at 9.45 p.m., and Mrs Green and her daughter, who shared a room at the front of the house on the first floor, went to bed at 11.00 p.m. Mrs Green, who claimed to be a light sleeper, said that she slept undisturbed by any unusual sounds until she was awakened by the police some five hours later.

Opposite New Cottage lived Walter Purkiss, the Manager of Essex Wharf, with his wife, children and servant. He and his wife, whose bedroom was on the second floor and fronted the street, went to bed between 11.00 p.m. and 11.15 p.m. Both were awake at various times during the night, but neither heard anything unusual.

In Winthrop Street, which ran parallel to Buck's Row, there was a slaughter-house called Barber's Yard because it was owned by a Mr Barber. At midnight Harry Tomkins[12] and a fellow worker named Charles Britten left Barber's Yard for a stroll to the end of the street, returning about 1.00 a.m. Neither saw or heard anything unusual at that time or during the night. Walter Purkiss said that he awoke about 1.00 a.m. Buck's Row was unusually quiet.

The police were able to establish Mary Ann Nichols's movements that night. She was seen walking in the Whitechapel Road at 11.00 p.m.; was seen leaving the Frying-pan Public House at 12.30 a.m.; and at 1.20 a.m. she was in the kitchen of the common lodging house at 18 Thrawl Street. She was seen by the deputy lodging house keeper who asked her for the 4d. for her bed. Nichols replied that she did not have the money and the deputy turned her out. Nichols laughed. 'I'll soon get my doss money,' she said. 'See what a jolly bonnet I've got now.' She indicated a little black bonnet which nobody had seen before.

At 2.30 a.m. Mary Ann Nichols was seen in Whitechapel Road outside a grocer's shop at the corner of Osborne Street, opposite Whitechapel Church. She was very drunk and leaning against a wall. Mrs Emily Holland[13], who had shared a room with Nichols at 18 Thrawl Street, was returning from going to see a fire at Ratcliffe – a great fire broke out at Ratcliffe dry dock shortly before 1.00 a.m. and another witness to it who featured in the Ripper saga was John Pizer, arrested as a man known as 'Leather Apron', at one time popularly thought to be the Whitechapel murderer. Emily Holland stopped to talk with Nichols for some seven or eight minutes and as they talked the clock of Whitechapel Church struck 2.30 a.m. Mrs Holland tried to persuade Nichols to return with her to the lodging in Thrawl Street, but Nichols refused. 'I've had my lodging money three times today and I've spent it. It won't be long before I'm back.' Nichols then staggered off towards Whitechapel.

At 3.15 a.m. PC John Thain, 96 J, passed the entrance to Buck's Row on his beat. At this moment PC John Neil, 97 J[14], passed the slaughter-house in Winthrop Street, where he saw Harry Tomkins and another horse slaughterer named James Mumford at work. PC Neil passed on and walked into and down Buck's Row. He did not see anything unusual or suspicious. About the same time Sergeant Kerby also passed down Buck's Row. He, too, saw nothing to arouse his suspicions[15].

At 3.20 a.m. Charles A Cross, a carman employed by Pickford and Co, left his home at 22 Doveton Street, Cambridge Road, Bethnal Green, and set off for his place of work in Broad Street. A little while later another carman, Robert Paul, who lived at 30 Foster Street, left his home and headed for his workplace in Corbett's Court, Whitechapel. Both men took a route through Buck's Row.

At 3.45 a.m. Charles Cross was the first to enter the little street. He was walking along the Essex Wharf side when he saw something lying against the gates leading to the stables next to New Cottage. He later told the inquest: 'I could not tell in the dark what it was at first; it looked to me like a tarpaulin sheet, but stepping into the road, I saw that it was the body of a woman. Just then I heard a man – about 40 yards off – approaching from the direction that I myself had come from. I waited for the man, who started to one side as if afraid that I meant to knock him down. I said, "Come and look over here, there's a woman." '

The other man was Robert Paul. He went with Cross. It was very dark, too dark to see that the woman had been brutally murdered or to see any blood. The woman's clothes were raised almost to her stomach. Cross felt her hands, which were cold and limp. 'I believe she's dead,' said Cross, but Paul, having felt her face and found it warm, tried to find a heartbeat and thought he detected a faint movement. 'I think she's breathing,' he said. 'But it's very little if she is.'

Paul wanted to try and sit the woman up. 'I'm not going to touch her,' replied Cross, and the two men, who were by now running late for work, decided to try and find a policeman.

Cross and Paul must have left Buck's Row within a matter of perhaps seconds of PC Neil entering the street and beginning his beat up the left hand side. He found the body of Mary Nichols in the position in which Cross and Paul had left it, but in the light from PC Neil's lamp it was clear that the woman was dead. Her eyes were open and glassy. Blood had oozed from a wound in her throat. Lying by her right side was the bonnet of which she had been so proud only a few hours before.

Within four or five minutes of leaving the body Cross and Paul met PC G Mizen, 56 H, at the corner of Hanbury Street and Baker's Row, 300 yards from Buck's Row. At the inquest PC Mizen testified that he had been approached by two men (Cross and Paul), one of whom (Cross) had said to him, 'You are wanted in Buck's Row by a policeman; a woman is lying there.' He maintained that neither man had told him that the woman was dead. Mizen's testimony has to be regarded with suspicion. Cross testified that he had told PC Mizen that the woman 'looks to me to be either dead or drunk' and that Paul had added, 'I think she's dead.' Cross said Mizen had merely replied, 'All right.' There seems to be no reason for disbelieving Cross, who seems to have presented his evidence in a very clear and succinct manner, his testimony being supported by Paul. Yet Mizen not only stated that neither man had told him that the woman was dead, he also claimed that they had said he was wanted in Buck's Row by a policeman. Asked at the inquest if he had told PC Mizen this, Cross replied, 'No. Because I did not see a policeman in Buck's Row.'

In any event, PC Mizen headed for Buck's Row. Cross and Paul continued on their way to work and parted company at the corner of Hanbury Street, Paul turning into Corbett's Court, leaving Cross to walk on alone to Broad Street, which he claimed to have reached at 4.00 a.m. Neither man had known the other prior to their meeting in Buck's Row over the corpse of Mary Ann Nichols.[16]

At 3.47 a.m. PC Thain, on his beat along Brady Street and walking away from Whitechapel Road, passed the entrance of Buck's Row again and was heard by PC Neil, who signalled with his lamp. Thain went down Buck's Row. 'For God's sake, Jack, go fetch a doctor,' said PC Neil.[17] PC Thain went at once to the surgery of Dr Rees Ralph Llewellyn[18] at 152 Whitechapel Road, about 300 yards from Buck's Row, first stopping off at the horse slaughterer's to pick up his cape and there mentioning the discovery of the body to Harry Tomkins.[19] In the meantime, PC Mizen arrived in Buck's Row, where he found PC Neil alone with the body. Neil sent him to fetch an ambulance.

At 4.20 a.m. Harry Tomkins and a colleague named James Mumford left the slaughterhouse and went to view the body in Buck's Row. They were later joined by Charles Britten. The men remained there until the body was taken away. For a time they were to fall under suspicion of having committed the murder, but after a long and detailed interview with the police they were able to give a satisfactory account of themselves.[20]

PC Thain now returned with Dr Llewellyn. PC Neil was at that time alone with Tomkins and Mumford. Whilst Dr Llewellyn was making a very cursory examination of the body, further policemen arrived, Sergeant Kerby and another officer of H Division.

Dr Llewellyn pronounced the woman dead and ordered that the body be taken to the mortuary in Old Montague Street. Having returned with the ambulance, PC Mizen helped PC Neil to put the body aboard the vehicle. Moving the body revealed a spot of congealed blood about six inches in diameter which had run towards the gutter. PC Thain also noticed a lot of blood on the back of the body and assumed that this had run down from the neck. He got a lot of blood on his hands when lifting the body into the ambulance.

It was roughly about this time that Patrick Mulshaw, a night porter watching some sewage works, was told by a passing man: 'Watchman, old man. I believe somebody is murdered down the street.' Mulshaw immediately went round the corner into Buck's Row, where he saw the deceased lying on the ground, surrounded by some working men and the police.

I do not know if this man was ever identified, but, though the expression 'old man' is a common one, it is interesting to note that Matthew Packer, who claimed to have sold some fruit to a later Ripper victim named Elizabeth Stride, said that a man had addressed him: 'Well, what's the price of the black grapes, old man?' And on being told, had replied: 'Well, then, old man, give us a half a pound of the black.'

At 4.30 a.m. Inspector John Spratling, J Division[21], was in the Hackney Road when he received news of the murder. He went at once to Buck's Row, arriving after the body had been taken to the mortuary. PC Thain, who was still at the murder scene, pointed out the spot where the body had been found. There was a slight stain of blood on the pavement. Inspector Spratling and PC Thain then went together to the mortuary in Old Montague Street. The keys to the mortuary had been sent for, but had not yet arrived. The body was still on the ambulance in the yard. Spratling was engaged in taking down a description of the body when the mortuary attendant, a pauper inmate of the Whitechapel Workhouse named Robert Mann, arrived with the keys and the body was moved indoors. Spratling continued to take down the description and it was in the process of doing so that he discovered that Nichols had suffered severe injuries to the abdomen. Inspector Spratling at once sent for Dr Llewellyn.

At 5.00 a.m. Inspector Spratling directed a PC named Cartwright to conduct a thorough search of the murder scene and surrounding neighbourhood, including the adjoining railway.

At 6.30 a.m. James Hatfield, another inmate of the Whitechapel Workhouse, arrived at the mortuary and despite instructions from Detective Sergeant Enright that the body of Nichols was not to be touched, Hatfield and Robert Mann stripped and washed the body, dumping Nichols's clothes in the yard. Inspector Spratling, who was present with PC Neil, noticed that Nichols's petticoats bore a stencil stamp of the Lambeth Workhouse. The matron of the workhouse was summoned, but she was unable to identify the body.

At 6.45 a.m. Inspector Helson, J Division, received news of the murder and went directly to the mortuary, arriving as the body was being stripped. From the mortuary he went to the murder scene.

Dr Llewellyn, who made a full *post-mortem* examination of the body at 10.00 a.m. on Saturday, 1 September, described Nichols's injuries as follows: on the right side of the face there was a bruise which looked as if it had been made either by a fist or by the pressure of a thumb; there was also a circular bruise on the left side of the face which was also probably caused by a fist or a thumb; there was a small bruise on the left side of the neck and an abrasion on the right. All the bruises appeared to have been caused at the same time and were evidently recent.

There were two cuts in the throat. One was four inches long and the other eight, both cuts reached through to the vertebrae. There were no other injuries on the body apart from bruising until the lower part of the abdomen. Here, two or three inches from the left side there was a jagged wound, very deep and having cut through the tissues. There were several incisions running across the abdomen. On the right side there were three or four cuts running downward. All the wounds had been inflicted with a sharp knife and appeared to have been made by a left-handed man.

In Dr Llewellyn's opinion the injuries had taken about 4-5 minutes to inflict and were the work of a person with some rough anatomical knowledge, for he had attacked all the vital parts. *The Times* on 18 September reported that 'no part of the viscera [i.e. internal organs] was missing'.

Not mentioned by Dr Llewellyn but widely reported in the press on 1 September was that one of Mary Ann Nichols's fingers bore the impression of a ring. The ring was missing. There were no marks on the finger to suggest that it had been wrenched off and it is not known if Nichols was wearing the ring on the night of her murder. However, it is known that the next victim of the Whitechapel murderer, Annie Chapman, was wearing two cheap brass rings on the night she was killed and that these appeared to have been forcibly removed from her finger.

Speculation during that Saturday afternoon gave rise to two theories; one was dismissed and the other should have been. The former was an initial police opinion that both Tabram and Nichols had been murdered by members of one of the gangs who were known to extort money from the Whitechapel prostitutes. One was the 'Old Nichol gang', so called from the district around Old Nichol Street, Bethnal Green; another, which gained brief notoriety, was called 'the High-rip' from Hoxton. By Saturday it was reported that the police gave no credence to this theory.

The other theory was that Nichols had not been murdered in Buck's Row, but somewhere else, from where she had been taken and dumped in Buck's Row. *The Times*, 1 September 1888, reported:

> Viewing the spot where the body was found, it seems difficult to believe that the woman received her deathwounds there . . . if the woman was murdered on the spot where the body was found, it is almost impossible to believe that she would not have aroused the neighbourhood by her screams.

This theory was revived in 1976 in a highly imaginative best-selling book. However, a report by Inspector Helson states that there was 'no doubt but that the murder was committed where the body was found'.[22]

That Saturday also saw the start of the long saga of whether or not a reward should have been sanctioned by the Home Secretary. Messrs Walter and Son, 11-13 Church Street, Spitalfields, were among the very first to write to Henry Matthews on the subject, receiving a reply in the negative a few days later.[23] It was a decision which Henry Matthews would have cause to regret.

CHAPTER FOUR

Saturday, 1 September
1888 – Friday 7 September 1888

IN THE EARLY afternoon of Saturday, 1 September, William Nichols, together with one of his sons, was taken to the mortuary. It was reported that he was greatly upset by the sight of his wife. 'I forgive you, as you are, for what you have been to me,' he said.

Later in the afternoon the inquest into Mary Ann Nichols's death was opened at the Working Lads' Institute. It was conducted by the Coroner for the South-Eastern Division of Middlesex, Wynne Edwin Baxter, who had just returned from a tour of Scandinavia. He turned up resplendently dressed in white and black checked trousers, a dazzling white waistcoat, a crimson scarf and a dark coat.

Wynne Baxter was born in Lewes, eight miles from Brighton. His grandfather had moved there about 1802 and had set up business as a printer. In 1837 he had founded the *Sussex Express*. Wynne Baxter was born in 1844 and after an education at Lewes Grammar School he became a solicitor, setting up practice at 13 Southwark Street, London. From 1868 he held a number of prominent positions in Lewes: Junior Headborough (1868), Junior High Constable (1878), High Constable (1880-1), Lord Mayor (elected 9 November 1881). He had married Kate Bliss, the daughter of the Mayor of Northampton, and had two sons, F T Baxter and Reginald Baxter. Among other things, he collected the works of Milton, was a member of the Archaeological Societies of Middlesex, Surrey, Kent, Sussex and Gloucestershire, and Secretary of the Royal Microscopical Society. He authored a Domesday book of Sussex, Surrey, Kent and Middlesex, and 'works on Van Heurch's miscosope and *Diatomaceae.*' He was also a prominent Freemason, a member of the South Saxon Lodge.

On 29 January 1880 he was appointed Coroner for the County of Sussex and in 1887 he was elected Coroner for East London and the Tower of London. Shortly afterwards this area was subdivided between three coroners, Baxter having jurisdiction over the South-Eastern Division.

According to Martin Fido, Baxter 'fought a very dirty election campaign . . . He advertised, canvassed, bribed, made deals to secure the withdrawal of other candidates in his favour, and used improper registration of voters to an alarming extent.' He was nevertheless elected and held the post until 1920. On 15 September of that year he suffered a heart attack and died at his home in Church Street, Stoke Newington, on 1 October. He was 76 years old and left an estate valued at £29,319.[1]

On the occasion of the inquest of Mary Ann Nichols the library of the Working Lads' Institute was almost full, interested spectators swelling the ranks of the police, press, jury and witnesses. After the jury, whose foreman was a Mr Horey, had been taken by Mr Banks, the Coroner's assistant, to view the body, Baxter, seated at the head of a long table with sheets of paper before him on which to write the witnesses' depositions, opened the inquest.

By 4 September news of the murders had crossed the Atlantic:

> Whitechapel has a murder mystery which transcends anything known in the annals of the horrible. It is Poe's *Murders in the Rue Morgue* and *The Mystery of Marie Roget* rolled into one story. It is nothing less than a midnight murderer, whose step is noiseless, whose strike is deadly, and whose cunning is so great that he leaves no trace whatsoever of his work and no clue to his identity. He has just slaughtered his third victim, and all the women in Whitechapel are terrified, while the stupidest detectives in the civilized world stand aghast and say they have no clue.

The newspaper went on to describe the murder and to state that the police were of the opinion that Nichols had been murdered by the same person reponsible for two earlier murders:

This man is called 'Leather Apron' and nobody knows him by any other name. He is a character halfway between Dickens's Quilp and Poe's Baboon. He is short, stunted and thickset. He has small, wicked black eyes and is half crazy. He is always hanging about the deep shadows that fill the intricate network of courts, passages and alleyways in Whitechapel. He does not walk, but always moves on a sharp, queer run and never makes any noise with his feet.[2]

It was a frightening picture of a monster on the loose. The real 'Leather Apron', if the man so accused was really the bearer of this soubriquet, presented a rather less alarming prospect.

On the afternoon of 6 September 1888 Mary Ann Nichols was buried at Ilford Cemetery in a polished elm coffin supplied by a Mr H Smith of Hanbury Street. The coffin was conveyed from the mortuary in a horse-drawn hearse, which was surrounded by policemen under the direction of Inspector Allison, H Division, to protect it from the horde of spectators. In another carriage was Edward Walker, two of Nichols's children and a grandchild.[3]

James Monro, Assistant Commissioner CID, had resigned his office, leaving his department in disarray as he took his Secret Service work to the Home Office. His official retirement was not until 31 August, so it happened that his successor, Robert Anderson, took office the day after the murder of Mary Ann Nichols. In his autobiography Anderson wrote:

I was at that time physically unfit to enter on the duties of my new post. For some time past I had not had an adequate holiday, and the strain of long and anxious work was telling on me. 'A man is as old as he feels', and by this test I was older at that time than when I left office a dozen years later. Dr Gilbart Smith, of Harley Street, insisted that I must have two months' complete rest, and he added that he would probably give me a certificate for a further two months' 'sick leave'. This, of course, was out of the question. But I told Mr Matthews, greatly to his distress, that I could not take up my new duties until I had had a month's holiday in Switzerland. And so, after one week at Scotland Yard, I crossed the Channel.[4]

The day Anderson left the country was the last day of life for another Whitechapel prostitute, for the murderer was about to strike again.

Before departing for Switzerland, Anderson recommended the appointment of a senior officer to supervise the inquiry into the murders.

The man selected to take charge of the investigation into the Whitechapel murders was Detective Chief Inspector Donald Sutherland Swanson. Anderson's recommendation has survived and is worth quoting in full.

I am convinced that the Whitechapel murder case is one which can be successfully grappled with if it is systematically taken in hand. I go so far as to say that I could myself in a few days unravel the mystery provided I could spare the time and give undivided attention to it. I feel therefore the utmost importance to be attached to putting the whole Central Office work in this case in the hands of one man who will have nothing else to concern himself with. Neither you nor I nor Mr Williamson can do this. I therefore put it in the hands of Chief Inspector Swanson who must be aquainted with *every detail*. I look upon him for the time being as the eyes and ears of the Commissioner in this particular case.

He must have a room to himself, and every paper, every document, every report, every telegram must pass through his hands. He must be consulted on every subject. I would not send any directions anywhere on the subject of the murder without consulting him. I give him the whole responsibility. On the other hand he should consult Mr Williamson, you or myself on every important particular before any action unless there is some extreme urgency.

I find that a most important letter was sent to Division yesterday without his seeing it. This is quite an error and should not occur again. *All the papers* in Central Office on the subject of the murder must be kept in his room and plans of the positions etc.

51

I must have this matter at once put on a proper footing so as to be a guide for the future in cases of importance.

Everything depends upon a careful compliance with these directions.[5]

These instructions contain a footnote of authorization in Sir Charles Warren's barely legible scrawl. From this document it would appear that Chief Inspector Swanson would have known more about the Whitechapel murders than anyone else, probably including his superiors.

Donald Sutherland Swanson was born in Geise in the Highlands of Scotland in 1848, the son of Mr John Swanson, a brewer, but he spent his boyhood days in Thurso, a small burgh in northern Caithness, on Thurso Bay, the most northerly town on the Scottish mainland. He was educated at the Miller Institution in Thurso, where he was reportedly 'a brilliant student' and a Greek and Latin scholar. He had first embarked on a teaching career, but saw no great future in it and set off for a career in London. He joined the Metropolitan Police on 27 April 1868, was appointed Chief Inspector in February 1888, and eventually achieved the rank of Superintendent CID. He married and had five children, three sons and two daughters. He died on 24 November 1924 at 3 Presburg Road, New Malden, Surrey, being buried at Kingston Cemetery.

To the end of his life Donald Swanson 'had a mind like a rapier. He was highly intelligent, very well read . . .' Those police officers who mentioned him in their reminiscences always spoke of him with praise. Of his own reminiscences, which would today be most highly valued, it was reported that 'viewing his work as a decidedly secret service, Mr Swanson was opposed to public reminiscences'.[6]

CHAPTER FIVE

Annie Chapman

(aka Annie Sivvey (Siffey), 'Dark Annie')
(found murdered on Saturday, 8 September, 1888)

ANNIE SMITH was born in September 1841. She had brothers,
one of whom was named Fontain or Fontin, and sisters, but
beyond this nothing is known about her life before she met and
married a coachman named John Chapman, who was in the
service of a gentleman who lived at Clewer, near Windsor,
until he was forced to retire through ill health. A Mrs Pearcer,
who lived in Hackney and was a friend of Annie Chapman,
told Timothy Donovan[1], the deputy of a lodging house in
Dorset Street, that John Chapman had at some stage in his
career been the valet of a nobleman who lived in Bond Street,
but had been forced to resign the position because of his wife's
dishonesty.[2]

John and Annie Chapman had two children, a boy and a
girl. At the time of Chapman's murder it was reported that the
boy was in a cripples' Home and the girl was at an unspecified
institution in France.

In 1884 or 1885 the couple had separated by mutual consent.
The reason is uncertain. A police report says they parted
because of 'her drunken and immoral ways'.[3] Her drunkenness
had certainly brought her to the attention of the Windsor
police, for a Superintendent Hayes reported that she had been
arrested there for drunkenness, though she had never been
brought before a magistrate.

John Chapman had regularly paid his wife a weekly
allowance of 10 shillings by post office order made payable at
the Commercial Street Post Office, but the payments had
ceased about eighteen months before Annie's murder. On
making inquiries from her brother-in-law, who lived in Oxford
Street, Whitechapel, Annie learned that her husband had died
on Christmas Day 1886 at Grove Road, Windsor.

Some time during 1886 Annie Chapman had been living at 30 Dorset Street, Spitalfields, with a sieve-maker named Jack Sivvey[4], but had more recently formed a relationship with a bricklayer's labourer named Edward Stanley, who at the time of Chapman's murder was living at 1 Osborne Place, Osborne Street, Whitechapel. He was known to certain people living at Chapman's lodging house as 'the Pensioner'. At the inquest into Chapman's death he said he had known Chapman for about two years and that he had known her when she was living in Windsor. Recently he had been seeing her at weekends, though the frequency of their meetings has not been established. Since May or June 1888 Annie Chapman had been living at Crossingham's lodging house at 35 Dorset Street.

Annie Chapman was 5 feet in height, had dark brown wavy hair, blue eyes and a thick nose. She was stout and well proportioned. The police report[3] states that she had two teeth missing in the lower jaw, but the teeth were not missing from the front. The doctor who examined Chapman's body and gave evidence at the inquest stated that Chapman was not missing any front teeth; the front teeth were perfect as far as the first molar and were very fine teeth indeed.

According to a friend named Amelia Farmer, Chapman had not been in the habit of frequenting the streets as a regular means of livelihood, but had crocheted antimacassars for sale and had at other times sold flowers and matches. However, like a great many other women in her position, Chapman appears to have resorted to prostitution as a means of making money.

The deputy of the lodging house at 30 Dorset Street where Chapman had lived with Jack Sivvey said that in his experience Chapman had not been given to drinking and that he was surprised to hear that she had reputedly been drinking to excess on the night of her murder. Amelia Farmer described her friend as a sober, steady-going woman who seldom took any drink (though she had a taste for rum). And Timothy Donovan, the keeper of Crossingham's lodging house, said Chapman was always very friendly with the other lodgers, that he had never had any trouble with her, and that although she used to get drunk on Saturday nights, she was sober the rest of the week.

In short, Annie Chapman had a taste for alcohol – as her arrest for drunkenness in Windsor testifies – but she was not an alcoholic, as Mary Ann Nichols almost certainly was. She does not appear to have resorted to prostitution prior to the death of her husband on 25 December 1886 and the cessation of the 10 shillings a week he had allowed her. Thereafter she had tried to sustain herself through doing crochet work or by selling flowers and matches. She got drunk on Saturday nights – but many people did and still do. Annie Chapman was also dying, far advanced in a disease of the lungs and the membranes of the brain.

Shortly before her death Annie Chapman was involved in a fight with a fellow lodger. The details are confused and confusing. According to Amelia Farmer, Chapman had told her that during the afternoon of Saturday 1 September she had been in the 'Ringers', a pub so named after the landlords Mr and Mrs Walter Ringer (the real name of the pub was the Britannia), at the corner of Dorset Street and Commercial Street. She was in the company of Ted Stanley (according to some accounts), a woman named Eliza Cooper and a man with the Runyonesque name 'Harry the Hawker', who was drunk. Chapman said that she had seen Cooper palm one of Harry's florins and replace it with a penny. She had mentioned this to Harry or otherwise drawn attention to Cooper's deceit and Cooper had struck her, blacking Chapman's eye and bruising her breast.[5]

That night Edward Stanley, who had been on duty with the 2nd Brigade Southern Division Hants Militia at Fort Elson, Gosport, since 6 August, returned to Whitechapel and met Chapman at the corner of Brushfield Street. They spent Saturday and Sunday nights together at 35 Dorset Street and parted company between 1.00 p.m. and 3.00 p.m. on the Sunday.

On Monday 3 September Amelia Farmer saw Chapman in Dorset Street. Chapman complained of feeling unwell and said that she intended to visit her sister. 'If I can get a pair of boots from my sister I shall go hop-picking,' she said.

On Tuesday 4 September Farmer saw Chapman near Spitalfields Church. Chapman again complained of feeling unwell and said she thought she would go to the casual ward for a day or two. She mentioned that she had had nothing to eat or drink that day, not even a cup of tea, and Farmer gave her 2d, cautioning her not to spend it on rum.

It is almost certain that Chapman did spend the next two days in the casual ward. Timothy Donovan said that in Chapman's room at the lodging house he had found a bottle of medicine which he thought indicated the truth of this. Certainly her friend Amelia Farmer did not see Chapman again until about 5.00 p.m. on 7 September. This was in Dorset Street. Chapman was sober and Farmer asked her if she was going to Stratford (where it was believed that she plied her trade). Chapman replied that she felt too ill to do anything. Farmer went about her business and on returning a few minutes later found that Chapman had not moved. Chapman said: 'It's no use my giving way. I must pull myself together and go out and get some money or I shall have no lodgings.'

Chapman was next seen at her lodging house at 35 Dorset Street, at about 11.30 p.m. when she asked Donovan for permission to go down to the kitchen.[6]

At 12.12 a.m. William Stevens, a painter who lodged at 35 Dorset Street, entered the kitchen and saw Chapman. He thought that she was the worse for drink. He saw Chapman take a box of pills from her pocket, but the box broke and she wrapped the pills in a torn piece of envelope which she took from the mantelpiece over the fire. Chapman then left the kitchen and Stevens thought that she had gone to bed. In fact she had probably gone to the 'Ringers' for a drink.

Chapman returned to the lodging house about 1.35 a.m. and was seen by John Evans, the night watchman. She told him she had been to Vauxhall to see one of her sisters and that she had just been out for a pint of beer. He asked her if she had the money for her bed and she said that she had not got enough, but that she would soon get it. She had then left the lodging house. Evans said that he saw her enter Paternoster Row and walk in the direction of Brushfield Street. That was the last time that Annie Chapman was definitely seen alive.[7]

The next possible sighting of Annie Chapman, which the police were unable to substantiate, was outside a pub near Spitalfields Market soon after it opened at 5.00 a.m. The only positive subsequent identification was when her body was found outside 29 Hanbury Street (formerly known as Brown Street), a building of largely wooden construction consisting of eight rooms. It was the home of seventeen people!

On the ground floor lived Mrs Annie Hardyman[8] and her 16 year old son. They both slept in the front room facing the street. This room doubled as a small shop which was used for selling cat meat. The rear room was used as a kitchen and was where the meat was cooked.

The first floor front room was occupied by Mrs Amelia Richardson who had lived in the house for fifteen years. She shared the room with her 14 year old grandson. She ran a business manufacturing packing cases and employed her son, John Richardson, and a man named John Tyler. She also rented the cellar, where the cases were made, and the yard of the house, which was also used for this purpose. The first floor back room was rented by Mr Walker and his son, who was described as weak-minded but very inoffensive.

The second floor front room was home to a carman named Thomson who worked for Goodson's in Brick Lane, together with his wife and adopted daughter. The back room was rented by Mr and Mrs Copsey, cigar makers.

The third floor front room was rented by an elderly man named John Davis, his wife, and three grown-up sons. An elderly woman named Sarah Cox lived in the rear room.

At the front of the building there were two doors, one leading into the shop and the other into a passage giving access to the stairs to various rooms and to a door leading into the yard. Neither the front door nor the yard door was kept locked, the occupants of the house leaving for and returning from work at various hours of the night and day.

The yard was about two feet below the level of the passage and was reached by two stone steps. The area was 13-14 feet square. There was a recess between the steps and the temporary fencing which separated the yard from that of the neighbouring house. When the yard door was opened it obscured this recess. It was in this recess that the body of Annie Chapman was found. At the bottom of the yard there was a shed. There was no exit from the yard except through the passage and back onto the street.

At 3.30 a.m. the carman, Thomson, who occupied the second

floor front room, left for work. He did not go into the yard.

Between 4.40 and 4.45 a.m. John Richardson, the son of Amelia Richardson, who lived at 2 John Street stopped by the house on his way to work at Spitalfields Market. It had become his habit to stop by the house when in the area because several months earlier somebody had broken the padlock on the cellar door and stolen a hammer and saw. He now stopped by to check the cellar door when in the area, though he did not usually call so early, the only times on which he had done so being market days.

Richardson's boots were hurting him. The problem was a strip of leather which needed to be cut off. Having checked that the padlock of the cellar door was secure, he pushed open the yard door. Standing on the top step, he cut the leather from his boot. He did not notice anything unusual in the yard and felt sure that he would have done so if there had been anything unusual there for him to see. He was not in the house for more than three or four minutes.

At 5.15 a.m. Albert Cadosch, a carpenter living at 27 Hanbury Street, next door to number 29, got up from bed and went into the yard of his house. As he returned across the yard he heard some people talking, apparently from the yard of number 29, but the only word he could catch was 'no'. On returning to the yard from his house he heard what sounded like something or someone falling against the fence. He did not take any notice because he thought it was just one of his neighbours. Cadosch then went off to work. As he was passing Spitalfields Church the time was about 5.32 a.m. He did not see anybody in Hanbury Street.

At 5.30 a.m. Elizabeth Long, who lived with her husband James Long, a park-keeper, at 32 Church Street[9], was walking down Hanbury Street on her way to Spitalfields Market. She was certain of the time because the brewer's clock had just struck. She was on the right hand side of the street – the same side as number 29 – and outside that house she saw a man and woman on the pavement talking, close against the shutters of number 29. Mrs Long could not see the man's face, which was turned away from her, but she had a good view of the woman, whom she subsequently identified as Annie Chapman. She heard the man say, 'Will you?' and the woman reply, 'Yes.'

Mrs Long then passed on her way.

Although she had not seen the man's face, Mrs Long stated that he looked like a foreigner, a description which in those days usually meant a Jew. He was about 40 years old and she thought he was wearing a dark coat, a deerstalker hat, and that he was of a 'shabby genteel appearance'. He was a little taller than the woman, which, if the woman was Chapman, would make the man between 5ft and 5ft 5ins.

Another woman, named Darrell or Durrell (who was not called to give evidence at the inquest and whose account may be a duplicate of that of Mrs Long and falsely attributed) also claimed to have been walking along Hanbury Street at 5.30 a.m. and to have seen the couple standing outside number 29. It was initially reported that she was very doubtful if she could recognise the woman again, but after a visit to the mortuary she maintained that the woman had been Annie Chapman.

At 5.45 a.m. John Davis, the elderly man who lived with his wife and three sons on the third floor of 29 Hanbury Street, got up, made himself a cup of tea, and at about 6.00 a.m. went downstairs and into the yard. He saw the body of Annie Chapman between the steps and the fence. 'I saw a female lying down, her clothing up to her knees, and her face covered with blood,' he said. 'What was lying beside her I cannot describe – it was part of her body. I did not examine the woman, I was too frightened at the dreadful sight.'

Just how dreadful that sight was – though it was by no means as dreadful as a sight yet to come – can be understood from the medical testimony given by Dr George Bagster Phillips at the inquest.[10] She was lying parallel to the fence, between the steps and the fence, her head about six inches in front of the level of the bottom step, about two feet from the rear wall of the house, and her feet pointing towards the shed at the bottom of the yard. The left arm had been placed across the left breast. The legs were drawn up, the feet resting on the ground and the knees turned outwards. The face and tongue were much swollen, the tongue protruding through the teeth, but not through the lips.

The body had been terribly mutilated. The throat had been cut through to the spine, the incisions through the skin being jagged and indicating that the throat had been cut from the left

59

side. It looked as though the murderer had attempted to cut through the spine to remove Chapman's head. From facial bruising the doctor was convinced that the killer had held Chapman by the lower jaw when he cut the throat.

Dr Phillips was very reluctant to give a detailed account of the injuries and mutilations and only did so after considerable pressure had been placed upon him by Wynne Baxter. None of the newspapers carried his report, but the evidence was revealed in the medical journal *The Lancet*.[11] The abdomen had been entirely laid open and the intestines, severed from their mesenteric attachments, had been lifted out and placed on the right shoulder of the corpse; whilst from the pelvis, the uterus and its appendages with the upper portion of the vagina and the posterior two-thirds of the bladder had been entirely removed.

Dr Phillips believed that the murderer had first strangled or suffocated Chapman because the face, lips and hands were livid, as in asphyxia, and not blanched as they would have been from loss of blood. The killer had then made a long incision in the neck through which the blood drained from the body, enabling him to make almost blood-free incisions and mutilation of the abdomen.

Of considerable importance with regard to the possible identity of the murderer, Dr Phillips was convinced that the mutilation of the body was done by an experienced hand. 'The doctor gives it as his opinion that the murderer was possessed of anatomical knowledge from the manner of the removal of the viscera, and that the knife used was not an ordinary knife, but such as a small amputating knife, or well-ground slaughterman's knife, narrow and sharp and blade of 6 – 9 inches in length.'[12] Indeed, Dr Phillips stated that he could not have performed all the mutilations, even on a passive victim, in under a quarter of an hour. To have done them in a deliberate way, as would fall to the duties of a surgeon, he thought that it would have taken him the best part of an hour.

Dr Phillips stated that the stiffness of the limbs was not yet marked, but was evidently commencing, and he thought that Chapman had been dead for at least two hours – which placed death at about 4.30 a.m. However, it had been a fairly cool morning and a great deal of blood had been lost, two factors which would have led to the body cooling rapidly, so the estimate of death was inexact.

The estimate of Chapman's time of death is obviously of crucial importance in the assessment of the testimony of Mr Cadosch, Mrs Long, and the woman Darrell/Durrell. At the inquest Wynne Baxter drew attention to the discrepancy in the times when Cadosch heard a sound in the yard of number 29 (which seems to have been accepted as being made by Chapman and her murderer) at 5.15 a.m. and the testimony of Mrs Long, who claimed to have seen Chapman at 5.30 a.m. Baxter, who heard the testimony of these witnesses at first hand, argued that Cadosch's estimate of the time was wrong, and Baxter was better able to assess the evidence than we are. However, could Baxter have been wrong?

It is not said how Mr Cadosch estimated the time when he heard the noise in the yard of number 29, but he said that he had passed Spitalfields Church a couple of minutes after the church clock struck 5.30 a.m. It is therefore possible that he either glanced up at the clock as he passed or that he heard the clock strike the half hour at some point after having left his house. Unless his estimate was completely awry, Cadosch could not have been in his yard at or after 5.30 a.m. as would have to have been the case if it was indeed Chapman whom Mrs Long had seen standing outside number 29 at 5.30 a.m.

I am inclined to the belief that Mrs Long's estimate of the time was in error, for if she had seen Chapman outside 29 Hanbury Street only a matter of minutes before 5.30 a.m. then it is easier to reconcile her testimony with that of Cadosch. Of course, the same error regarding the time would have had to have been made by the woman Darrell/Durrell, and one must doubt whether both women could have made such a mistake. However, Darrell/Durrell raises a further question. If she and Mrs Long both passed 29 Hanbury Street at approximately the same time, why did they not comment on seeing each other? Perhaps they did and it was never reported; maybe they did not think it was of any significance; or perhaps Mrs Long and the woman Darrell/Durrell are one and the same person – in which case attention should be given to the statement by the woman Darrell/Durrell in which she expressed doubts about her ability to identify the woman seen

61

outside number 29.

The police were forced to dismiss the evidence of Mrs Long, though for different reasons from those given above.

> If the evidence of Mrs Long is correct, that she saw the deceased at 5.30 a.m., then the evidence of Dr Phillips as to the probable time of death is incorrect. He was called and saw the body at 6.20 a.m. and he then gives it as his opinion that death occurred about two hours earlier, viz 4.20 a.m. hence the evidence of Mrs Long which appeared to be so important to the Coroner, must be looked upon with some amount of doubt, which is to be regretted.[3]

In fact, Dr Phillips did qualify his estimate by saying that the coolness of the morning and the great loss of blood would have made an accurate estimate of the time of death difficult. One could accept an error of about one hour, allowing for the noise heard by Mr Cadosch to have been made by Chapman and her murderer.

Having found the body, Davis returned through the passage and went out into the street. Henry John Holland (4 Aden Yard, Mile End Road) was on his way to work when he was summoned by Davis, who said, 'Come and look in the back yard!' Davis then spotted two men waiting outside the Black Swan Public House at 23 Hanbury Street. They were employees of a packing case manufacturer, Joseph and Thomas Bayley, who ran their business from 23a, the rear of the pub. 'Men! Come here!' shouted Davis. 'Here's a sight. A woman must have been murdered!' The two men, James Green (36 Acton Street, Burdett Road) and James Kent (20 'B' Block, King David Lane, Shadwell), followed Davis and Holland into the yard.

The time was now shortly after 6.00 a.m. Mrs Hardyman, on the ground floor, was awakened by footsteps in the passage. She woke her son and told him to go and see what was going on. He did so and returned to say that a woman had been killed in the yard.

The sequence of events is now very confused. James Kent went for a policeman, but could not immediately see one and instead went for a brandy, which he probably needed. He then went to fetch a piece of canvas with which to cover up the body. James Green appears to have returned directly to the workshop at 23a, whilst Henry John Holland, having dashed off to find a policeman, found one in Spitalfields Market. The constable, however, was on fixed point duty – under strict instructions not to leave his position under any circumstances – and told Holland to find another officer. Holland was so incensed that that afternoon he reported the constable at Commercial Street Police Station.

What is certain is that shortly after 6.00 a.m. Inspector Chandler, H Division[13], was on duty at the Commercial Street Station when he received information that a woman had been murdered in Hanbury Street. He proceeded to number 29, where he found plenty of people in the passage, but none in the yard.

Inspector Chandler sent for the Divisional Surgeon, Dr George Bagster Phillips, whose surgery was at 2 Spital Square, and to the Commercial Street Station for the ambulance and further assistance. Constables duly arrived and Chandler cleared all bystanders from the passage. From a neighbour he acquired some sacking with which he covered the body of Annie Chapman.

Dr Phillips arrived at Hanbury Street at 6.30 a.m. He viewed the body and ordered that it be taken to the mortuary in Old Montague Street, at the corner of Eagle Street, a cul-de-sac which ended in the green doors of the mortuary. The body was conducted there by Sergeant Edmund Berry, 31 H, in the same shell as was used to convey the body of Mary Ann Nichols. News of the murder had spread quickly and when the body was brought through the passage of the house to the street it was greeted by a crowd estimated to number several hundred and described as very excitable.

After the removal of the body, Inspector Chandler searched the yard. He found a piece of coarse muslin, a small pocket haircomb, a screwed up piece of paper containing two pills, and a portion of envelope which on one side had the letter 'M' in a man's handwriting and a post office stamp 'London, 28 August 1888'. On the reverse was the seal of the Sussex Regiment. According to the police report this portion of the envelope had

63

been picked up by Chapman in the lodging house[14].

On 14 Sepember Inspector Chandler made inquiries of the 1st Battalion, Sussex Regiment, at the North Camp, Farnborough, and learned that stationery bearing the regimental seal was on sale in the canteen and used by most of the men. Inquiries among the men failed to produce anyone who admitted to knowing or writing to anyone in Whitechapel. The pay books were also scrutinized, but none of the signatures matched the writing on the portion of envelope.

Inspector Chandler then spoke to Messrs Summer and Thirkettle, Postmasters at Lynchford Road Post Office. They told him that the letter had been posted there, but they did not know by whom. They told him that writing paper and envelopes bearing the regimental stamp were on sale to the public at the post office, so the letter could have been posted by anyone in the district.

Chandler believed that the envelope had been picked up by Chapman in the lodging house and he also said the lodging house was frequented by many strangers, so the envelope could have belonged to anyone.

At 7.00 a.m. Robert Mann, the pauper inmate of the Whitechapel Union who had charge of the mortuary and who received the body of Nichols, now received the body of Annie Chapman. Inspector Chandler arrived at the mortuary at about the same time and after checking that everything was secure, he left the body in the charge of PC Barnes, 376 H.

Two nurses from the infirmary, Mary Elizabeth Simonds and Frances Wright, were directed to undress the body (Mann left the mortuary whilst this was done). At the inquest Simonds said that she had been instructed by Inspector Chandler to do this. Chandler denied that he had ever issued any such instructions and the Coroner's Officer said that it had been done by order of the clerk of the Guardians. The nurses stripped the body and placed the clothes in a pile in the corner, though they left a handkerchief around the neck of Chapman. They then washed the body.

Meanwhile, Detective Sergeant Thicke[15], Sergeant Leach and other detective officers had arrived in Hanbury Street, and a telegram had been sent to Inspector Abberline at Scotland Yard. Sergeant Thicke went to the mortuary and took a description of the body, which was later circulated, and Abberline consulted with Inspector Helson, J Division, and Acting Superintendent West, who was in charge of H Division. They agreed that Annie Chapman had been murdered by the same man who had killed Mary Ann Nichols.

CHAPTER SIX

Saturday, 8 September 1888 – Sunday, 30 September 1888

(John Sanders, William Henry Pigott, John Pizer, Joseph Issenschmidt, Charles Ludwig, and others)

IT WOULD BE tedious to record every incident which took place during the course of the month. I have therefore only related incidents which were considered important at the time or which have assumed some importance since. Other events have been chosen because they convey a flavour of the atmosphere prevailing at the time.

Before examining the events of September 1888 in detail, it would be useful to gain some understanding of the broad line of action of the police following the murder of Annie Chapman. According to the police report, they searched the rooms and questioned the residents of 29 Hanbury Street and their neighbours; inquired at all common lodging houses about any bloodstained or otherwise suspicious individuals; made inquiries in an attempt to find Chapman's rings; and investigated all people who behaved suspiciously in the street or who were the subject of letters received from members of the public. But by far the most interesting remark in the report is: 'Enquiries were also made to trace three insane medical students who had attended London Hospital. Result two traced, one gone abroad.'[1]

This report is dated 19 October 1888, but it referred to investigations undertaken by the police at the time of Annie Chapman's murder. However, since the investigations into the murder of Mary Ann Nichols had been combined with those of Chapman's, it is possible that the three insane medical students had come to the attention of the police before Chapman's murder.

The police report was written in response to a request made on 13 October 1888 by Henry Matthews to Charles Warren for a report of all the measures which had been taken for the detection of the Whitechapel murderer. On 19 October, presumably under direction from Warren, Chief Inspector Donald Swanson copied and dated reports on each of the murders up to that date and these were submitted to Matthews. It is the report of Chapman which contains the reference to the medical students. These reports, together with a minute by Robert Anderson and a covering letter by Warren were sent to Matthews on 24 October 1888. Matthews wrote various notes and queries on the reports. Against the reference to the medical students he wrote 'When?', meaning 'when did the third student go abroad?'

Another document in the Home Office files[2] is a memorandum concerning a letter received from Sir Charles Warren. The memorandum contains notes and queries from a variety of people, including one to a Mr Murdoch from somebody who signed himself W T B. It reads:

> Please see Mr Wortley's pencil memo on Sir C Warren's letter. Shall the police be asked at the same time for report as to what has become of the 3rd insane medical student from the London Hosp.? about whom [the name under the name of Dr — is omitted]) there is a good deal of gossip in circulation.

A draft copy of the resulting letter to Warren, dated 29 October 1888, refers to the same question:

> Another question has arisen on the report forwarded by the Commissioner. Reference is made to three insane medical students, and it is stated that two have been traced and that one has gone abroad. Mr Matthews would be glad to be informed of the date when the third student went abroad and whether any further inquiry has been made about him.[2]

The reply to this query is to be found in the Scotland Yard files in a letter dated 1 November 1888 from Inspector Abberline to Sir Charles Warren:

> With regard to the latter portion of your letter I have to

state that searching enquiries were made by an officer in Aberdeen Place, St John's Wood, the last known address of the insane medical student named 'John Sanders', but the only information that could be obtained was that a lady named Sanders did reside with her son at number 20, but left that address to go abroad about two years ago.[2]

Nobody named Sanders lived at 20 Aberdeen Place in 1888 or in 1886 (or, indeed, prior to that date). John Sanders lived with his family at 20 Abercorn Place, St John's Wood. The Marylebone census of 1881 lists the Sanders family at that address and the Post Office London directories list Mrs Sanders as living there from 1874 to 1896 inclusive.

Laura T Sanders was the widow of an Army Surgeon and the mother of six children, four girls and two boys, all of whom were listed in the 1881 census as living at home. John W Sanders, who would have been 27 years old in 1888, was born in Milton, Kent, and was a medical student.

The only material about John Sanders possessed by the London Hospital Medical College is contained in the College Register Sheets. These state that he entered the Medical College on 22 April 1879; that he was an out-patient dresser during November and December 1880 and January 1881. There is then a very faint and barely legible pencil entry which reads: 'Away with Dr – for several months in 1882'. The name of the doctor is barely readable. The best reading that I have been able to obtain is 'Dr Swete'. John Sanders's name also appears in the Examination Book, but is marked: 'Retired because of ill health'.

I have only been able to find a reference to one Dr Swete who was practising in 1882. This was Edward Horatio Walker Swete, whose address in the 1888 *Medical Directory* and the 1889 *Medical Register* is given as Baskerville House, Worcester. Dr Swete's son, Horace Lawton Swete, was also a doctor, but did not practise until 1887.

According to an obituary (neither the source nor the date is given), Edward Horatio Walker Swete opened an establishment known as Dunmarklyn in Weston-super-Mare as a home for patients requiring 'special treatment'. He is listed as living there in the 1871 census, but neither he nor the home are mentioned in an 1872 directory. Nor does he appear on the 1881 census. By 1883 Dunmarklyn had become a school. The files of the Woodspring Central Library in Weston-super-Mare contain a note that in 1870 he was Honorary Medical Superintendent at the Royal West of England Sanitorium. This establishment had a fairly broad brief for the patients it would take, namely any convalescent who did not have an infectious disease. It is perhaps significant that the Sanitorium was officially opened in 1882, the year when John Sanders is reported to have been 'away with Dr Swete(?)'. I can find no evidence that he had any specific interest in mental illness. The only slightly indicative report is a reference in his obituary to a partnership formed about 1900 with a Dr Vernon when they opened an institution at Glentworth House, Weston-super-Mare, 'for medical-electro treatment'.

It would be very interesting to know why the police took an interest in these three men – and the fact that their inquiries were specifically mentioned in the report for the Home Secretary would alone indicate that they had a particular interest in them and that they were not simply among individuals who were the subject of general inquiries. Fortunately, this surmise is supported by the reference in the Home Office papers to John Sanders being the subject of 'a good deal of gossip'. This gossip does not appear to have reached the press, from which it must be assumed that it was circulating among the police and Home Office personnel at a fairly high level, which may indicate the importance given to Sanders as a suspect.

The only possible clue to the source of the information about Sanders is in *From Constable to Commissioner,* the autobiography of Sir Henry Smith[3], who was Chief Superintendent of the City Police at the time of the Ripper investigations. He wrote:

After the second crime I sent word to Sir Charles Warren that I had discovered a man very likely to be the man wanted. He certainly had all the qualifications requisite. He had been a medical student; he had been in a lunatic asylum; he spent all his time with women of loose character, whom he bilked by giving them polished farthings instead of sovereigns, two of those farthings having been found in the pocket of the murdered woman. Sir Charles failed to find him. I thought he was likely to be in Rupert Street, Haymarket. I sent up two men, and there he was, polished farthings and all, but he proved an alibi without shadow of doubt.

Was this man John Sanders or one of the two medical students reported in the files as having been found?

Finally, soon after the discovery of Annie Chapman's body an unnamed woman reported that she had been accosted in Spitalfields by a man who struck her several times and ran off when she started to scream. She said that the man had given her two brass medals, passing them off as sovereigns. It was reported that the police were investigating[4]. Whether or not this had the slightest bearing on the subject under discussion remains to be seen.

The day of Chapman's murder was when Robert Anderson departed for his month's rest in Switzerland, having recommended that Chief Inspector Donald Swanson take charge of the investigations. Another recommended appointment made that day was by Acting Superintendent West, who reported: 'Every possible inquiry is being made with a view to tracing the murderer, but up to the present without success. Local Inspector Reid being on his annual leave, the enquiries have been entrusted to Inspector Chandler and Police Sergeants Thicke and Leach CI Dept. I would respectfully suggest that Inspector Abberline, Central, who is well acquainted with H Division, be deputed to take up this enquiry as I believe he is already engaged in the case of the Buck's Row murder which would appear to have been committed by the same person as the one in Hanbury Street.'[5].

It soon became implanted in the public mind that the murders were so hideous that no Englishman could have sunk to such bestial depths and that they therefore had to be the work of a foreigner, by which a Jew was usually, though not exclusively, meant. That Saturday 'in several quarters in East London the crowds who had assembled in the streets began to assume a very threatening attitude towards the Hebrew population of the district . . . Happily the presence of a large number of police in the streets prevented a riot actually taking place', reported the *East London Observer*[6]. The Jews continued to be the focus for abuse throughout the week. The *Jewish Chronicle* reported: 'Without doubt the foreign Jews in the East End have been in some peril during the past week owing to the sensationalism of which the district has been the centre.'[7]

Greater interest in the crimes was beginning to be taken across the Atlantic. The *New York Times* carried a particularly florid report:

London, Sept. 8. – Not even during the riots and fog of February 1886, have I seen London so thoroughly excited as it is tonight. The Whitechapel fiend murdered his fourth victim this morning and still continues undetected, unseen, unknown. There is a panic in Whitechapel . . . The murder in all its details was inhuman to the last degree, and, like the others, could have been the work only of a bloodthirsty beast in human shape.

All day long Whitechapel has been wild with excitement . . . The London police and detective force is probably the stupidest in the world.

Such a series of murders has not been known in London for a hundred years . . . The murders are certainly the most ghastly and mysterious known to English police history. What adds to the weird effect they exert on the London mind is the fact that they occur while everybody is talking about Mansfield's 'Jeckyll and Hyde' at the Lyceum.

Aside from this local sensation Europe's little budget of trivial happenings seems hardly worth relating this week to a people who have such a genuine topic of interest as a Presidential campaign of their own.[8]

The correspondent of the *New York Times* certainly had a gift for building the murders to the height of sustained horror, only to reduce them to a 'local sensation' among a 'little budget of trivial happenings'. It is nevertheless interesting to note that in 1888, as in 1988, the United States was absorbed by the carnival of a presidential campaign – it was won by the

Republican Benjamin Harrison.

A second point of similarity is that in 1988 there is considerable debate about whether or not the portrayal of violence on television causes people to commit acts of violence in reality. Much the same concerns were raised in 1888 by the Whitechapel murders. The *Eastern Argus* complained of 'pictures of murders and assassinations' which had been pasted to various walls in the parish and asked if the Vestry had 'no control over this frightful method of inflaming the minds of weak and passionate men?'[9]

Others firmly laid the blame on serials in cheap magazines.

> It is only those whose duties cause them to be mixed up with the lower and criminal classes who can really appreciate how great is the evil influence of this pernicious literature . . . It is, to my mind, quite possible that the Whitechapel murders may be the fruit of such pernicious seed falling upon a morbid and deranged mind.[10]

That Saturday morning at 10 o'clock Amelia Farmer, Chapman's friend, having read a description of the murdered woman in a newspaper, went to the police station and said that she thought she knew her. At 11.30 a.m. she was taken to the mortuary and made a positive identification.

As Amelia Farmer gazed down on the mortal remains of her friend, several miles away, on the Rectory Field, Blackheath, the Blackheath Cricket Club were playing at home. In the Blackheath team was a man named Montague John Druitt, who in later years was to become the leading suspect.

At 7.00 a.m. on Sunday 9 September 1888 a strange man entered the Prince Albert Tavern (known locally as the 'Clean House') at the corner of Brushfield Street and Stewart Street. The landlady, Mrs Fiddymont, was talking to a friend, Mary Chappell, who lived in Stewart Street, when the man asked for half a pint of ale. It was noticed that there were spots of blood on the back of his right hand, dried blood between his fingers and a narrow streak of blood below his right ear. The man aroused further suspicion by hurriedly drinking his beer and leaving the pub.

Mary Chappell left the pub by a different door and drew

the man to the attention of a builder named Joseph Taylor who lived at 22 Stewart Street. Taylor pursued the man and drew abreast. The man looked at him. 'His eyes were as wild as a hawk's,' said Taylor, who said the man had a ginger moustache and short sandy hair. He did not further pursue the man, but watched him go as far as Dirty Dick's in Halfmoon Street. Taylor swore that he had seen the man coming out of a lodging house in Wilton Street very differently dressed, by which he seems to have meant more smartly dressed.

The *Yorkshire Post* reported:

> The police, who give information very unwillingly, and who do not accept the theory that the crime has been committed by the man designated 'Leather Apron', are indisposed to believe that the person seen by Mrs Fiddymont had any connection with the crime. They are unwilling, indeed, to accept any assistance or suggestion from any private source and work upon a plan of their own, which consists of frequent visits to common lodging-houses of the neighbourhood and a strict watch at night in all the streets in the vicinity.[11]

The unwillingness of the police to give information was such a common and frequent complaint that it must be regarded as true, but the police were certainly interested in and seem to have seriously suspected the man who entered Mrs Fiddymont's pub.

Meanwhile, throughout that Sunday large numbers – newspapers spoke of thousands – of well-dressed people turned up in Hanbury Street. Costermongers had set up stands and were enjoying a brisk trade selling fruit and refreshments. Sometimes the road became so crowded that the police had to charge at the spectators. Throughout Saturday and Sunday the people living either side of number 29 did business by making a small charge to view the yard where the murder had taken place or simply to view the crowds. People also visited the house in Dorset Street where Chapman had lodged.

At 4.00 p.m. in Gravesend a man named William Henry Pigott approached four young men and asked them where he could get a drink of water. They told him, but instead of following their instructions he jumped on a tramcar. At this time he was carrying a black bag. He was next seen by a Mrs Beitchteller who kept a fish shop. He did not now have the black bag, but instead carried a paper parcel, which he left at the shop and which was later recovered by Sergeant Berry of the local police, who found it contained two shirts, both marked with blood. Pigott told Mrs Beitchteller that he was going across the water to Tilbury, but instead he went to the Pope's Head tavern. Here his conversation, which apparently concerned his great hatred of women, attracted attention. He was reported to the police and a PC Vollensworth was sent to investigate. He found Pigott in a dazed state, unable to give a satisfactory account of himself, and having a wounded hand, which he refused to explain. Pigott was duly arrested.

At the police station Pigott made a rambling statement to the effect that on Friday night he had wandered the streets of the East End and at 4.00 a.m. on Saturday, whilst walking down Brick Lane, he had seen a woman fall in a fit. Whilst trying to pick her up he had been bitten on the hand by the woman and angered by the pain he had struck her. He had then seen two policemen approaching and had run off.

The divisional surgeon, Dr Whitcombe, was summoned and he examined the two shirts which had now been recovered from the fish shop. He pronounced that these were stained with blood and gave it as his opinion that blood had recently been wiped from Pigott's shoes.

Inspector Abberline was summond to Gravesend on Monday morning and returned to London with Pigott. A large crowd had gathered at Gravesend Railway Station to see Abberline and his prisoner depart, but since news of the arrest had not reached London their arrival at London Bridge passed almost unnoticed and they had a relatively quiet journey by four-wheeled cab to Commercial Street Police Station, where they arrived at 12.48 p.m.

At 2.30 p.m. Pigott was one of seventeen men placed in an identity parade before Mrs Fiddymont and other witnesses who unanimously declared that Pigott was not 'Leather Apron'. The police nevertheless decided to detain him and after a couple of hours his behaviour became so strange that Dr Phillips was summoned. He reported that Pigott's behaviour was not inconsistent with the onset of homicidal mania. Pigott was removed to the workhouse lunatic yard preparatory to being committed to an asylum.

Pigott was described as 52 years old, the son of a man who some years earlier had held a position with the Royal Liver Society. He had earlier been a publican, having paid some £8,000 for a pub in Hoxton. His movements at the time of the murders were eventually accounted for, but his ultimate fate is not recorded[12].

Pigott is a fairly typical example of the kind of person wandering around the streets at that time.

There were others. On 11 September Drs Cowan (10 Sandseer Road) and Crabb (Holloway Road) arrived at Holloway Police Station and reported that a man named Joseph Issenschmidt, who was then lodging at 60 Milford Road and who was known to them as a lunatic, was probably the perpetrator of the murders. The police went to the address given by the doctors and there spoke to a Mr George Tyler. He said that he had met Issenschmidt on 5 September and had provided him with accommodation. Issenschmidt left the house frequently over the next few days and was absent during the night in which Annie Chapman was murdered. The police then went to 97 Duncombe Road, Upper Holloway, where they spoke to Mrs Issenschmidt. During this and a subsequent interview they learned that she and Issenschmidt had been married for 21 years; that Issenschmidt was a journeyman butcher whose business at 59 Elthorne Road had failed; that as a result of this he had become very depressed, habitually stayed away from home, and had eventually spent ten weeks at Colney Hatch Asylum, being released in the middle of December 1887 as cured. He had obtained a job, but left it at Whitsun 1888.

By 17 September Issenschmidt was confined at the asylum at Bow. Sergeant Thicke visited the Medical Superintendent there and ascertained that Issenschmidt admitted to having told various women in Holloway that he was 'Leather Apron'. He claimed that he had only been teasing them, and he assumed his present predicament was caused by one of them having reported him to the police. He had also explained his frequent absences from his lodgings by saying that he was often at

75

market to collect sheeps' heads, feet and kidneys, which he dressed and sold to restaurants and coffee shops in the West End. He said that he had left his wife after an argument. On 18 September Abberline wrote:

> He has been previously confined in an asylum, and is said to be at times very violent. Although at present we are unable to procure any evidence to connect him with the murders he appears to be the most likely person that has come under our notice to have committed the crimes . . .

On 19 September Abberline submitted a report:

> I beg to add that the man Issenschmidt who was detained at Holloway on 12 inst., and handed over to the parochial authorities as a lunatic, is identical with the man seen in the Prince Albert, Brushfield Street, at 7.00 a.m. on the morning of the murder of Annie Chapman, by Mrs Fiddymont and other persons. This house is only about 400 yards from the scene of the murder . . . He is now confined in the Bow Infirmary Asylum, Fairfield Road, Bow, and Dr Mickle has been seen with a view to arrange for Mrs Fiddymont and other witnesses to see him, but the doctor thinks this cannot be done at present with safety to his patient. As time is of the greatest importance in this case, not only with regard to the question of identity, but also for the purpose of allaying the strong public feeling that exists, I would respectfully suggest that either the Chief Surgeon or one of the Divisional Surgeons may be requested to see Dr Mickle, the resident medical officer, to make if possible some arrangements for the witnesses to see Issenschmidt.

It was reported in the press that Issenschmidt was released as a harmless lunatic, though some years later he was readmitted to Colney Hatch and a photograph taken of him at that time shows him as very ferocious-looking. There is no mention in the files as to whether or not he was the man seen by Mrs Fiddymont. However, Abberline's report testifies to the interest taken by the police in Mrs Fiddymont's testimony.

Since the press seem to have taken increasingly little interest in Mrs Fiddymont and she is not mentioned again in the police files, it would seem that the man she saw was probably Issenschmidt and that he was probably not the Whitechapel murderer.[13]

Another individual of interest was Charles Ludwig who on Tuesday, 18 September 1888, was charged at Thames Police Court with being drunk and threatening to stab. Ludwig, who was about 40, 5ft 6 ins. in height, with a grizzled beard and moustache, had arrived in London from Hamburg some 15 months earlier and had met a hairdresser, C A Partridge, who had a shop in the Minories, at a German Club in Houndsditch. He gained employment with Mr Partridge and later took lodgings with a German tailor named Johannes in Church Street, Minories. Ludwig's habits eventually made him unwelcome and he moved to a hotel in Finsbury. Here he at one time produced several razors and acted in such a manner that he alarmed several other residents. On the day following the murder of Chapman he turned up at the hotel to wash his hands, claiming to have been injured. According to a witness, Ludwig had blood on his hands.

Early on the morning of 18 September, PC John Johnson, 866 City, was on duty in the Minories when he heard a cry of 'Murder!' come from Three Kings Court, which was only a few yards away from the hairdressing shop where Ludwig worked for Mr Partridge. PC Johnson responded to the cry and found Ludwig with a one-armed prostitute named Elizabeth Burns ('One-armed Liz'[14]), who appeared to be very frightened and said, 'Oh, policeman, do take me out of this.'

PC Johnson sent the man off and escorted Elizabeth Burns to the end of his beat, when she said, 'He frightened me very much when he pulled a big knife out.'

'Why didn't you tell me that at the time?' retorted PC Johnson. Burns replied that she had been much too frightened at the time. PC Johnson then made every effort to find the man, alerting other policemen as he met them.

Ludwig had in fact gone to a coffee stall in Whitechapel High Street. Standing at the coffee stall was Alexander Freinberg (an 18 year old Pole who had anglicized his name to Alexander Finlay and lived at 51 Leman Street). Ludwig turned to him. 'What you looking at?' he said in broken English. Freinberg apologised. 'Oh, you want something,' replied Ludwig, obviously seeking trouble, and pulled out a long penknife. Freinberg grabbed a dish from the coffee stall and prepared to throw it at Ludwig's head. Ludwig backed off and Freinberg summoned PC Gallagher, 221 H, who arrested Ludwig. On his appearance at the Thames Police Court later that morning Ludwig was remanded at the request of Inspector Abberline[14].

Considering that the likes of Pigott, Issenschmidt and Ludwig were wandering the streets of the East End – and they were by no means the only people picked up by the police who were violent and/or unstable – clearly weakens the theories that the Whitechapel murderer was someone like J K Stephen (a cousin of Virginia Woolf advanced as a suspect by Michael Harrison) or Frank Miles (a friend of Oscar Wilde, briefly advanced by Colin Wilson in his introduction to Rumbelow's book), for why seek the murderer among celebrities when there were any number of forgotten lunatics actually living in Whitechapel who are far more likely.

The subject of the greatest speculation, of course, was the mysterious 'Leather Apron', a soubriquet by which the Whitechapel murderer might have passed into history and possibly been forgotten if somebody had not written some letters and signed them 'Jack the Ripper'. Alternatively, the *East London Advertiser*'s nickname, 'The Red Terror', might have caught on[15].

The *Manchester Guardian* published the following description of the man known as 'Leather Apron' on 10 September:

> He is 5ft 4ins or 5ft 5ins in height and wears a dark, close fitting cap. He is thickset and has an unusually thick neck. His hair is close clipped. His age is about 38 to 40. He has a small black moustache. The distinguishing feature of costume is a leather apron, which he always wears, and from which he gets his nickname. His expression is sinister and seems to be full of terror for the women who describe it. His eyes are small and glittering. His lips are usually parted in a grin, but excessively repellent. He is a slipper maker by trade, but does not work. His business is blackmailing women late at night. A number of men in Whitechapel follow this interesting

profession. He has never cut anybody, so far as is known, but always carries a leather knife, presumably as sharp as leather knives are wont to be. This knife a number of women have seen. His name nobody knows, but all are united in the belief that he is a Jew or of Jewish parentage, his face being of a marked Hebrew type. But the most singular characteristic of the man is the universal statement that in moving about he never makes any noise. What he wears on his feet the women do not know, but they agree that he moves noiselessly. His uncanny peculiarity to them is that they never see him or know of his presence until he is close by them. 'Leather Apron' never by chance attacks a man. He runs away on the slightest appearance of rescue. One woman whom he assailed some time ago boldly prosecuted him for it, and he was sent up for seven days. He has no settled residence but has slept oftenest in a four-penny lodging house of the lowest kind in a disreputable lane leading from Brick Lane. The people in this lodging house denied that he had been there, and appeared disposed to shield him. 'Leather Apron's' pal, 'Micheldy Joe', was in the house at the time, and his presence doubtlessly had something to do with the unwillingness to give information. 'Leather Apron' was last seen at this house some weeks ago, though this account may be untrue. He ranges all over London, and rarely assails the same woman twice. He has lately been seen in Leather Lane, which is in Holborn.

This account has the appearance of being a journalistic invention and on the same day as it was published the *Manchester Guardian* gave the opinion that 'Leather Apron' was a more or less mythical personage. A Central News reporter stated that among the various goups of people huddled on the pavements over the weekend of Annie Chapman's murder:

The words most frequently heard in their conversation are 'Leather Apron'. The term has become a by-word of pavement and gutter, and one more often hears it accompanied by a guffaw than whispered in a tone which would indicate any fear of the mysterious individual who is supposed to live under that soubriquent. Whilst a large number of persons – including many members of the police force – firmly believe in the existence and almost certain guilt of the aproned one, the talk of the footways indicates that a large number of other inhabitants of the East End are sceptical as to his personality[16].

Among the people who claimed to know 'Leather Apron' was Timothy Donovan, the keeper of the lodging house at 30 Dorset Street, who not only claimed to 'know him well', but also to have once turned him out of the lodging house when he attacked a woman there[17].

At 8.00 a.m. on Monday 10 September 1888, Sergeant Thicke, accompanied by two or three other officers, went to 22 Mulberry Street, a street running off Commercial Road; almost opposite, on the other side of Commercial Road was Berner Street where another victim of Jack the Ripper would be murdered. A Jew named John Pizer[18] opened the door. 'You are just the man I want,' said Sergeant Thicke.

According to John Pizer:

> I asked him what for. He replied, 'You know what for. You will have to come with me.' I said, 'Very well, I will go with you with the greatest of pleasure.' The officer said, 'You know you are Leather Apron,' or words to that effect. Up to that time I did not know that I was known by that name. I have been in the habit of wearing an apron when coming from my employment, but not recently. When I arrived at the police station I was searched. They took everything from me, according to custom I suppose. They found nothing that could incriminate me, thank God, or connect me with the crimes that I have unfortunately been suspected of.[19]

John Pizer was the son of Israel Pizer and his wife August (née Cohen), the eldest of five known children – John, Jeannette, Gabriel, Barnett, and Samual G. He is generally stated to have been Polish, which was probably the case, though the 1871 and 1881 censuses state that all the children with the exception of John, who is not listed, and Samuel, who was born in Stepney, were born in Germany. However, in the 1881 census their mother, August, gave Germany as her birthplace, yet in the 1871 census both she and her mother, Leah, gave their birthplace as Russia/Poland, where Israel Pizer was also born. It is odd that neither census mentions John Pizer.

John was described as 'of about 5ft 4ins., with a dark-hued face, which was not altogether pleasant to look upon by reason of the grizzly black strips of hair nearly an inch in length, which was increased if anything by the drooping, dark moustache and side whiskers. His hair was short, smooth and dark, intermingled with grey, and his head was slightly bald on top. The head was large, and was fixed to the body by a thick, heavy-looking neck . . .' Pizer was also described as splay-footed, quietly spoken and insignificant[20].

Pizer was taken to Leman Street Police Station. A search of 22 Mulberry Street produced five long-bladed knives and several old hats. Pizer's friends protested his innocence and maintained that he was of a very delicate constitution.

A man named Emanual Delbast Violenia, described as half-Spaniard, half-Bulgarian, had gone to the police and explained that he was staying in Hanbury Street with his wife and children, having tramped from Manchester to London in anticipation of being able to emigrate to Australia. He had taken a lodging in Hanbury Street and early on Saturday morning he had seen a man and a woman quarrelling in that street and had heard the man threaten to knife the woman. At 1.00 p.m. on 10 September Inspector Cansby and Sergeant Thicke conducted a line-up of a dozen men, mostly Jews, at Leman Street. One of the men was John Pizer and Violenia unhesitatingly identified him as the man he had seen threaten the woman.

Pizer later told a newspaper reporter that Violenia was 'a stalwart man of negro caste, whom I know to be a boot finisher' – by which he presumably meant that he had discovered he was a boot finisher after the identification – who had placed a hand on his shoulder. 'I do not know you,' said Pizer. 'You must be mistaken.'

Violenia was then taken to the mortuary to view Chapman's body. It was reported that he could not identify the body as that of the woman he had seen in the company of Pizer. During that afternoon he was subjected to three hours of intensive cross-questioning and was found to contradict himself time after time. At 8.00 p.m. the officers agreed that his story was a complete fabrication. He was reprimanded for having wasted valuable police time.

Pizer was also questioned, but he was able to provide an alibi for his whereabouts on the nights of the murders of Nichols and Chapman. On the night of the former he had been staying at the Round House, the name by which Crossman's lodging house in Holloway Road was known. He had had supper there at about 11.00 p.m. on Thursday and had then gone out as far as the Seven Sisters Road, at which time he had seen the reflection of what was then called 'the Great London Docks Fire'.

There were two dock fires that night. The first broke out at about 9.00 p.m. in a huge warehouse at the London Docks. By 11.00 p.m. it was waning, though firemen were still at work at midnight. The second fire was reported at 12.55 a.m. It was at Ratcliffe Dry Dock, Stepney. Several warehouses caught fire, including one containing 800 tons of coal, and it took until morning to bring it under control. John Pizer said that he did not leave his lodging house until 11.00 a.m. at which time the London Docks fire was waning. This may have been the fire whose glow he saw in the sky. On the other hand, he did not return to his lodgings until 1.30 a.m., so it may have been the second, larger fire that he saw. On returning to his lodging he spoke to the lodging house keeper and to a police constable. His story was investigated and substantiated.

On the night of Annie Chapman's murder Pizer had been at home. He had arrived home at 10.45 p.m. that Thursday night, chatted with his sister's 'young man', then gone to bed. Apart from going into the yard of the house, Pizer had not poked his nose outdoors until he was arrested. At the inquest the following questions were put to Pizer by Wynne Baxter:

BAXTER: Why were you remaining indoors?
PIZER: Because my brother advised me.
BAXTER: You were the object of suspicion?
PIZER: I was the object of a (pause) false suspicion.
BAXTER: It was not the best advice that could be given you.
PIZER: I had proofs that I should have been torn to pieces.

Pizer later complained to the press that he would '. . . see if I cannot legally proceed against those who have made statements about me. The charges against me have quite broken my spirits, and I fear that I shall have to place myself under medical treatment.'

Pizer did in fact take out libel actions and it was reported that he received large sums, but this was denied by the *East London Advertiser*[21], which stated that 'more than one of them has been compromised, and for moderate amounts. Two or three of them, however, are still outstanding. The report that he has already received £5,000 is preposterously wide of the mark. £500 would, I should say, be a serious exaggeration.'

The story of John Pizer is an interesting one which may repay a careful review, in trying to gain some grasp of what those policemen involved in the case were thinking.

On 5 September 1888 *The Star* published a major feature on 'Leather Apron'. On 6 September it reported that Constables 47 J and 173 J (Bethnal Green Division) had actually had the 'crazy Jew' in their hands the previous Sunday (2 September). We do not know who this person could have been[22]. On 7 September Inspector Helson reported to Scotland Yard:

> The inquiry has revealed the fact that a man named Jack Pizer, alias Leather Apron, has for some considerable period been in the habit of illusing prostitutes in this, and other parts of the Metropolis, and careful search has been and is continued to be made to find this man in order that his movements may be accounted for on the night in question, although, at present, there is no evidence whatever against him.[23]

From this we know that Pizer was the subject of police inquiries prior to 7 September and that information about him had been received from someone who knew him well enough to call him by the familiar 'Jack'.

John 'Jack' Pizer was arrested by Sergeant Thicke on 10 September. On 11 September the *Daily News* reported:

> Detective Sergeant Thicke, H Division, who has long done duty in the district, receiving information which led

him to believe that a man known by the name of Leather Apron was to be found in Plummer's Row, also called Mulberry Street, succeeded in apprehending the man, whom he lodged in Leman Street Police Station. The man's name is Piser, a Jew, who certainly bears a remarkable resemblance to the published description of Leather Apron.

Martin Fido, who unearthed this interesting report, has pointed out that Mulberry Street was not also called Plummer's Row; Mulberry Street and Plummer's Row ran parallel with one another and were neighbouring streets. 'Since the *Daily News* mistakenly and unnecessarily identified Plumber's [sic] Row with Mulberry Street, it is certain that Plumber's [sic] Row was mentioned in the evidence identifying Leather Apron's whereabouts.'[24]

On 19 September Inspector Abberline wrote:

In the course of our inquiries amongst the numerous women of the same class as the deceased it was ascertained that a feeling of terror existed against a man known as Leather Apron who it appeared have [sic] for a considerable time past been levying blackmail and illusing them if his demands were not complied with. Although there was no evidence to connect him with the murders it was however thought desirable to find him and interrogate him as to his movements on the night in question, and with that view searching inquiries were made at all common lodging houses in various parts of the Metropolis, but through the publicity given in the 'Star' and other newspapers the man was made aquainted with the fact that he was being sought for and it was not until the 10th Inst. that he was discovered, when it was found that he had been concealed by his relatives. On being interrogated he was able, however, to give such a satisfactory account as to his movements as to prove conclusively that the suspicions were groundless.[25]

It has been suggested that Pizer stayed indoors because of the anti-Jewish feelings prevailing in the East End following the murder of Annie Chapman, but it is significant that he acted on his brother's advice on the night of Thursday 6 September, which, as Abberline pointed out in the above report, was the day following publication of the 'Leather Apron' feature in *The Star*. If Pizer was not 'Leather Apron' and did not know that he was referred to by this nickname, why did he hide indoors?'

Finally, there is a further report. *The Echo* on 20 September, a week after John Pizer had been allowed to clear himself formally at Chapman's inquest, reported:

> Inspector Reid, Detective Sergeant Enright, Sergeant Goadby [sic] and other officers then worked on a slight clue given them by 'Pearly Poll'. It was not thought much of at the time; but what was gleaned from her and other statements given by Elizabeth Allen and Eliza Cooper of 35 Dorset Street, Spitalfields, certain of the authorities have had cause to suspect a man actually living not far from Buck's Row. At present, however, there is only suspicion against him.

The impression received from all this information is that the police believed that John Pizer was known as 'Leather Apron' and that he was – or perhaps thought that he was – the man whom various prostitutes had accused of extorting money from them. However, he was not guilty of the Whitechapel murders and may not have been *the* 'Leather Apron'. The man against whom the police entertained suspicions and for whom they were still looking by 20 September apparently lived not far from Buck's Row, possibly in Plummer's Row. However, on 23 October, Robert Anderson, Assistant Commissioner CID, submitted a report in which he stated '. . . that five successive murders should have been committed without our having the slightest clue of any kind is extraordinary . . .'[26]. Whether or not the police believed that they had a lead in September, it would seem to have dried up by late October.

Other events during the month can be quickly summarized: Samuel Montague, MP for Whitechapel, having read about the murders, went to Leman Street Police Station and there asked an inspector if he knew whether the Government intended to offer a reward for information leading to the arrest

85

and conviction of the murderer. The Inspector said that he did not know. Montague then said that he believed that the Home Secretary was away from London and that there might therefore be some delay in his authorizing a reward. Montague asked for the police to offer a reward of £100 which was to be donated by himself. The Inspector said that he would submit the proposal to the Commissioner.

In the absence of Sir Charles Warren, who was still on holiday in the South of France, the Assistant Commissioner, Sir Alexander C Bruce[27], informed the Home Office. Attached to his letter there is a memorandum on which a Home Office official noted:

> The Home Office rule is against offering rewards . . . It is generally agreed that the Whitechapel murderer has no accomplices who could betray him. Any person, other than an accomplice, who possesses information, would be certain, in the present state of public feeling, to give it without prospect of a reward. On the other hand the offer of a reward would be almost certain to produce *false* information.

E Leigh Pemberton wrote to Warren on 13 September stating that the practice of offering rewards had been discontinued and that had it been thought necessary to make an exception in this case then the Secretary of State would have offered one on behalf of the Government[28]. Warren accordingly wrote to Montague on 17 September, but by this time Montague's offer was public knowledge and it was too late for it to be withdrawn[29].

Sir Charles Warren returned from France on Monday 10 September. The following day the Metropolitan Police issued the following very curious description of a man wanted for questioning in connection with the murder of Annie Chapman:

> Description of a man who entered the passage of a house at which the murder was committed of a prostitute at 2.00 a.m. on the 8th – age 37; height 5ft 7ins. rather dark beard and moustache. Dress: shirt, dark jacket, dark vest and

trousers, black scarf, and black felt hat. Spoke with a foreign accent.[30]

From whom did the police obtain this description? As far as is known nobody saw Annie Chapman between her leaving her lodging house and the reported sighting at 5.30 a.m. by Mrs Long of a man and woman talking outside 29 Hanbury Street – Mrs Long did not see the man, so she could not have given such a detailed description; she did not see the man and the woman enter the house; and, of course, she was not in Hanbury Street at 2.00 a.m. The only person we know of who could have given the description is Emanual Delbast Violenia, in which case the description is worthless, since Violenia's evidence was discredited and he was dismissed by the police the night before the description was published. Was there therefore a witness of whom we know nothing?

The Times of 11 September also gave birth to the 'lodger' theory and to the notion which has persisted to this day, namely that the Whitechapel murderer was not a member of the working classes. In the mistaken belief that the murderer would have been covered in blood, the newspaper argued that he 'came not from the wretched class from which the inmates of common lodging houses are drawn. More probably, it is argued, he is a man lodging in a comparatively decent house in the district, to which he would be able to retire quickly . . .'

On Tuesday 11 September 1888, Inspector Chandler, as a result of a request from the Coroner for a plan of the yard of 29 Hanbury Street and the neighbouring house, called at number 25. Here a little girl named Laura Sickings pointed out some marks in the yard. On examination these marks seemed to be blood – a bloody train, running for some five or six feet to the yard door of number 25 which gave rise to the belief that the murderer had escaped from number 29 by climbing over the fence and making his way to the street through the passage from the yard of number 25. Also found was a curious sprinkle of blood on a wall which gave the impression of someone having knocked a blood-soaked coat against it. Further, in the yard of Mr Bayley, the packing case manufacturer who occupied the yard of the Black Swan pub, was found a crumpled piece of paper almost saturated with blood. It was supposed that the murderer had found the paper in the yard of number 25, wiped his hands on it, and thrown it over the fence into Bayley's yard. The police who had searched the yard on the day of the murder were certain that the paper had not been there at that time. On 14 September the paper was subjected to analysis and it was reported that the stains were certified to be human blood[31].

During the morning of Friday 14 September, Annie Chapman was buried at Manor Park Cemetery. The burial had been arranged in the utmost secrecy by the undertaker, Mr H Hawes of Hunt Street, Mile End.

As the month progressed the police, Home Secretary, Coroner, and even Dr George Bagster Phillips, came in for criticism:

> It is clear that the Detective Department at Scotland Yard is in an utterly hopeless and worthless condition; that if there were a capable Director of criminal investigations, the scandalous exhibition of stupidity and ineptitude revealed at the East End inquests, and immunity enjoyed by criminals, murder after murder, would not have angered and disgusted the public feelings as it has done.

On the subject of the Government the same source was equally critical:

> We have had enough of Mr Home Secretary Matthews, who knows nothing, has heard nothing, and does not intend to do anything in matters concerning which he ought to be fully informed, and prepared to act with energy and despatch. It is high time that this hapless Minister should be promoted out of the way of some more competent man.[31]

Wynne Baxter was criticised by a correspondent in *The Times* for prolonging the inquest[32], whilst George Bagster Phillips received censure for not giving a full account of the injuries suffered by Annie Chapman, another correspondent pointing out that 'by the Statute de Coronatere, the coroner is bound to inquire the nature, character and size of every wound on a dead body . . . Originally this was done *super visum corpus* . . .

88

The object of the inquest is to preserve the evidence of the crime, if any . . .'[33]

Finally, on Wednesday 26 September 1888, Wynne E Baxter concluded the inquest into the death of Annie Chapman. During his summing up he proposed a theory about the motive of the murderer:

> The body had not been dissected, but the injuries had been made by someone who had considerable anatomical skill and knowledge. There were no meaningless cuts. The organ had been taken by one who knew where to find it, what difficulties he would have to contend against, and how he should use his knife so as to abstract the organ without injury to it. No unskilled person could have known where to find it or have recognised it when found. For instance, no mere slaughterer of animals could have carried out these operations. It must have been someone accustomed to the *post-mortem* room. The conclusion that the desire was to possess the missing abdominal organ seemed overwhelming.

In other words, Baxter argued that Annie Chapman had been murdered by a surgically skilled person with the specific purpose of obtaining the uterus. He then went on to reveal that he had recently learned that a few months earlier an American had visited several medical institutions in London wishing to procure specimens of the uterus, for which he was prepared to pay £20 apiece, his purpose being to preserve them in glycerine and issue one specimen with each copy of a publication on which he was working. The request had been turned down, but Baxter suggested that the American's request 'might have incited some abandoned wretch to possess himself of a specimen'.[34]

The theory gained immediate acceptance in the press, *The Times* on 27 September carrying a long commentary on the subject, but the response of the medical press was markedly different. The *British Medical Journal* retorted: 'This story, however, presents several inherent improbabilities, which will occur to every medical reader, and we cannot accept it as explaining much that still remains mysterious in this crime'[35].

The Lancet shared this view, saying that the purpose for which the organ was required was 'too grotesque and horrible for a moment to be entertained . . . The whole tale is almost past belief; and if, as we think, it can be shown to have grown in transmission, it will not only shatter the theory that cupidity was the motive of the crime, but will bring into question the discretion of the officer of the law who could accept such a statement and give it such wide publicity.'[36]

The *Law Journal*, as was to be expected, was less interested in the medical testimony than in the handling of the inquest. It thought that Baxter 'on the whole promoted the true function of the coroner's inquest'. However, it maintained that he should have summoned his informant so that his testimony could be given under oath; Baxter, who was not under oath, had repeated hearsay, an act which 'was technically out of order'[37].

Wynne Baxter's statement was nevertheless correct in its essentials. The *British Medical Journal* had investigated and found that though Baxter's informant had misinterpreted much of what he had overheard, a foreign physician some eighteen months or more earlier had indeed made inquiries regarding the possibility of acquiring specimens of the uterus[38]. Baxter's theory therefore had a certain though very loose validity.

The Central News Agency had by this time received a letter dated 25 September 1888, which not only bequeathed the soubriquet 'Jack the Ripper' to posterity – for this was the first time that it appeared – but was also the harbinger of a deluge of letters from some very twisted people. The Central News Agency did not make this letter public until 30 September.

In his autobiography Sir Robert Anderson wrote: 'I will only add here that the "Jack-the-Ripper" letter which is preserved in the Police Museum at New Scotland Yard is the creation of an enterprising London journalist.'[39] In his own copy of Anderson's book, Chief Inspector Donald Swanson noted in pencil that the identity of the journalist was 'known to Scotland Yard *head* officers of CID[40]. Sir Melville Macnaghten (see page 58) similarly ascribed authorship to a journalist. There seems to be no substantial reason for disbelieving Anderson and had his words only been noted a long time ago then much wasted handwriting analysis could have been more profitably applied elsewhere.

Anderson, of course, was still on holiday abroad. He wrote: 'The newspapers soon began to comment on my absence. And letters from Whitehall decided me to spend the last week of my holiday in Paris, that I might be in touch with my office'[41].

Anderson's holiday was to be shorter than he had anticipated.

CHAPTER SEVEN

Elizabeth Stride

(aka 'Long Liz')
(found murdered on Sunday, 30 September 1888)

ELIZABETH STRIDE was born Elisabeth Gustafsdotter on 27 November 1843. She was a daughter of a farmer named Gustaf Ericsson and his wife Beata Carlsdotter, whose farm was called Stora Tumlehed and was in the parish of Torslanda, north of Gothenburg in Sweden.

Her life prior to arriving in Britain has been well established. She was baptised on 5 December 1843, and in 1859 was confirmed in the church of Torslanda. On 14 October 1860 she took out a certificate of altered residence from the parish of Torslanda and moved to the parish of Carl Johan in Gothenburg, where she worked as a domestic for workman Lars Frederick Olofsson who had four children. On 2 February 1862 she moved again, taking out a new certificate, this time to the Cathedral parish of Gothenburg, but the details of her home address or place of work are not known. She still gave her profession as a domestic.

In March 1865 she was registered as a prostitute by the police of Gothenburg, and on 21 April gave birth to a still-born girl. In October and November she twice entered hospital for the treatment of venereal diseases.

On 7 February 1866, she took out a certificate from the Cathedral parish to the Swedish parish in London and on 10 July 1866, she was entered on the London register[1].

Charles Preston, who was living at the same lodging house as Elizabeth Stride at the time of her death, understood her to say that she had come to Britain in the service of a foreign gentleman[2] and Michael Kidney, with whom she had lived on and off until shortly before her death, said that Stride had come to Britain as a servant to a family at Hyde Park. He added that he believed her to have had relatives on her mother's side in Britain.[3]

On 7 March 1869 she married John Thomas Stride at the Parish Church, St Giles in the Fields. The service was conducted by Rev Will Powell and witnessed by Daniel H Wyatt and N Tayler. The marriage certificate gives Elizabeth Stride's maiden name as Gustifson and her father is described as Augustus Gustifson, labourer. She gave her address as 67 Gower Street.

John Thomas Stride gave his address and occupation as 21 Munster Street, Regent's Park, carpenter. He was the son of William Stride, a shipwright, and was born about 1821. He died on 24 October 1884 at the Sick Asylum, Bromley. The death certificate gives his age as 63 and his address as the Poplar Union Workhouse.[4]

Stride told several people that she and her husband had kept a coffee shop in Chrisp Street, Poplar. I have not been able to find any record of a coffee shop registered in the name of Stride in Chrisp Street, but a John Thomas Stride appears in Kelly's trade directory for 1870 as keeping a coffee room in Upper North Street, Poplar. In 1872 he moved to 178 Poplar High Street, and remained there until the business was taken over by John Dale in 1875.

At about 8.00 p.m. on Tuesday 3 September 1888, the saloon steamer *Princess Alice* collided in the Thames with a large screw steamer, *Bywell Castle,* and sank with the terrible loss of 600 – 700 lives. *The Times* called it 'one of the most fearful disasters of modern times'.[5] Stride claimed that she and her husband had been employed aboard the *Princess Alice* and that her husband and two children had died in the tragedy.

At the inquest Wynne Baxter took a harsh approach to Sven Olsson of the Swedish Church in London when he commented on Stride's *Princess Alice* story. 'Do you remember that there was a subscription raised for the relatives and sufferers by the *Princess Alice*?' asked Baxter. Olsson said that he did not. 'I can tell you there was,' said Baxter. 'And I can tell you another thing – that no person of the name of Stride made any application. If her story had been true, don't you think she would have applied?' Olsson, who quite rightly could not justifiably speculate about what Stride may or may not have done, said that he did not know.[6]

93

Notwithstanding the fact that nobody named Stride appears among the passengers or crew of the *Princess Alice,* several newspapers on 8 October 1888, carried what could seem to have been a news agency story:

> With reference to the identity of Elizabeth Stride, the Woolwich newspapers of the time of the Princess Alice disaster have been referred to, and it has been found that a woman of that name was a witness at the inquest and identified the body of a man as her husband, and of two children then lying in Woolwich Dockyard. She said she was on board and saw them drowned, her husband picking up one of the children, and being drowned with it in his arms. She was saved by climbing the funnel, where she was accidently kicked in the mouth by a retired arsenal police inspector, who was also clinging to the funnel. The husband and two children are buried in Woolwich Cemetery.[7]

Several searches of the Woolwich newspapers have failed to produce Elizabeth Stride's story. Curiously, and presumably coincidentally, among those who died aboard the *Princess Alice* was Mr W A Fisher of 43 Chrisp Street; Chrisp Street being where Stride claimed to have had a coffee shop.

By 1882 Elizabeth Stride was living at 32 Flower and Dean Street in Spitalfields[8]. By 1885 she had taken up with a waterside labourer named Michael Kidney and was living with him at 33 Dorset Street. He said that Stride sometimes left him and went off on her own. They had lived apart for about five months in the three years they had lived together[9].

On 20 and 23 May 1886, the records of the Swedish Church show that Elizabeth Stride applied for and received financial aid. At that time she gave her address as Devonshire Street, off Commercial Road[10]. She received further aid on 15 and 20 September 1888, and on Tuesday 25 September, Michael Kidney saw her for the last time. They had parted in Commercial Street. He had expected Stride to be at home when he returned from work, but she was not there. He was not particularly alarmed. Stride had gone off before. 'It was drink that made her go away,' he said. 'She always returned without me going after her.'[11] According to a woman named Catherine Lane, Stride said that she had left Kidney after a row[12], but at the inquest Kidney denied this.

On Thursday 27 September 1888, Elizabeth Stride took lodgings at 32 Flower and Dean Street. She had stayed there before, but not within the previous three months.

On the afternoon of Saturday 29 September 1888 Elizabeth Stride cleaned the rooms at 32 Flower and Dean Street for the lodging house deputy, Elizabeth Tanner, and received a payment of 6d. Mrs Tanner knew Stride only by the nickname 'Long Liz'. She described her as a very quiet woman who sometimes stayed out late at night and did cleaning work for the Jews. She said Stride spoke without any trace of an accent. Mrs Ann Mill, a bedmaker at the lodging house, said that Stride worked when she could get work and added that 'a better hearted, more good natured cleaner woman never lived'.[13]

Elizabeth Tanner next saw Stride at 6.30 p.m. in the Queen's Head, a public house in Commercial Street. Stride evidently did not stay there for very long because she was seen in the lodging house between 7.00 p.m. and 8.00 p.m. by Charles Preston and Catherine Lane. Stride was preparing to go out. Before leaving she gave Lane a piece of velvet to look after until she came back. She also borrowed a clothes brush from Charles Preston. She then left[14]. Thomas Bates, the watchman at the lodging house, said that she looked quite cheerful.

40 Berner Street, the scene of Stride's murder, was an ordinary house which had been converted for use as a social club, the International Workers' Educational Club, which had been founded in 1884 by a group of Jewish socialists. One who knew the Club intimately described it as:

> an old wooden building . . . The Club was spacious with a capacity of over 200 people and contained a stage. Here were performed by amateurs, mostly in Russian language, plays by well known Russian revolutionists – Chaikovsky, Volchovsky, Stepniak . . . Invariably, on Saturday and Sunday, there was a truly international gathering of Russian, Jewish, British, French, Italian,

Czech, Polish and other radicals . . . Quite often the renowned radical poet, William Morris was seen there reading his splendid verses . . . Like Faneuil Hall in Boston, Berner Street Club was the 'Cradle of Liberty' for the workers' emancipation from economic slavery[15].

The Club also became the patron of the leading Jewish radical journal *Arbeter Fraint* (*Worker's Friend*), which had been founded by Morris Winchevsky (real name Leopold Benedikt) and first appeared on 15 July 1885. *Arbeter Fraint* was then published every month from 29a Fort Street, off Brushfield Street, but when, in June 1886, the Club took over the paper, it began to appear weekly, being supplied with a brick-built printing and editorial office in the yard behind the Club. *Arbeter Fraint* attracted many bright young immigrant writers and intellectuals, among them the editor, Philip Kranz[16].

The Club did not have a savoury reputation with people living in the neighbourhood. Abraham Heahbury, who lived at 28 Berner Street, told a journalist that 'there are generally rows there . . . There was a row there last Sunday night. It went on until two in the morning and in the end two people were arrested.' Barnett Kentorrich, of 38 Berner Street, which adjoined the Club, said, 'The club is a nasty place.' And a young man who was in the crowd when the reporter was making inquiries, said, 'You see, the members are "bad" Jews – Jews who don't hold their religion – and they annoy those who do in order to show their contempt for the religion . . .' Such was the outsiders' view of the Jewish radicals who used the Berner Street 'Cradle of Liberty'.

On the ground floor there was a single window and a door. The door gave access to a hallway which ran the full length of the house. One door led off the hall into the front room, used as a dining room; in the middle of the hall there was a staircase leading to the first floor; beyond the staircase was a door leading into the rear ground floor room, used as a kitchen. Beyond this there was a further door, this one leading into a passage which ran along the side of the house.

On the first floor there was a room used for entertainments. 'Plain benches without backs stretched through it crosswise and along the walls . . . On the walls hung a number of portraits: Marx, Proudhon, Lassalle overthrowing the golden calf of capitalism . . . At the front the room was enclosed by a small stage . . .'[17] The room had three windows, all looking out on the rear yard of the building.

At the side of the house there was a gateway, 9 – 12ft wide, with two wooden gates folding backwards from the street. One of the gates had a small door set in it. Beyond the gates there was a passage which ran the length of the house and which gave access to the rear entrance, opposite which there were two lavatories. The passage led into a yard known as Dutfield's Yard, after Mr Arthur Dutfield, van and cart manufacturer, who carried on business there. On the left-hand side of the yard there was a single house occupied by two or three tenants. Opposite the gates was a workshop occupied by Walter Hindley, sack manufacturer. The only access or egress was through the gates. Adjoining the workshop was an unused stable and next to this the rear of the Club, onto which had been built a stone office consisting of two rooms, one used by the editor of *Arbeter Fraint* and the adjoining one used as a composing room. There was no light of any kind in the passage or the yard. The only illumination came from the Club, the *Arbeter Fraint* offices and the house in the yard.

That night, Saturday 29 September 1888, there was a meeting and discussion in the large first floor room. About 90 – 100 people attended. It ended between 11.30 p.m. and midnight. Most of the people left the Club by the street door, 20 – 30 people remaining behind. About a dozen were downstairs. The rest were in the upstairs room, either talking in small groups or singing.

Some 200 yards from the murder scene was Settles Street and it was here, shortly before 11.00 p.m., that J Best of 82 Lower Chapman Street, and John Gardner of 11 Chapman Street, saw a man with a woman whom they felt certain was Stride, outside the Bricklayer's Arms. 'They had been served in the public house, and went out when me and my friends came in,' said Mr Best. 'It was raining very fast and they did not appear willing to go out. He was hugging her and kissing her, and as he seemed a respectably dressed man, we were rather astonished at the way he was going on with the woman . . .' Best and his friends chaffed the man. Eventually 'he and the woman went off like a shot soon after eleven.'[18]

The man seen by Best, Gardner, and their friends was described as 5ft 5ins. in height. He was well dressed in a black morning suit and coat. He sported a thick, black moustache, but was otherwise clean shaven. He also did not have any eyelashes. He wore a black billycock hat.

An elderly man named Matthew Packer who sold fruit from the front room of 44 Berner Street claimed that between 11.00 p.m. and midnight on the night of the murder he sold some grapes to a man and a woman. He later identified the woman as Elizabeth Stride and on 1 October the newspapers reported several people as saying that Stride was clutching a bunch of grapes when her body was found.

It is very difficult to assess the truth of Mr Packer's story and the truth of whether or not Stride was clutching any grapes. Louis Deimschutz, who discovered the body, told a reporter for the *Evening News* that Stride's hands were tightly clenched. When they were opened by the doctor, sweets were seen to be clenched in one hand, grapes in the other[19]. However, Abraham Heahbury, who was one of the first on the scene said only that, 'In her hand there was a little piece of paper containing five or six cachous[20]'. Another witness early at the scene, Edward Spooner, told the inquest that Stride had only a 'piece of paper doubled up in her right hand.'[21] Also, at the inquest Dr Phillips said that 'neither on the hands nor about the body did I find any grapes, or connection with them. I am convinced the deceased had not swallowed either the skin or seed of grape within many hours of death'. However, he did say that on the larger of two handkerchiefs found on the body he found stains which he believed to be of fruit.[22]

The facts as far as I have been able to establish them are that the Vigilance Committee, which had been set up by local traders, together with several newspapers, had hired a couple of private detectives, a Mr Grand and Mr J H Batchelor of 283 Strand. These men learned that before the police had washed down the passage where Stride's body was found, a Mrs Rosenfield and her sister Miss Eva Harstein of 14 Berner Street had seen a blood-caked grape stalk and some white flower petals in the passage. On 2 October the private detectives searched the drain in the yard and found a grape stalk among the refuse swept away after the passage had been examined by the police.

They then questioned Packer, who said that he had sold some grapes to a man and a woman. On 4 October 1888, they took Packer to the mortuary, where he identified the woman to whom he had sold the grapes as Elizabeth Stride. That evening the *Evening News* and other newspapers gave emphasis to Packer's story, particularly to Packer's claim that he had not been questioned by the police.

Sergeant Stephen White had in fact interviewed Packer about 9.00 a.m. on the morning of the murder, 30 September, when he said: 'I saw no one standing about, neither did I see anyone go up the yard. I never saw anything suspicious or heard the slightest noise. And I knew nothing about the murder until I heard of it this morning[23].'

Packer subsequently changed his story several times. He said to the majority of newspapers that he had sold the grapes at 11.00 p.m.; the *Evening News* on the 4 October twice reported that he had sold the grapes at 11.45 p.m.; and in the other accounts he sold the grapes at midnight.

Chief Inspector Swanson, in a report to the Home Secretary, wrote: 'It was not until after the publication in the newspapers of the description of the man seen by the PC (this was PC William Smith, see below) that Mr Packer gave the foregoing particulars to two private enquiry men . . . Packer, who is an elderly man, has unfortunately made different statements so . . . any statement he made would be rendered almost valueless as evidence[24].'

Whether or not Elizabeth Stride was clutching any grapes when found cannot be known for certain, nor is it certain that it was to Stride that Mr Packer sold grapes that night. But if he did sell grapes to Stride, he was not the last person to see her alive, so his testimony is not vitally important and in the circumstances must be regarded as so unreliable as to be best set aside.

At about 11.45 p.m. a labourer named William Marshall was standing at the door of his lodging at 64 Berner Street. Outside number 63 a man and a woman were standing. He did not pay them any attention until he saw them kiss and overheard the man say, 'You would say anything but your prayers.' The couple then went down the street. Marshall described the man as wearing a small black coat and dark trousers; round cap with a peak of the type that sailors wore; he looked to be middle aged, about 5ft 6 ins. in height, rather stout; he was clean shaven and did not carry gloves or a stick[25].

Also about this time, Morris Eagle, a Russian who lived at 4 New Road, off Commercial Road, and was a traveller in jewellery, left the Club, where he had that night occupied the Chair and opened the discussion, to take his sweetheart home. He left by the street door.

At 12.30 a.m. on Sunday 30 September 1888 PC William Smith, 452 H[26], passed up Berner Street on his beat. He saw a man and a woman. He later immediately identified the body of Elizabeth Stride as being that of the woman he had seen. She was wearing a red flower pinned to her jacket. The man was aged about 28, was 5ft 7ins. in height, of dark complexion and sporting a small dark moustache. He was wearing a black diagonal coat, hard felt hat, white collar and tie[27].

Mrs Fanny Mortimer, the wife of a carman named William Mortimer, who lived at 36 Berner Street, told a reporter of the *Evening News* that at about 12.45 a.m. she 'heard the measured, heavy stamp of a policeman passing the house on his beat. Immediately afterwards she went to the street door' and remained standing there for ten minutes. She saw no one enter or leave the yard gates. She returned indoors and bolted the door some five or six minutes before Stride's body was discovered[28].

If it was a policeman who passed her house then Mrs Mortimer must have gone to her door shortly after PC Smith passed at 12.30 a.m. Several newspapers later reported this to have been the case, saying that Mrs Mortimer had been at her door for the half hour between 12.30 a.m. and 1.00 a.m. This was not the case. As we shall see, there are three pieces of testimony which fix when Mrs Mortimer was in her doorway.

Also at 12.30 a.m. Charles Letchford, who lived at 39 Berner Street, walked up the road. 'Everything seemed to me to be going on as usual,' he said[29].

William West, who lived at 2 William Street and was overseer of the *Arbeter Fraint* printing office, left the Club at about 12.30 a.m. by the side entrance and went into the printing office to return some literature. The editor, Philip Kranz, was there reading. West returned to the Club, again by the side entrance, and looked towards the gates. He saw nothing unusual. However, he admitted to being short-sighted and said that if the body had been there he might not have noticed it[30].

At 12.35 a.m. Morris Eagle, having accompanied his young lady home, returned to the Club with the intention of having some supper. He found the front door locked, so went through the gates and down the passage to the rear door. It was very dark by the gates and he could not be sure that a body was not lying there, but he did not see anything. On entering the Club he went upstairs and joined a friend who was singing a Russian song.

A man named Joseph Lave, who had only recently arrived in Britain from the United States (though he was born in Russia) and was living at the Berner Street Club until he could find permanent lodging, told a representative of the press that about twenty minutes before the discovery of the body he had gone into the yard to get a breath of fresh air. 'I walked for five minutes or more,' he said, 'and went as far as the street. Everything was very quiet at the time, and I noticed nothing wrong.'[31]

We now come to an important piece of testimony – possibly the most important testimony with regard to the murder of Elizabeth Stride in particular and to the Whitechapel murders in general. The witness never gave evidence at the inquest and his testimony remained largely unknown until the Home Office files were opened to public inspection. The information is therefore missing from almost every book on the subject of the Ripper murders.

According to the Home Office file[32]:

Israel Schwartz of 22 Helen Street, Backchurch Lane, stated that at this hour, on turning into Berner Street from Commercial Street, and having got as far as the gateway where the murder was committed, he saw a man

101

stop and speak to a woman, who was standing in the gateway. The man tried to pull the woman into the street, but he turned her round and threw her down on the footway and the woman screamed three times, but not very loudly. On crossing to the opposite side of the street, he saw a second man standing lighting his pipe. The man who threw the woman down called out, apparently to the man on the opposite side of the road, 'Lipski', and then Schwartz walked away, but finding that he was followed by the second man, he ran as far as the railway arch, but the man did not follow so far.

Schwartz cannot say whether the two men were together or known to each other. Upon being taken to the mortuary Schwartz identified the body as that of the woman he had seen . . .

Later in the report:

It will be observed that allowing for differences of opinion between the PC and Schwartz as to the apparent age and height of the man each saw with the woman whose body they both identified, there are serious differences in the description of dress . . . so that at least it is rendered doubtful whether they are describing the same man.

If Schwartz is to be believed, and the police report of his statement casts no doubt upon it, it follows if they are describing different men that the man Schwartz saw and described is the more probable of the two to be the murderer . . .

The word 'Lipski', as Abberline explained in a report to the Home Office[33], was used to insult Jews, having become so since the murder of a woman in 1887 by a Jew named Lipski. In the same report Abberline wrote:

I questioned Israel Schwartz very closely at the time he made the statement as to whom the man addressed when he called Lipski, but he was unable to say. Also, it was never ascertained whether the man lighting his pipe ran after Schwartz or ran because he, too, was alarmed by the man who had thrown the woman to the ground.

Henry Matthews, the Home Secretary, made two interesting comments on the report by Swanson. One was that the use of the word 'Lipski' increased his belief that the murderer was a Jew. Matthews made this comment before he had received Abberline's explanation of what the word meant – an explanation which perhaps indicates that the man seen by Schwartz was not a Jew, for would one Jew have used a racially derogatory expression to another? But what reason did Matthews have for suspecting that the murderer was a Jew in the first place? Had Matthews, too, succumbed to the absurd anti-semitic argument that the murders were too horrible to have been committed by a gentile Englishman, or were there more tangible reasons for his statement?

The second observation was: 'The police apparently do not suspect the second man Schwartz saw and who followed Schwartz.'

There is no further mention of this second man in the police or Home Office files and we do not know whether he ever made contact with the police.

Schwartz described the man who assaulted Elizabeth Stride (for it was almost certainly Stride whom Schwartz had seen) as about 30, 5 ft 5 ins., with a fair complexion, dark hair, small brown moustache, full face and broad shoulders. He was wearing a dark jacket and trousers, and a black cap with a peak.

The second man was described as 35, 5 ft 11 ins., with fresh complexion, light brown hair and brown moustache. He was dressed in a dark overcoat and an old black hard felt hat with a wide brim.

As far as I have been able to ascertain Schwartz's testimony was only reported in one newspaper, the *Star*[34]. Such is the importance of Schwartz's testimony, it is worth quoting the article in full:

Information which may be important was given to the Leman Street police yesterday by an Hungarian concerning this murder. This foreigner was well-dressed, and had the appearance of being in the theatrical line. He could not speak a word of English, but came to the police station accompanied by a friend, who acted as

103

interpreter. He gave his name and address, but the police have not disclosed them. A *Star* man, however, got wind of his call, and ran him to earth in Backchurch Lane. The reporter's Hungarian was quite as imperfect as the foreigner's English, but an interpreter was at hand, and the man's story was retold just as he had given it to the police. It is, in fact, to the effect that he saw the whole thing.

It seems that he had gone out for the day, and his wife had expected to move, during his absence, from their lodgings in Berner Street to others in Backchurch Lane. When he came homewards about a quarter before one he first walked down Berner Street to see if his wife had moved. As he turned the corner from Commercial Road he noticed some distance in front of him a man walking as if partially intoxicated. He walked on behind him, and presently he noticed a woman standing in the entrance to the alleyway where the body was found. The half-tipsy man halted and spoke to her. The Hungarian saw him put his hand on her shoulder and push her back into the passage, but feeling rather timid of getting mixed up in quarrels, he crossed to the other side of the street. Before he had gone many yards, however, he heard the sound of a quarrel, and turned back to learn what was the matter, but just as he stepped from the kerb a second man came out of the doorway of the public house a few doors off, and shouting out some sort of warning to the man who was with the woman, rushed forward as if to attack the intruder. The Hungarian states positively that he saw a knife in the second man's hand, but he waited to see no more. He fled incontinently, to his new lodgings.

He described the man with the woman as about 30 years of age, rather stoutly built, and wearing a brown moustache. He was dressed respectably in dark clothes and felt hat. The man who came at him with a knife he also describes, but not in detail. He says he was taller than the other, but not so stout, and that his moustaches were red. Both men seem to belong to the same grade of society. The police have arrested one man answering the description the Hungarian furnishes. This prisoner has

104

not been charged, but is held for inquiries to be made. The truth of the man's statement is not wholly accepted.

Bearing in mind that Chief Inspector Swanson wrote to the Home Office that the police report of Schwartz's testimony 'casts no doubt' on the honesty of his statement, we may safely disregard the final observation of the *Star*'s reporter. However, Schwartz's story as reported in the *Star* differs in several important respects from that given in the police reports. First, the man does not appear to have been the same as the one seen with Stride by other witnesses that night, although it is possible that the couple had separated and the man was in the process of returning to Stride when observed by Schwartz. Secondly, the man pushed Stride *into* the passage; there is no mention of him throwing Stride to the pavement. Thirdly, there was a quarrel between the woman and the man. Fourthly, the second man carried a knife, whereas to the police Schwartz said that this man had simply been lighting his pipe. Fifthly, this second man apparently shouted at the first – which is interesting; if the second man shouted 'Lipski', then it suggests that the man who attacked Stride was or appeared to be Jewish; there is also the possibility that the second man's intention was to go to the aid of Stride. Finally, no further mention is made of the second man having run after Schwartz.

It is difficult to know what to make out of these different reports, but the police evidently placed sufficient importance on Schwartz's testimony to refer to it at length in reports to the Home Office. Also, Schwartz does not appear to have testified at the inquest – or, if he did, his testimony was not reported in the press. This may mean that his evidence was regarded as unreliable, yet the reports to the Home Office were written *after* the inquest. The inference must therefore be that the police decided not to make Schwartz's testimony public. Either that or Schwartz refused to testify. Either way, as we shall see, his failure to testify is significant.

Further testimony was given by a dock labourer named James Brown, who lived at 35 Fairclough Street. He was returning with his supper from a chandler's shop at the corner of Fairclough Street and Berner Street when he saw a man and a woman standing outside the board school in Fairclough

Street. The woman had her back to the wall, and the man had his arm against the wall, looking as if he was impeding her. As Brown passed, he heard the woman say: 'No. Not tonight. Some other night.' Brown turned to look. He was almost certain that the woman was Elizabeth Stride. The man, he said, was about 5 ft 7 ins., stoutish, and wore a long coat which very nearly reached his heels. Brown walked on. He had very nearly finished eating when he heard cries of 'Police!' and 'Murder!' He estimated that this was about a quarter of an hour after he had got in.[35] Brown may not in fact have seen Elizabeth Stride. At 11.45 p.m. a woman who was probably Stride was seen by William Marshall with a man who fitted the description of the man whose assault on a woman was observed by Schwartz. The woman seen by Marshall and Schwartz had a flower pinned to her jacket. Brown did not see any flower and his description of the man differs from that of the man seen by Marshall and Schwartz. Moreover, the man and woman seen by Brown were standing in a particularly dark place, shrouded by the shadows. Brown merely glanced at them and had no reason to pay any great attention to them, whilst Marshall had watched a couple in reasonable visibility for nearly ten minutes, and Schwartz, frightened by the assault that he had witnessed, had good reason to remember the man and woman he had seen. Finally, we know that for twenty minutes, from about 12.40 a.m. an unnamed young girl was standing with her boyfriend in an unspecified 'bisecting thoroughfare'. This couple are briefly mentioned in the *Evening News* of 1 October 1888 and they could have been the couple seen by Brown.

To return briefly to the testimony of Mrs Fanny Mortimer, many newspapers report her as saying that she had been standing outside her house from 12.30 a.m. until 1.00 a.m. She said that she had gone to the door shortly after hearing the measured tread of a policeman passing by and that she had bolted the door some four or five minutes before she heard a man named Louis Diemschutz pass by in his pony and cart.

The only policeman known to have passed up Berner Street was PC William Smith at 12.30 a.m. If Mrs Mortimer had indeed been standing outside her house from that time then she would have seen Morris Eagle return to the Club at 12.35 a.m., Joseph Lave on his stroll at or about 12.40 a.m., and the assault on Stride at 12.45 a.m. That she saw none of these people suggests that she is either a worthless witness or that she was wrong about the time.

That Mrs Mortimer got the time wrong is almost certain. A report in the *Evening News,* 1 October 1888, referring to Mrs Mortimer, says, 'It appears that shortly before a quarter to one o'clock she heard the measured heavy tramp of a policeman passing the house on his beat. Immediately afterwards she went to the street door with the intention of shooting the bolts, though she remained standing there ten minutes before she did so.'

Mrs Mortimer herself said that the only man she had seen in Berner Street 'was a young man carrying a black shiny bag who walked very fast down the street from the Commercial Road. He looked up at the club, and then went round the corner by the board school . . .'[36]. This man was Leon Goldstein of 22 Christian Street and he presented himself at Leman Street Police Station on the day after the murder. He said that he had passed through Berner Street shortly before the discovery of Stride's body, that his bag contained empty cigarette boxes and that he had left a coffee house in Spectacle Alley a short time before[32]. Goldstein's statement puts Mrs Mortimer in the street for ten minutes immediately prior to 1.00 a.m. This may be confirmed by Charles Letchford, who passed through the street at 12.30 a.m. and said that his sister had been standing outside her house for ten minutes from 12.50 a.m. It would seem probable that Mrs Mortimer was Letchford's sister.

Louis Diemschutz was a traveller in cheap jewellery who for the past six years had acted as Steward of the Berner Street Club. He was returning from Westow Market at Westow Hill, Crystal Palace, which he usually visited on Saturdays. He returned to the Club in his pony and cart at 1.00 a.m. or a minute or two later – he noticed the time at a tobacco shop in Commercial Road – to drop off some goods with his wife before taking his pony on to its stables in George Yard.

> My pony is rather shy and as I turned into the yard it
> struck me that he bore too much towards the left hand
> side against the wall. I bent my head to see what it was

shying at, and I noticed that the ground was not level. I saw a little heap which I thought might be some mud. I touched the heap with the handle of my whip, and then I found that it was not mud. I jumped off the trap and struck a match. When I saw that it was the body of a woman I ran indoors.'[37]

Elizabeth Stride was lying on her back close to the wall by the gates of the Club, her feet pointing towards the street. Her face was turned towards the wall. Her left arm was extended and there was a packet of cachous – a pill used by smokers to sweeten the breath – in her hand. A number of the cachous were in the gutter. Her right arm was over her belly. She was *not* clutching any grapes. The hand and wrist of the right hand were covered in blood. The legs were drawn up, with the feet close to the wall. There was mud on the left side of the face and matted in the hair. Over both shoulders there was a bluish discolouration which in the opinion of Dr Frederick Blackwell had been caused 'by two hands pressing on the shoulders'.

Stride's throat had been cut. The incision was 6 inches in length and commenced 2½ inches in a straight line below the angle of the jaw; ¾ of an inch deep over an undivided muscle, then becoming deeper. The cut was very clean and deviated a little downwards. The left carotid artery had been severed, from which death had resulted.

When the post-mortem was conducted the doctors reported that Stride's stomach contained cheese, potato, and farinacious powder. There was no trace of grape skin or pip. The medical opinion was certain that Stride had *not* eaten any grapes that night. The doctors also noted that all Stride's teeth on the left lower jaw were absent.

Dr Phillips, who had charge of the post-mortem, gave it as his opinion that Stride had been seized by the shoulders and forced onto the ground. Her murderer had been on her right side (i.e. facing the wall) and had cut her throat from left to right. He thought that the murderer had 'a knowledge of where to cut the throat' and stated that he would not necessarily have been bloodstained, the commencement of the wound being away from the murderer, so the blood would have flowed away from him and into the gutter.

Dr Phillips's opinion did not account for Stride's bloodstained hand and wrist, nor was he able to account for them in any other way, but Dr Blackwell, who had examined the body and participated in the post-mortem, suggested that the murderer had taken hold of the back of a scarf Stride had worn around her neck, pulled her head back, then severed the windpipe as he sliced her throat. The action of grabbing the back of the scarf would have caused Stride to grasp the front of the scarf, thus getting blood on her hand when her throat was cut.

The body was not mutilated. The conclusion was that either Stride was not murdered by Jack the Ripper or her killer was interrupted before he could inflict the injuries from which he obtained his soubriquet.

Diemschutz went directly to an upstairs room and informed some people there of his discovery. Among those present was Morris Eagle. In company with a man named Isaac M Kozebrodsky, familiarly known as Isaacs, he went down to the yard. 'As soon as I saw the blood I got very excited and ran away for the police. I did not touch the body. When I got outside I saw Jacobs and another man going for the police in the direction of Fairclough Street, and I went to the Commercial Street, all the time shouting 'Police!' On getting to the corner of Grove Street I saw two constables and told them that a woman had been murdered. They returned with me to the yard.'[38]

Meanwhile, Louis Diemshutz and another man had run off in search of a policeman, but had failed to find one. At the corner of Fairclough Street and Christian Street they passed Edward Spooner who lived at 26 Fairclough Street, who asked them what was going on. On being told, Spooner returned with them to Berner Street. There were about fifteen people in the yard. Somebody struck a match and Spooner lifted the chin of the woman. He said that she had a piece of paper doubled up in her hand (the packet of cachous) and that there was a white and red flower pinned to her jacket. He thought that maybe five minutes had passed between his arrival and the return of Morris Eagle with two policemen.[39]

The policemen were PC Henry Lamb, 252 H, and PC Edward Collins, 12 HR. Having viewed the body, PC Lamb sent PC Collins for the doctor and Morris Eagle off to fetch assistance from the police station. By now there were about twenty or thirty people in the yard. Among them was Abraham Heahbury of 28 Berner Street. Like Spooner, he saw the packet of cachous, but no grapes.

PC Collins reached 100 Commercial Road, the residence of Drs Kay and Blackwell. Dr Blackwell was asleep in bed but his assistant, Edward Johnston, having first informed him of what had happened, immediately returned with Collins to the murder scene. According to Edward Johnston, Dr Blackwell arrived at Berner Street at precisely 1.16 a.m. Dr Blackwell estimated that Stride had been dead for 20 – 30 minutes by the time he arrived – placing death between 12.45 a.m. and 1.00 a.m.

Following the arrival of Dr Blackwell other officers and medical men appeared at the murder scene in rapid succession. Chief Inspector West and Inspector Pinhorn were followed at 1.25 a.m. by Dr Phillips. Inspector Reid, H Division, arrived shortly aferwards, and was in turn followed by Superintendent Arnold.

In the course of the next few hours the police examined Dutfield's Yard, the Club, the houses in the yard and the *Arbeter Fraint* offices. Everyone was searched and had their clothes examined. Nothing significant was found. Inspector Reid did make one curious statement at the inquest which was reported without comment in *The Times*, 6 October 1888. He said that on searching the building in the yard he discovered that 'a door of a loft was found locked on the inside, and it was forced. The loft was searched, but no trace of the murderer could be found.' Nor, apparently, was there any trace of the person who bolted the door from the inside!

At 4.30 a.m. the body of Elizabeth Stride was removed to the mortuary. By 5.00 a.m. the police had concluded their initial inquiries. At 5.30 a.m. PC Collins washed away all traces of blood.

Eye-witness testimony is notoriously unreliable. People will give different accounts of the same event even when that event is closely observed. Significant variations in the descriptions of the man and woman seen together that night should therefore be expected and the least reliable witnesses must be PC William Smith and James Brown, for both paid the couple scant attention and had no reason to remember them. Brown was further disadvantaged by the fact that the couple were standing in a particularly dark place, and shrouded by the shadows. On the other hand, Marshall watched the couple for about ten minutes and the frightening assault witnessed by Schwartz may have engraved the faces of the woman and her assailant on his memory. The descriptions of the man given by Marshall and Schwartz also bear the strongest similarity.

It seems reasonable to think that Stride was in the company of the same man from 11.45 p.m. until 12.45 a.m.; and if this was the same man as was seen to leave the Bricklayer's Arms in the company of a woman identified as Stride by Best and Gardner, then she may have been in his company from before 11.00 p.m. If it is felt that Stride was out to service as many clients as she could and would not therefore have stayed with one man for most of the night, let it not be forgotten that Martha Tabram went on a pub crawl with a soldier for most of the night on which she was murdered. Nor was Stride desperate for money, for she could always have returned to Michael Kidney and his bed for as long as she wanted to stay.

A further problem in the evidence of James Brown is that he claimed to have seen Elizabeth Stride at 12.45 a.m., the same time as Schwartz claimed to have seen her being assaulted, and his description of the man seen in her company – particularly his long overcoat – differs markedly from the description of the assailant given by Schwartz. They obviously could not have seen Stride in two places at the same time and with different men, so one or the other was clearly mistaken about the time, though not necessarily by more than three or four minutes. But if Brown saw Stride *after* the assault witnessed by Schwartz, then her assailant could not have been her murderer.

Consideration must be given to Martin Fido's appealing argument that the man seen by Schwartz was a mugger. His argument, which in view of the story in the *Star* carries a certain weight, is largely based on two premises: that Stride had been working that night yet had no money on her, from which he infers that it had been stolen; and that Brown overheard the woman say, 'No, not tonight. Some other night.' Fido, who infers that she was turning away a client, asks why, if she was working, was she refusing to turn a trick? The answer, he suggests, was that Stride was more interested at that moment in following her assailant so that she could learn his address

111

and return later with some male companions.[40]

If the man seen by Schwartz was the same as the one seen in Stride's company one hour earlier, he is unlikely to have been a mugger. A mugger would not have spent an hour or maybe more in the company of his intended victim. But be this as it may, Fido's argument is built entirely on the unsubstantiated premise that Stride had been working and that she therefore had money on her in the first place.

As I have said, there is no certainty that the woman seen by Brown was Elizabeth Stride. He had a fleeting look at her as she stood swathed by the shadows. The assessment in the files of Schwartz's evidence by the police does not mention Brown, from which we might infer that they did not regard his evidence as particularly important – although he was called to testify at the inquest, which Schwartz was not. This may not be significant in terms of the value of their respective testimony; many people appeared at the inquests who had no information of value to give. That Schwartz did not appear could indicate that his testimony was too highly prized to be made public. Rather than build a theory on a sequence of 'ifs', I would rather assume that Brown did not see Stride. But even if he did, and given that she seems to have been in the company of the same man for at least an hour, I would submit that it is more likely that Brown's description of the man is wrong than that the man was a different person from the one seen by Marshall and Schwartz.

It is therefore possible – but by no means certain – that Israel Schwartz was the last person to see Stride alive and may have seen Jack the Ripper.[41]

CHAPTER EIGHT

Catharine Eddowes

(aka Kate Kelly)
(found murdered on Sunday, 30 September 1888)

CATHARINE EDDOWES[1] was born on 14 April 1842, at Graisley Green, Wolverhampton. She was the daughter of a tinplate worker named George Eddowes and his wife Catharine née Evans)[2].

There is some dispute about her early years. One newspaper reported that her father and his brother William, who were employed as tinplate workers at the Old Hall Works in Wolverhampton, had at the time of the tinmen's strike, about 1848, taken their families to London, walking the whole distance. In London the brothers eventually found employment, but whilst George and his wife settled, William took his family back to Wolverhampton and resumed work at Old Hall. This report stated that in the early 1860s Catharine Eddowes returned to Wolverhampton to visit her family. Her relatives recalled the visit very clearly and described her 'as a very good looking and very jolly sort of girl'.[3]

A somewhat different story was given by a Wolverhampton paper. It says that when George Eddowes completed his apprenticeship at the Old Hall Works he married a cook at a local hostelry and took her to London to make their fortunes. Instead George fathered twelve children. His wife died in or about 1851 and George died a few months later. Catharine Eddowes was returned to Wolverhampton and the care of an aunt who lived in Biston Street.

The article said that when aged 21 or 22 and still living in Wolverhampton with her aunt, Catharine became involved 'with an old pensioner of the name of Thomas Conway'. The couple went to Birmingham and then on to other towns, making a living selling 'cheap books of lives written by the old pensioner'. In the course of their travels they returned to

113

Wolverhampton, where Catharine gave birth to a child. They then made their way to London. The newspaper also reported that Catharine Eddowes tried to return to her aunt's house 'after running away with the pensioner', but was refused admittance and was forced to seek refuge in a lodging house in Bilston Street. This incident was presumably on the occasion of her visit to Wolverhampton in the early 1860s. Catharine was 'spoken of by her friends in the district as having been an intelligent, scholarly woman, but of fiery temperament'.[4] Her education was gained at the Dowgate Charity School[5].

Catharine certainly took up with a man named Thomas Conway who was receiving a pension from the 18th Royal Irish Regiment[6], but there is no evidence that they ever got married. They had three children, Annie (born c.1865), George (born c.1868), and another son (born c.1873), but by 1880 their relationship had broken down completely, Catharine's predilection for alcohol being the cause. Her daughter, Annie, said that 'before they actually left each other she was never with him for twelve months at a time, but would go away for two or three months . . .'[7]. Annie also said that she had fallen out with her mother because of the latter's drinking.

Eddowes's sister, Mrs Elizabeth Fisher, who lived at 33 Hackliffe Street, Greenwich, told a different story of what had caused the relationship to break up: 'My sister left Conway because he treated her badly. He did not drink regularly, but when he drew his pension they went out together, and it generally ended in his beating her . . .'[8]

This may simply have been a case of Mrs Fisher defending her sister, but on the other hand Thomas Conway was hardly likely to have admitted to wife-beating.

Eddowes moved into a lodging house and there met John Kelly. He jobbed around the markets, but for more than twelve years he had been employed fairly constantly by a fruit salesman named Lander. He was found to be a 'quiet and inoffensive' character with 'fine features' and 'sharp and intelligent eyes', but he was a sick man, having a kidney complaint and a bad cough[9].

It may have been out of respect for the dead, but those who knew her did not give Eddowes a bad character. Frederick William Wilkinson, the deputy of Cooney's Lodging House, where she and Kelly stayed, said that Eddowes 'was not often in drink and was a very jolly woman, often singing'. As far as he knew she was not in the habit of walking the streets, she was generally in the lodging between 9.00 p.m. and 10.00 p.m., and he had never known or heard of her being intimate with anybody but John Kelly[10]. Kelly himself did not know that Eddowes ever went out for immoral purposes, but said that she sometimes drank to excess, though was not in the habit of doing so[11]. Another sister, Eliza Gold, who lived at 6 Thrawl Street, said that Eddowes was of sober habits[12].

Every year Eddowes and Kelly went to Kent for the hop-picking season. In the 1880s the acreage assigned to hops in Britain averaged 66,000 and hop-picking gave a regular 'holiday' in the countryside to thousands of city-dwellers. In 1890 it was estimated that between 50,000 and 60,000 people went to pick hops in a good season[13]. In 1888 Kelly and Eddowes went to Hunton, near Maidstone in Kent. 'We didn't get on any too well and started to hoof it home,' said Kelly. 'We came along in company with another man and woman who had worked in the same fields, but who parted with us to go to Cheltenham when we turned off towards London. The woman said to Kate, ''I have got a pawn ticket for a flannel shirt. I wish you'd take it since you're going up to town. It is only for 2d, and it may fit your old man.' So Kate took it and we trudged along . . . We did not have money enough to keep us going till we got to town, but we did get there, and came straight to this house. Luck was dead against us . . . we were both done up for cash . . .'[14].

They reached London on the afternoon of Friday 28 September. Kelly managed to earn 6d. Eddowes took 2d and told Kelly to use the remaining 4d to get a bed at their lodging, Cooney's Lodging House at 55 Flower and Dean Street. Eddowes said that she would get a bed in the casual ward in Shoe Lane.

In an interview given to the *East London Observer,* the Superintendent of the casual ward said that Eddowes was well known there, but that this was the first occasion that she had stayed there for some time. Eddowes explained that she had been hopping in the country, but she said 'I have come back to earn the reward offered for the apprehension of the Whitechapel murderer. I think I know him.' The Superintendent cautioned Eddowes to take care that he did not murder her. 'Oh, no fear of that,' replied Eddowes[15].

I have been unable to find any corroborative statement from John Kelly, to whom Eddowes would surely have confided, that she knew or had any suspicions about the identity of Jack the Ripper, and I am inclined to believe that either she was joking or that this statement was invented by the casual ward Superintendent or the journalist involved. The only cause for doubt is that on the following day, Saturday 30 September, Catharine Eddowes told Kelly that she was going to see if she could get some money off her daughter in Bermondsey. Now, Eddowes's daughter gave testimony to the effect that her mother was a persistent scrounger. If this is true, Eddowes would surely have known that she no longer lived in Bermondsey. Eddowes must also have known the futility of trying to trace her daughter's whereabouts, for she would surely have attempted to track her down several times over the years. So did Eddowes sincerely intend to go to Bermondsey, or did she have reasons of her own for being away from Kelly for a few hours? Did she really have an idea about the identity of Jack the Ripper?

Eddowes returned to 55 Flower and Dean Street at 8.00 a.m. on Saturday 29 September 1888, having been turned out of the casual ward because of some unspecified trouble there. Kelly had a pair of boots and he decided to pawn them, which he did with a broker named Smith who had premises in Church Street. It was Eddowes in fact who took them into the shop and pledged them in the name of 'Jane Kelly' for 2/6. With this money Kelly and Eddowes bought some food, tea and sugar. Between 10.00 a.m. and 11.00 a.m. they were seen by Wilkinson, the lodging house deputy, eating breakfast in the lodging house kitchen.

By the afternoon they were again without money and, as I have said, Eddowes said she was going to see if she could get some money from her daughter. She parted with Kelly in Hounsditch at 2.00 p.m., promising to be back no later than 4.00 p.m. 'I never knew if she went to her daughter's at all,' said Kelly. 'I only wish to God she had, for we had lived together for a long while, and never had a quarrel.'[14]

On duty in Aldgate High Street, PC Louis Robinson, 31

City[16], saw a group of people gathered outside number 29 at 8.30 p.m. On going over he found the object of their interest to be Catharine Eddowes, drunk and crumpled in a heap on the pavement. He asked if anybody knew her, but nobody did. He heaved her to her feet and lent her against the shutters of number 29, but she slipped sideways. PC Robinson then summoned the assistance of PC George Simmons, 959 City, and together they took Eddowes to the Bishopsgate Police Station.

On arriving at the Police Station, Eddowes was asked her name, but she said, 'Nothing.' She was placed in a cell by the station Sergeant, James Byfield[17]. At 8.50 p.m. PC Robinson looked in on her. She was asleep and smelt strongly of drink. At 9.45 p.m. PC George Henry Hutt, 968 City[18], took charge of the prisoners. He visited them several times during the course of the night.

At 12.55 a.m. Sergeant Byfield instructed PC Hutt to see if any of the prisoners were fit to be released. Eddowes was found to be sober and was brought from the cells. On being asked her name, she said 'Mary Ann Kelly' and gave her address as 6 Fashion Street. She was then released.

Catharine Eddowes left the station at precisely 1.00 a.m. – which was when Elizabeth Stride's body was discovered in Berner Street. 'I shall get a damned fine hiding when I get home,' she said. Hutt replied, 'And serve you right. You had no right to get drunk.'

Hutt pushed open the swing door of the Police Station. 'This way, missus,' he said. Eddowes went into the passage leading to the street door. 'Please pull it to,' said Hutt. 'All right,' replied Eddowes. 'Good night, old cock.' Eddowes pulled the door almost closed and was seen to turn left. This took her in the opposite direction to her quickest route back to Flower and Dean Street. It looked as if she was heading for Houndsditch, which led back to Aldgate High Street, where she had been found drunk. On going down Houndsditch she would have passed an entrance to Duke Street, at the bottom of which was a narrow lane called Church Passage which led into Mitre Square. It was estimated that it would have taken Eddowes no longer than about eight minutes to reach Mitre Square.

At 1.30 a.m. PC Edward Watkins, 881 City [19], passed

through Mitre Square on his beat. He was positive that Eddowes's body was not there at that time [20].

At 1.35 a.m. Joseph Lawende, a commercial traveller in the cigarette trade who lived at 45 Norfolk Road, Dalston [21], and who had business premises in St Mary Axe, together with Joseph Hyam Levy, a butcher of 1 Hutchinson Street, Aldgate, and Mr Harry Harris, a furniture dealer of Castle Street, Whitechapel, left the Imperial Club at 16 – 17 Duke Street. At the corner of Duke Street and Church Passage they saw a man and a woman talking. According to a report by Chief Inspector Swanson dated 6 November 1888 [22], Levy and Harris 'took but little notice and state they could not identify man or woman'. However, Lawende was able to describe the man and later identified Eddowes's clothes as the same as those worn by the woman he had seen.

Harry Harris did not appear at the inquest into Eddowes's death and all sources agreed that he did not pay any attention to the couple and had no information to offer. However, Lawende and Levy did attend the inquest and their testimony is of sufficient importance to warrant quoting in detail:

LAWENDE:	I was at the Imperial Club with Mr Joseph Levy and Mr Harry Harris. We could not get home because it was raining. At half past one we left to go out, and left the house about five minutes later. I walked a little further from the others. We saw a man and a woman at the corner of Church Passage, in Duke Street, which leads into Mitre Square.
CORONER: (Mr Langham)	Were they talking at the time?
LAWENDE:	She was standing with her face towards the man. I only saw her back. She had her hand on his chest.
CORONER:	What sort of woman was she?
LAWENDE:	I could not see her face, but the man was taller than she was.
CORONER:	Did you notice how she was dressed?

118

LAWENDE:	I noticed she had a black jacket and black bonnet. I have seen the articles at the Police Station, and I recognise them as the sort of dress worn by that woman.
CORONER:	What sort of woman was she?
LAWENDE:	About five feet in height.
CORONER:	Can you tell us what sort of man this was?
LAWENDE:	He had a cloth cap on, with a peak of the same material.
MR CRAWFORD: (solicitor for the police)	Unless the jury particularly wish it, I have special reason for not giving details as to the appearance of this man.
JURY:	No.
CORONER:	You have given a special description of this man to the police?
LAWENDE:	Yes.
CORONER:	Do you think you would know him again?
LAWENDE:	I doubt it, sir.
MR CRAWFORD:	The Club is 16 and 17 Duke Street, about 15 or 16 feet from where they were standing at Church Passage. By what did you fix the time?
LAWENDE:	By seeing the club clock and my own watch. It was five minutes after the half hour when we came out, and to the best of my belief it was twenty-five to when we saw these persons.
CORONER:	Did you hear anything said?
LAWENDE:	No, not a word.
CORONER:	Did either of them appear in an angry mood?
LAWENDE:	No.
CORONER:	Was there anything about them or their movements that attracted your attention?
LAWENDE:	No, except that Mr Levy said the court

119

	ought to be watched, and I took particular
	notice of a man and woman talking there.
CORONER:	Was her arm on his breast as if she was
	pushing him away?
LAWENDE:	No, they were standing very quietly.
CORONER:	You were not curious enough to look back to
	see where they went?
LAWENDE:	No.[23]

Lawende gave his testimony on 5 October, yet the police had already issued a brief description of the man which, among other newspapers, was published in *The Times* on 2 October: 'He was described as of shabby appearance, about 30 years of age and 5ft 9ins. in height, of fair complexion, having a small fair moustache and a cap with a peak.' A fuller description is found in the Home Office files. The man is described as 30, 5ft 7ins. or 5ft 8ins., fair complexion, fair moustache, medium build, pepper-and-salt coloured loose jacket, grey cloth cap with peak of the same colour, reddish handkerchief tied in a knot round the neck, with the appearance of a sailor. Detective Chief Inspector Donald Swanson noted: 'For the purpose of comparison, this description is nearer to that given by Schwartz than to that given by the PC [i.e. PC Smith in Berner Street]'[24]. Lawende is also referred to by Major Henry Smith in his autobiography, *From Constable to Commissioner*, but on the basis of present evidence he appears to be a highly unreliable source. A number of details are wrong and the description he gives of the man seen by Lawende differs in several respects from that given by Lawende at the inquest and by Swanson in the Home Office files[25]. Let us turn to the testimony of Joseph Hyam Levy.

LEVY:	I was with the last witness and Harris at the
	Imperial Club on the 29th, and left with
	them about half past one. It might be about
	three or four minutes past the half hour
	when we came out. I saw a man and woman
	standing at the corner of Church Passage,
	but I did not take any further notice of them,
	thinking that persons standing at that time
	in the morning in a dark passage were not up

120

	to much good. So I walked on. I was at home at twenty minutes to two.
CORONER:	What height was the man?
LEVY:	He might be about three inches taller than the woman.
CORONER:	Can you give any description of either of them?
LEVY:	I cannot. We went down Duke Street into Aldgate leaving the man and woman still talking behind. I can only fix the time by the club clock.
FOREMAN:	Was the place badly lighted?
LEVY:	There is a much better light there now than there was then. I can say that. I said when I came out of the club to Mr Harris, 'I don't like going home by myself when I see these sorts of characters about. I'm off.'
JUROR:	Is it an unusual thing to see a man and woman there at that hour of the morning?
LEVY:	It is unusual for me to be out at that time. I am usually at home at eleven.
CRAWFORD:	What was there terrible in their appearance?
LEVY:	I did not say that.
CRAWFORD:	Your fear was about yourself?
LEVY:	Not exactly.
CRAWFORD:	You simply buttoned up your coat and hurried on?
LEVY:	Yes.[23].

There is a feeling that Levy was being slightly evasive. He saw a man and a woman talking together, doing nothing to attract attention or cause alarm, yet they alarmed Levy, who refused or was unable to say why when pressed by Mr Crawford[26]. Then there is Lawende's testimony to the effect that he paid attention to the couple because Levy had said that the court ought to be watched, yet Levy, who made the suggestion, apparently hurried past without paying any attention to the couple at all.

Beyond question there was something very strange going on after the murders of Elizabeth Stride and Catharine Eddowes. On 1 October the *Evening News* reported: 'The police are

121

extraordinarily reticent with reference to the Mitre Square tragedy.' The *Yorkshire Post* on the same date reported: 'The police apparently have strict orders to close all channels of information to members of the press.' Even the *New York Times* on 1 October was moved to complain of the police that 'they devote their entire energies to preventing the press from getting at the facts. They deny to reporters a sight of the scene or bodies, and give them no information whatever.' Then, suddenly, on 2 October the *Manchester Guardian* reported:

> The barrier of reticence which has been set up on all occasions when the representatives of the newspaper press have been brought into contact with the police authorities for the purpose of obtaining information for the use of the public has been suddenly withdrawn, and instead of the customary stereotyped negatives and disclaimers of the officials, there has ensued a marked disposition to afford all necessary facilities for the publication of details and an increased courtesy towards the members of the press concerned.

It is possible that the police opened channels of communication both to direct attention away from areas which they regarded as sensitive, and because they had those sensitive areas reasonably secured. This is suggested by the fact that the press apart from the *Star* never got close to Israel Schwartz and also by a very interesting statement in the *Evening News* of 9 October. Referring to Lawende and Levy, the paper says:

> They [the police] have no doubt themselves that this was the murdered woman and her murderer. And on the first blush of it the fact is borne out by the police having taken exclusive care of Mr Joseph Levander [sic], to a certain extent having sequestrated him and having imposed a pledge on him of secrecy. They are paying all his expenses, and one if not two detectives are taking him about. One of the two detectives is Foster. Mr Henry Harris [sic], of the two gentlemen our representative interviewed, is the more communicative. He is of the opinion that neither Mr Levander nor Mr Levy saw

122

anything more than he did, and that was only the back of the man. Mr Joseph Levy is absolutely obstinate and refuses to give the slightest information. He leaves one to infer that he knows something, but he is afraid to be called on the inquest. Hence he assumes a knowing air.

The Metropolitan Police kept Israel Schwartz under wraps, or so it would appear, whilst the City Police certainly had Lawende under close observation and, it would seem, had silenced Levy. 'Although Lawende maintained that he could not again recognize the man, and Levy maintained that he paid the man no attention, on the face of it, it would appear that the police believed that Schwartz, Lawende and possibly Levy had seen Jack the Ripper!

Five minutes after Lawende, Levy and Harris passed the man and woman at the entrance to Church Passage, PC James Harvey[27] passed down Duke Street and went down Church Passage as far as the entrance of Mitre Square. 'I saw no one. I heard no cry or noise,' he told the inquest. 'I was at the end of Church Passage about 18 or 19 minutes to 2.' He was certain of the time because he had checked the post office clock[20].

At 1.45 a.m. PC Watkin's beat again brought him into Mitre Square and he discovered the body of Catharine Eddowes in a dark corner. Without touching the body, PC Watkins ran across to the warehouse of Messrs Kearley and Tonge on the opposite side of the square to obtain the assistance of the night-watchman, George James Morris, a former policeman.

PC Watkins called out, 'For God's sake mate, come out and assist me.' Morris grabbed a lamp and went outside. 'What's the matter?' he asked. 'Another woman has been cut to pieces,' said PC Watkins. The two men went over to where Eddowes's body lay. Morris took one brief look at the body, then ran out of the square into Mitre Street and then into Aldgate .At that moment PC James Harvey was on his beat in Aldgate, returning towards Duke Street. He stopped Morris and was told of the discovery. PC Harvey then summoned PC Holland, 814 City[28], who was across the street. Together they went to Mitre Square. PC Holland then went to fetch Dr George William Sequeira at 34 Jewry Street, Aldgate[29]. He arrived at 1.45 a.m.

Catharine Eddowes was horribly mutilated. Her face had been severely cut, her eyes, nose, lips and cheek having been attacked with calculated ferocity; her throat had been cut; and as in the case of Nichols and Chapman her abdomen had been the killer's primary target. The left kidney and, again, the uterus were missing.

There was disagreement among the doctors about whether the mutilation revealed anatomical knowledge and/or skill. When at the inquest Dr Sequeira was asked whether the injuries indicated that the killer possessed great anatomical skill, he replied, 'No. I do not.' Another doctor, Dr William Sedgwick Saunders[30], who was also present at the post-mortem, when asked the same question, also replied that he did not think that the murderer possessed anatomical skill.

On the other hand, when Dr Frederick Gordon Brown was asked the same question, he expressed the opinion that the killer would have possessed 'a good deal of knowledge as to the position of the organs in the abdominal cavity and the way of removing them.' He agreed, however, that the required knowledge would have been possessed by a person accustomed to cutting up animals.[31]

Dr George Bagster Phillips agreed with Brown. According to Detective Chief Inspector Swanson, Phillips 'reported that there were missing the left kidney and the uterus, and that mutilation so far gave no evidence of anatomical knowledge in the sense it so far evidenced the hand of a qualified surgeon, so that the police could narrow their inquiries into certain classes of persons. On the other hand, as in the Metropolitan Police cases, the medical evidence showed that the murder could have been committed by a person who had been a hunter, a butcher, a slaughterman, as well as a student in surgery or a properly qualified surgeon[32].

At 1.55 a.m. Inspector Edward Collard[33], on duty at Bishopsgate Police Station, received news of the murder in Mitre Square. He at once sent a constable to fetch the police surgeon, Dr Frederick Gordon Brown[34], then headed for Mitre Square. He timed his arrival at 2.03 a.m. Dr Brown arrived a few minutes later, being followed by Superintendent McWilliam[35] and Superintendent Foster[36].

Major Henry Smith writes in his autobiography that he also visited the scene of the crime:

> The night of Saturday, September 29, found me tossing about in my bed at Cloak Lane Station, close to the river and adjoining Southwark Bridge . . . Suddenly the bell at my head rang violently. 'What is it?' I asked, putting my ear to the tube. 'Another murder sir, this time in the City.' Jumping up, I was dressed and in the street in a couple of minutes[37].

The doctors examined the body. A Sergeant Jones found three small black metal buttons of the type used on women's boots; also found were a common thimble and a small mustard tin containing two pawn tickets, one in respect of John Kelly's boots, the other for the flannel shirt which Emily Burrell had given to Eddowes when they parted company on the road back from hop-picking in Kent.

Meanwhile, another important episode occurred in the murder investigation – and one which was to assume considerable importance with the publication in 1976 of Stephen Knight's imaginative *Jack the Ripper: The Final Solution*. At 1.55 a.m. Detective Daniel Halse[38], Detective Robert Outram[39], and Detective Edward Marriott[40], were at the corner of Houndsditch, by Aldgate Church. They had been searching alleys, passages, the halls of lodging houses, and other places where it was thought possible that Jack the Ripper might strike. On receiving news of the murder the three men went at once to Mitre Square, where Detective Halse gave instructions for the immediate vicinity to be searched and for all people in the streets to be stopped and questioned. He then went via Middlesex Street to Wentworth Street, where he stopped and questioned two men. From Middlesex Street he passed through Goulston Street. The time was 2.02 a.m. He returned to Mitre Square, and went from there to the mortuary.

At 2.20 a.m. PC Alfred Long, 254 A[41], who had been temporarily drafted to assist H Division, passed through Goulston Street on his beat. He noticed nothing to excite his attention. He again passed through Goulston Street at

2.55 a.m. This time he noticed a piece of apron on the floor of a common stairs leading to 118 – 119 Goulston Street Buildings. The apron was stained with blood. The torn piece of material positively matched the apron worn by Catharine Eddowes. There was and is no doubt that Jack the Ripper passed through Goulston Street and stopped by the stairs to wipe his hands or his knife.

On the wall above where the apron lay there was a message written in white chalk. There was a difference of opinion about the precise wording of the message. PC Long maintained that it read 'The Juwes are the men that will not be blamed for nothing', Whilst Detective Halse said that it read 'The Juwes are the men that will be blamed for nothing.'

The writing on the wall is not of any great significance because it was never certainly established that it was written by the murderer. The only real point of interest at our present state of knowledge is that the murderer had that night struck near to clubs largely frequented by Jews, but how this and the writing is to be interpreted is difficult to say.

The writing was erased at the express command of Sir Charles Warren, Goulston Street being within the jurisdiction of the Metropolitan Police, and apparently against the wishes of the City Police. Warren was not alone in wanting the writing removed. Superintendent Arnold[42] explained in a report to the Home Office:

> Knowing in consequence of suspicion having fallen upon a Jew named John Pizer alias 'Leather Apron', having committed a murder in Hanbury Street a short time previously, a strong feeling existed against the Jews generally, and as the building upon which the writing was found was situated in the midst of a locality inhabited principally by that sect, I was apprehensive that if the writing were left it would be the means of causing a riot and therefore considered it desirable that it should be removed . . . An inspector was present by my instructions with a sponge for the purpose of removing the writing when the Commissioner arrived on the scene.[43]

Sir Charles Warren also submitted a report in which he

explained that he had decided to take the responsibility for erasing the writing upon himself, that he had wholly agreed with Superintendent Arnold's reasoning and 'was much gratified with the promptitude with which Superintendent Arnold was prepared to act in the matter if I had not been there.'[44]

That the writing on the wall was erased at the express command of Sir Charles Warren assumed considerable importance when a BBC Television series in 1975, *The Ripper File*, argued that the word 'Juwes' featured in high-level Masonic rituals. It was further argued that since Warren was a senior Mason, the writing was removed because it implicated the Freemasons by revealing Jack the Ripper to be a senior member.

The reasoning has an inherent weakness. The erasure did not prevent the spelling of the word becoming known or its supposed significance from being apparent to anyone acquainted with Masonic ritual. The erasure therefore achieved none of the objectives for which Warren is accused of having it erased. Moreover, even if the writing had been left, who other than senior Masons would have known the significance of the word, and would senior Masons have been less anxious than Warren to keep the Masonic connection unrevealed?

Such inherent improbabilities did not dissuade Stephen Knight from weaving such a well-written fantasy about the Masonic conspiracy that many people were convinced that he had produced the truth. It has now been thoroughly discredited.[45]

'Juwes' is supposed to be the collective name for Jubelo, Jubela and Jubelum, who, during the building of Solomon's Temple, murdered the Grand Master, Hiram Abiff. They featured in British Masonic rituals until 1814, but they were dropped during the major revision of the ritual between 1814 and 1816. By 1888 it is doubtful if many British Masons would even have known their names. In the United States, however, the names were and are used. But in neither country were Jubelo, Jubela and Jubelum known officially or colloquially as the 'Juwes'. They were always referred to as 'the ruffians'. 'Juwes' is not and never has been a Masonic word, nor has 'Juwes' or any word approximating to it ever appeared in

British, Continental or American Masonic rituals. It is a mystery why anyone ever thought that 'Juwes' was a Masonic word.

Sir Charles Warren

James Monro

Sir Robert Anderson

Sir Melville Macnaghten

Chief Inspector Donald Swanson

Dr Thomas Bond *(By courtesy of the Board of Trustees of the Victoria and Albert Museum)*

Wynne E Baxter

Buck's Row, scene of the murder of Mary Ann Nichols

Berner Street, scene of the murder of Elizabeth Stride

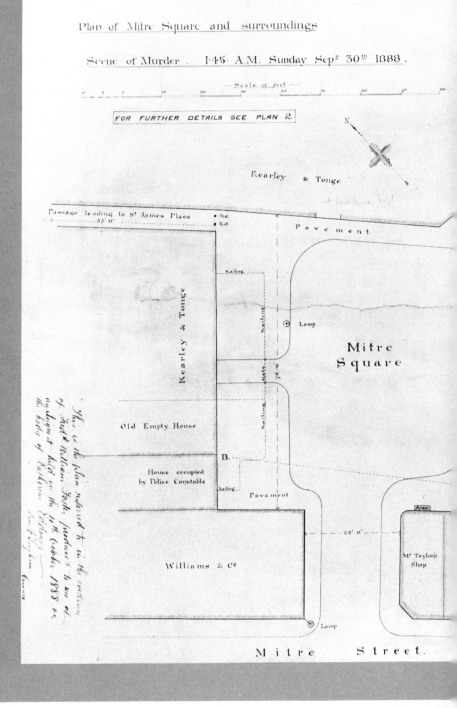

Plan of Mitre Square and surroundings

Scene of Murder . 1·45 A.M. Sunday Sep.ʳ 30ᵗʰ 1888 .

Scale of feet

FOR FURTHER DETAILS SEE PLAN 2

N

Kearley & Tonge

Passage leading to St James Place

Pavement

Kearley & Tonge

Railing

Lamp

Mitre
Square

Old Empty House

B.

House occupied
by Police Constable

Pavement

Williams & Cᵒ

Area

Mʳ Taylor's
Shop

Lamp

Mitre Street.

Diagram and sketches relating to
(Reproduced by kind permission of the Departm

Sketch taken from point B. on plan looking towards A.

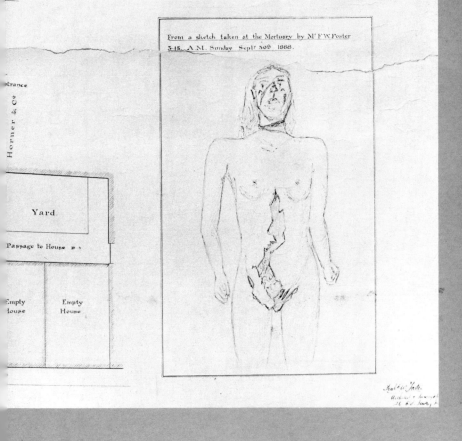

From a sketch taken at the Mortuary by Mr F.W. Foster
3.45. A.M. Sunday Sept 30th 1888.

Horner & Co

trance

Yard.

Passage to House

Empty
House

Empty
House

Entrance to Miller's Court, off Dorset
Street, scene of the murder of Mary Jane Kelly
(*Reproduced by kind permission of
W H Allen & Co Ltd*)

29 Hanbury Street, scene
of the murder
of Annie Chapman

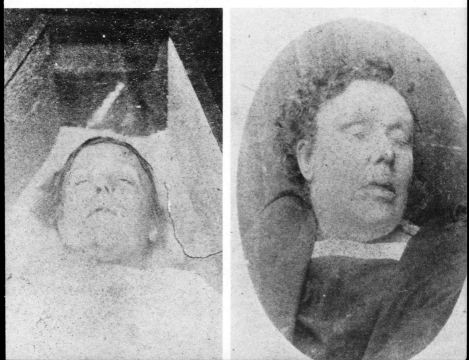

25 Sept. 1988

Dear Boss

I keep on hearing the police have caught me but they wont fix me just yet. I have laughed when they look so clever and talk about being on the right track. That joke about Leather Apron gave me real fits. I am down on whores and I shant quit ripping them till I do get buckled. Grand work the last job was. I gave the lady no time to squeal. How can they catch me now. I love my work and want to start again. You will soon hear of me with my funny little games. I saved some of the proper red stuff in a ginger beer bottle over the last job to write with but it went thick like glue and I cant use it. Red ink is fit enough I hope ha ha. The next job I do I shall clip the ladys ears off and send to the police officers just for jolly wouldnt you. Keep this letter back till I do a bit more work then give it out straight. My knifes so nice and sharp I want to get to work right away if I get a chance. Good luck

yours truly

Jack the Ripper

Dont mind me giving the trade name

POST CARD

Mr Boss
Central News
Office
London City

Letter and postcard from someone purporting to be Jack the Ripper

Previously unseen mortuary photographs of Mary Ann Nicholls and Annie Chapman

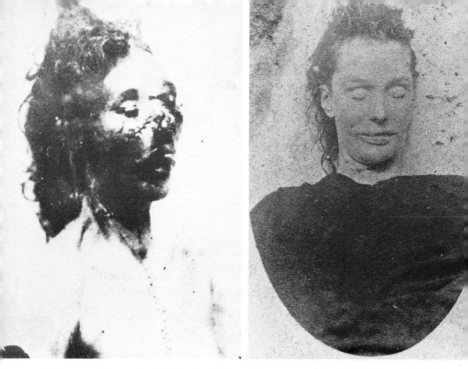

Mortuary photograph of Catharine Eddowes *(Crown copyright. Public Records Office)*
and a previously unseen photograph of Elizabeth Stride,
released by the Metropolitan Police in 1988

Mary Kelly as found in Miller's Court
(Crown copyright. Public Records Office)

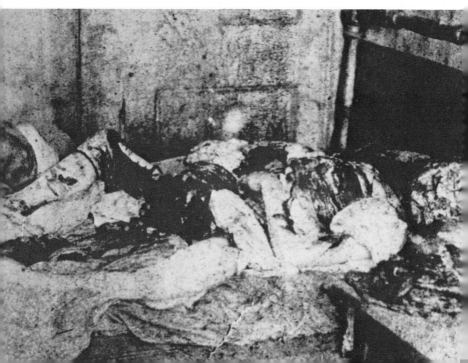

CHAPTER NINE

Sunday, 30 September 1888 – Thursday, 8 November 1888

LONG BEFORE daybreak on Sunday, 30 September, crowds of people descended on Berner Street. Police had to be posted along the street and further constables were drafted in to protect the mortuary. The entrances to Mitre Square were closed by order of the police and a large number of constables under the charge of Inspector Izzard and Sergeants Dudman and Phelps were kept on the spot to preserve order. The *East London Observer* later reported the scene:

> The appearance of East London early on Sunday morning as soon as the news of the murders was shown – and, indeed, all day – almost baffled description. At 10.00 a.m. Aldgate and Leadenhall Street, Duke Street, St James's Place, and Houndsditch were all literally packed with human beings – packed so thick that it was a matter of utter impossibility to pass through. The babel of tongues as each inquired of the latest particulars, or the exact locality of the Aldgate murder, or speculated on the character or whereabouts of the murderer, was simply deafening. Every window of every inhabited room in the vicinity was thrown open, for the better view of the inmates; and seats at these windows were being openly sold and eagerly bought. On the outskirts of this vast chattering, excited assemblage of humanity, coster-mongers, who sold everything in the way of edibles, from fish and bread to fruit and sweets, and newspaper vendors whose hoarse cries only added to the confusion of sounds heard on every hand, were doing exceedingly large trades.[1]

Major Smith and Sir Charles Warren were reported to have discussed the crimes at length and to have visited the scenes of the murders during the course of the day.

That afternoon, at 3.00 p.m., a meeting of nearly 1,000 people took place in Victoria Park under the chairmanship of Mr Edward Barrow of the Bethnal Green Road. There were several speeches regarding the conduct of Sir Charles Warren and Home Secretary Matthews and a resolution was unanimously passed that 'it was high time both men should resign and make way for some other officers who would leave no stone unturned for the purpose of bringing the murderer to justice . . .'[2] Similar meetings and similar resolutions were passed at four other locations in London that day. The Home Secretary, Henry Matthews, was particularly castigated for not offering a reward for the apprehension of the murderer. George Lusk, the Chairman of the Whitechapel Vigilance Committee virtually accused Matthews of having one law for the rich and another for the poor, pointing out that a reward had been offered for the capture of the murderer of Lord Frederick Cavendish, the victim of the Phoenix Park murder. A reward 'would convince the poor and humble residents of the East End that the Government authorities are as much anxious to avenge the blood of these unfortunate victims', wrote Lusk.

A press agency report published in many newspapers warned: 'With each fresh murder in the Whitechapel series public alarm has been accentuated and unless something can soon be done to restore confidence in the detective powers of the police panic will be the result.'[3]

Of course, the widespread complaints about the police in the British press was grist to the mill of the *New York Times*'s London correspondent, who had previously never missed an opportunity to criticise the police. 'The assassin is evidently mocking the police in his barbarous work. He waited until the preceding inquests were quite finished, and then murdered two more women.'[4]

Perhaps it was proximity to the events that prevented the London newspapers from exercising rational thought. It took traditional Northern common sense to voice a defence of the police, but the voice was too small to be heard over the baying of the press in London.

The police then are at fault, because the circumstances transgress their experience. The criminal annals of this country offer no parallel to these hideous and apparently purposeless Whitechapel murders, and with no precedent to guide them, perhaps it is not surprising that the police are at fault.[5]

When the City Police on 1 October offered a reward of £500 for 'such information as shall lead to the discovery and conviction of the murderer or murderers', and the Lord Mayor, acting on the advice of the City Commissioner, offered in the name of the Corporation of London a further reward of £500[6], the criticism of the Metropolitan Police and the Home Secretary mounted.

It is rather hard upon Mr Matthews that he, who has never proposed legislation for the reform of the City, nor indeed done anything by personal initiation of a remarkably useful character, should now be placed in this difficulty by that unreformed Corporation he has done his best to protect. But if the £500 reward offered by the City for the apprehension of the Whitechapel murderer should be claimed, it may go hard with Mr Matthews in regard to his refusal.[7]

This was the opinion of the *Daily Telegraph* leader column.

The Home Secretary now in office is a source of miserable weakness and discredit to the present administration. In the House of Commons he has been nothing more nor less than a fantastic failure. In the provinces he is scarcely known, even by name; and when the provincials do become aware of him, it is only to mistrust him and to express disrespectful and indignant astonishment that a Government, otherwise so capable and so popular, should drag with it a dead weight of so much vacillation, so much ineptitude, and so many frankly naive confessions of crass ignorance concerning things of which the most commonplace Home Secretary ought to be fully cognisant.

131

The *Star* decreed that 'Mr Matthews is a feeble mountebank, who would pose and simper over the brink of a volcano . . . Every London newspaper but *The Times* is for getting rid of our never-at-Home Secretary.'[8]

It was even rumoured that the Tories were after Matthews's head. It was reported that Matthews did not want to resign and that the Prime Minister did not want his resignation, but that the wind through 10 Downing Street might change 'if Mr Matthews's view against offering a reward for the apprehension of the Whitechapel murderer were obstinately adhered to against that of the Prime Minister and other colleagues'[9].

The irony is that neither Matthews nor Warren were ever wholly opposed to the Government offering a reward. The decision not to offer rewards had been taken by Sir W V Harcourt, the Home Secretary in Gladstone's Liberal Government, and Matthews had simply acted on the advice of his advisors, following a precedent which had not even been set by his own party.

Warren had apparently either stated his opinion that the offer of a reward would bring no practical result, or offered no opinion on the subject. Matthews reasonably assumed that he had Warren's support. It therefore came as a considerable shock to him when Warren advocated a reward of £5,000! Ruggles-Brise seems himself to have seen the implications and at once sent a messenger to Matthews, who was out of town. Matthews wrote back immediately. The letter has not to my knowledge been published before and is worth quoting in full for the light it sheds on the private opinion of Matthews, in contrast to the 'public' one in the Home Office files. It was dated 5 October 1888.

Dear Brise,
I am sure you meant well and were acting in what you believed to be my interests tonight, but I think on consideration you will see that your action was very embarrassing. Your messenger arrived here after 8 o'clock and sent in with your box a message that he had to catch a train at 9. I had to leave my guests in the middle of dinner, – to read all the papers you sent and to scribble an answer in about 20 or 25 minutes. In as much as you

asked me to reverse a decision twice publicly announced – a decision about which I had had a long conference with Sir C W day before yesterday and Mr Monro yesterday with the result that the latter approved and that the former did not disapprove – I am not using too strong a word when I say that the appeal under such circumstances of hurry was at least embarrassing. I have never myself shared to the full extent the HO prejudice against rewards; nor have I thought Harcourt's reasoning on the subject at all conclusive. I am disposed to regret now that in the first instance I did not sacrifice to popular feeling and offer a considerable reward. But in as much as I did yield to the official view and refuse to make an offer and subsequently repeated the refusal, I feel that my hands are tied. Unhappily the first HO letter (to Montague M.P. I think) was so worded as to make a change of front still more difficult. Sir C W on Wednesday told me he thought a reward was of no practical use; – that it would serve as 'eye-wash' for the public and nothing else; – and that after the Lord Mayor's offer it was unnecessary. He appears, on your report, to have modified his opinion to a considerable extent. He certainly the day before yesterday did not say a word to urge the offer of a reward upon me – although I distinctly asked him what was his view. He gave not the slightest hint of the enormous reward that you suggest, quoting him.

I feel very strongly that to make such an offer now, after what has passed, so far from conciliating public opinion (and that is admittedly the only reason for the step) would cover me with ridicule and contempt – as having given way to popular pressure – with nothing to justify or call for change, which would itself be the strongest condemnation of my previous action.

There must be done something publicly. Why cannot the police apply to the magistrates for search warrants against all the houses in which they think it probable or possible that the murderer may be concealed? If warrants are refused, that would be a new circumstance. I agree with Sir C W that he cannot act on Sir J Ellis' suggestion and search houses illegally, with all the fearful consequences that might follow from resistance. Again, the police can legally search all probable hiding places without warrant – if they can get the consent of the landlord or a person having control of the premises. A house to house search (of suspicious places) with the consent of the landlord, or under warrant, would be helpful – and would give some satisfaction to the public. If it resulted in nothing (as it probably would) there would be some sort of ground for offering a reward.

You say nothing about the suggestion of my offering a free pardon to anyone not the actual perpetrator of the murders. I could do that more easily, and with less discredit, than would follow from offering a reward. Has Sir C W considered the effect of such an offer? There may be persons who conceal and harbour the murderer and who are therefore afraid to speak – I mentioned this to Pemberton, but not to Warren, on Wednesday.

Your letter does not at all enable me to grasp how and why Sir C W has changed his mind since Wednesday. I imagine that you yourself have been out of Town and perhaps hardly know of what has taken place, and what the HO have written. At any rate your letter shows no indication of your having grasped that I have taken a certain line on grounds of principle and reason and that I shall incur more public censure by abandoning it without some very good reason, than by adhering to it. If I could without discredit satisfy public feeling I would be very glad to do so. But I have already and irretrievably incurred the odium of resisting a popular outcry for a useless measure and I should only make matters worse by yielding to it without some reason that could be defended in argument.

If Sir C W felt able to write to me officially that the police had exhausted every means at their command – that they had not only failed, but had no expectation of succeeding in tracing the murderer – and that therefore, as a last resort, he felt bound to suggest recourse to an expedient which experience proves to be unsatisfactory and even mischievous, namely the offer of a reward – I might act on such a letter − provided I might make it public. But I think it is too soon *for the credit of the police* to take such a step yet. They do not seem to have exhausted the resources of detective energy. The fear of another murder tomorrow or Sunday is really too shadowy to be grounds for action.

I have marked this letter 'private' because I intend it for you alone. Use its contents discreetly in talking with Sir C W. I could hardly act on a letter from him nakedly recommending a large reward without more. For his own credit and that of the force it is imperative that some visible evidence of effort − of ingenuity − of vigorous and intelligent exertion − should be on record. Anybody can offer a reward and it is the first idea of ignorant people. But more is expected of the CID Sir C W will not save himself, or put himself right with the public, by merely suggesting that. This conversation with you looks as if he wanted to hedge at my expense.

I wish you had come here instead of writing − I should have preferred an interview to this long letter written late at night and very incoherently.

6 October

I have thought it best to write a note myself to Warren upon his of the 4th. Will you keep a copy and send it to him at once.

Sir Charles Strand's note. He is a barrister − was a solicitor − and has intelligence and quickness. If he can be useful, I think he is trustworthy. Anderson was to return today.

I return Sir C W's letter − keep it.
Yours etc.
H.M.[10]

In other words, whilst it was generally agreed that the offer of a reward was a palliative to public feeling, Matthews was neither opposed to rewards or in wholehearted agreement with Harcourt's reasoning on the subject. He had nevertheless followed a precedent, in the belief that in doing so he was supported by Warren, though he was inclined now to regret his decision and was willing to offer a reward if there was a way of doing so which did not reflect badly on him. Matthews's nice touch was to suggest that he would agree to offer a reward if Warren publicly declared the utter failure of the police to capture Jack the Ripper.

Warren countered on 6 October by saying that from the outset his 'opinion had not been asked on this subject' and he had assumed the decision not to offer a reward was a matter of Government policy on which his comments were unrequired. However, in the light of the reward offered by the City, 'if other murders of a similar nature take place shortly, and I see no reason to suppose that they will not, the omission of the offer of a reward on the part of the Government may exercise a very serious effect upon the stability of the Government itself'.

It seems reasonably clear that Warren forsaw a public reaction against the Government if any further murders took place, anticipated Parliamentary questions and perhaps Matthews's downfall. He realised that Matthews would publicly state that he had acted with the agreement of the Commissioner, which Matthews had not initially done, and that Warren would fall with Matthews. He therefore stated in his letter to Matthews that in the event of Parliamentary questions, Matthews was to say that Warren was in favour of a reward being offered[11].

Whilst the question of a reward occupied the Home Secretary and Warren, the other major cause of unrest, rightly perceived by Warren when he ordered the writing on the wall to be erased, was anti-semitism. From this distance in time and without knowing the people involved, it is difficult to say whether they were just bigoted or bigoted *and* incredibly stupid. At a meeting on 8 October of the Young Men's Christian Association, Revd Dr Tyler stated his opinion that crime was decidedly on the decrease and that Buck's Row was in a better condition than it had been twenty or thirty years before. Crime, he said, was 'largely brought about by the wholesale importation of the scum of other countries'.[12]

A man named Edward Dillon Lewis wrote a letter to *The Times* in which he argued that the murderer had to be a foreigner because that type of murder was unknown as having been committed by an Englishman, and because the celerity with which the crimes had been committed was inconsistent with 'ordinary English phlegmatic nature'[13].

There were many other anti-Jewish stories in circulation and reported in the press. People had some extraordinary ideas.

It would serve no purpose to examine in detail the efforts of the police following the murders of Stride and Eddowes. Chief Inspector Swanson summarized police activity in a report to the Home Office on 19 October. Some 80,000 handbills requesting information about any suspicious people were distributed; an extensive house-to-house search was conducted, over 2,000 lodgers being questioned and examined; the Thames Police made inquiries of sailors aboard ships in the docks or on the river; inquiries were made among Asiatics in the various opium dens in London. Approximately 300 people were questioned as a result of communications from members of the public; 76 butchers and slaughterers were questioned; and inquiries were made concerning the presence in London of some Greek gipsies. But perhaps the most fascinating comment in Swanson's report was that 'three of the persons calling themselves Cowboys who belonged to the American Exhibition were traced and satisfactorily accounted for themselves'[14].

These cowboys must have belonged to Buffalo Bill Cody's Wild West Show which arrived in London as part of Queen Victoria's Golden Jubilee celebrations. The show had sailed aboard the steamship *State of Nebraska* in the spring of 1887, and returned to the United States in the spring of 1888, but some of the cowboys are known to have liked Britain and stayed behind.

It is difficult to equate the London of Jack the Ripper with the age of the American Wild West, yet only seven years before the Whitechapel murders, in July 1881, Billy the Kid had been shot dead; in October of that same year Wyatt Earp and Doc Holliday fought it out with the Clantons in the gunfight at the OK Corral; and in April 1882 Bob Ford shot and killed Jesse James!

As Matthews remarked in his letter to Brise, Robert Anderson was summoned back from his holiday, returning to London on 6 October. In his autobiography he wrote:

On my return I found the Jack-the-Ripper scare in full swing. When the stolid English go in for a scare they take leave of all moderation and common sense. If nonsense were solid, the nonsense that was talked and written about those murders would sink a *Dreadnought*. The subject is an unsavoury one, and I must write about it with reserve.

He went on to explain:

I spent the day of my return to town, and half the following night, in reinvestigating the whole case, and next day I had a long conference on the subject with the Secretary of State and the Chief Commissioner of Police. 'We hold you responsible to find the murderer,' was Mr Matthews's greeting to me. My answer was to decline the responsibility. 'I hold myself responsible,' I said, 'to take all legitimate means to find him.' But I went on to say that the measures I found in operation were, in my opinion, wholly indefensible and scandalous; for these wretched women were plying their trade under definite Police protection. Let the Police of that district, I urged, receive orders to arrest every known 'street woman' found on the prowl after midnight, or else let us warn them that the Police will not protect them. Though the former course would have been merciful to the very small class of woman affected by it, it was deemed too drastic, and I fell back on the second.[15]

It was on 6 October that Elizabeth Stride was buried 'quietly and at the parish's expense'. Catharine Eddowes was buried on 8 October. Her body was laid in a polished elm coffin with oak mouldings, and it was borne in an open-glass hearse drawn by a pair of horses. There followed the mourning coaches and her cortège was conducted to the cemetery by the police, the route being thronged with crowds of people. All the expenses were met by a Mr Hawks, an undertaker[16].

There were also the usual run of people arrested on suspicion and released after questioning, and a few men who confessed to having committed the crimes[17]. A journalist dressed in women's clothes in the hope of attracting Jack the Ripper aroused the curiosity of a crowd in Lewisham who declared that he was a man and he had to be taken to the police station for his own protection[18]. A group of spiritualists claimed to have summoned the spirit of Elizabeth Stride and to have learned from her that the killer was a middle-aged man who lived off Commercial Street or Commercial Road and was one of a gang of twelve[18]. Sir Charles Warren investigated the possibility of using bloodhounds. Robert James Lees, supposedly possessed of psychic gifts, offered his services to the police and was 'called a fool and a lunatic'; on his second visit he was called 'a madman and a fool'; his third visit received the 'same result' and a promise that the police would write to him if his services were required[19].

Probably the most significant event of the month took place shortly after 5.00 p.m. on 16 October, when a letter and a cardboard box were delivered to George Lusk, the Chairman of the Whitechapel Vigilance Committee. The letter read: 'From Hell. Mr Lusk. Sir, I send you half the kidne I took from one woman, prasarved it for you, tother piece I fried and ate; it was very nice. I may send you a bloody knif that I took it out if you only wate a while longer. [signed] 'Catch me when you can Mr Lusk.'

Lusk was at first inclined to think that it was a hoax, but other members of the Committee decided to take the contents of the box to a doctor whose surgery was nearby, Dr Reed of 56 Mile End Road. After Dr Reed had examined it they took it to Dr Openshaw of the London Hospital, then passed it to the police, where it was examined by Dr Gordon Brown.

According to a report submitted to the Home Office by Chief Inspector Swanson:

> The result of the combined medical opinion they have taken upon it, is, that it is the kidney of a human adult; not charged with fluid, as it would have been in the case of a body handed over for the purpose of dissection to a hospital, but rather as it would be in the case where it was taken from the body not so destined. In other words similar kidneys might and could be obtained from any dead person whom a post mortem had been made from any cause by students or dissecting room porter.[20]

There is a considerable body of additional testimony – Martin Fido quotes an interview with Dr Sedgwick Saunders in the *Evening News*[21] – that the kidney was a hoax. This was also the opinion of the press[22]. It is difficult to reconcile the weight of expert medical opinion with Major Smith's assertion that it was the kidney removed from Catharine Eddowes, and Smith's account is inaccurate insofar as he says that the kidney was sent to the offices of the Central News, the manager of which sent it directly to Smith. Whatever the truth of the kidney's origins, only Smith maintained that it came from Eddowes, and Smith's account can be shown to be unreliable[23].

By 22 October the sensation had died down and there was 'very little excitement'[24] in the district.

CHAPTER TEN

Mary Jane Kelly

(aka Marie Jeanette Kelly, 'Fair Emma', 'Ginger')
(found murdered on Friday, 9 November 1888)

MARY JANE KELLY[1] is generally regarded as having been the last victim of Jack the Ripper. This view was held by Sir Robert Anderson[2] and Sir Melville Macnaghten[3]. Mary Jane Kelly has therefore assumed far greater importance than any other victim. Did the murders stop because Mary Kelly was all along the woman whom the killer was seeking? Did the murderer commit suicide or leave the country, or did his mental state degenerate to such an extent that he was confined by family or friends to a lunatic asylum?

It was said that Mary Jane Kelly was about 25 years old, 5 ft 7 ins. tall, stout, with blonde hair and blue eyes, and a fair complexion. Sir Melville Macnaghten described her as 'said to have been possessed of considerable personal attractions'[4].

According to Joseph Barnett, the man with whom Kelly had lived for 18 months until a few days before her death, she claimed to have been born in Limerick, though it is not clear whether she meant County Limerick or Limerick town. As a young child she moved with her family to Wales, where her father, John Kelly, had a job in an ironworks in Carnarvonshire or Carmarthenshire. She claimed that she had six or seven brothers and one sister. A friend named Lizzie Albrook said that Kelly had also spoken of a relative who was on the stage in London[5].

Kelly's landlord, John McCarthy[6], said that Kelly sometimes received letters from Ireland, he thought from her mother, but Joseph Barnett said that Kelly never corresponded with her family, although he said that she had once been visited by a brother who served in the 2nd Battalion Scots Guards. The 2nd Battalion was stationed in Dublin at the time, so perhaps the reporter misunderstood McCarthy to say mother when he in fact said brother[7].

Barnett and a Mrs Carthy, with whom Kelly once lived, both said that Kelly had come from a good family; Barnett described them as 'fairly well off' and Mrs Carthy as 'well-to-do-people'[8]. Kelly was stated to have been 'an excellent scholar and an artist of no mean degree'[8], whilst a friend, Maria Harvey, described her as 'much superior to that of most persons in her position in life'[9]. An unnamed woman who claimed to have lived at Cooley's Lodging House at the same time as Kelly, said that she was a fluent Welsh speaker[10].

Tom Cullen[11] claims that Mary Jane Kelly was nicknamed 'Black Mary'. He says that 'of all the mythomaniacs we have encountered so far, Mary Jane Kelly, or Black Mary, as they called her, was the worst. She seemed incapable of stating a fact without embroidering upon it.' Cullen goes on to record the observations of Dennis Barrett who 'as a boy, knew Black Mary by sight. ". . . She had her pitch outside the Ten Bells pub in Commercial Street, and woe to any woman who tried to poach her territory – such a woman was likely to have her hair pulled out in fistfuls." In short, Black Mary was a bit of a terror.'

Cullen goes on to say that 'Black Mary was no stranger to the Britannia. Many was the time she had rushed into this pub, after rolling some drunken sailor, to swap shawls with one of the other whores there. Thus disguised, she would take to the streets again, knowing that the police would be looking for her under a different description.'

By all accounts Mary Jane Kelly was an attractive woman, a cut above the average for the district, so the chance of her escaping detection by the simple ruse of changing shawls was slim. Whether or not Cullen found this information in a printed source or took it from sources such as Dennis Barrett, the description of Kelly's character is not borne out by other testimony. Nor is there any evidence to support Cullen's claim that Mary Jane Kelly was a mythomaniac of extraordinary proportions. What she said of her life cannot be proved, but neither can it be disproved.

Joseph Barnett said that he had 'always found her of sober habits'; landlord John McCarthy said that 'when in liquor she was very noisy; otherwise she was a very quiet woman'[12];

Caroline Maxwell said that Kelly 'was not a notorious character'[13]; Catherine Pickett said 'She was a good, quiet, pleasant girl, and was well liked by all of us.'[14]

Allowing for their views to have been moderated by respect for the deceased, it is difficult to reconcile what people at the time said about Kelly with Cullen's assertion that she was 'a bit of a terror'.

Barnett said that Mary Jane Kelly, when aged about 16 (c.1879), had married a collier named Davies, who was killed in a mine explosion two or three years later[15]. Kelly then went to Cardiff, where she stayed with a cousin and lived as a prostitute. At the inquest Barnett said that Kelly 'was in an infirmary there for 8 or 9 months'[16]. Mr Hemingway, Chief Constable in Cardiff, told a reporter that he had no recollection of any woman answering Kelly's description and 'so far as he was aware the woman had not come under notice of the police'[17].

Stephen Knight states that Kelly moved from Cardiff to London.

> She arrived in 1884 . . . Shortly after arriving in London she found her way to an East End convent which provided her with board and lodging in return for the coppers she earned doing domestic work. In 1885 she found a permanent position at the tobacconist's in Cleveland Street[18].

There seems to be a long-standing tradition among the nuns of the Providence Row Women's Refuge that Kelly was there, but I have been unable to locate any confirmatory documentary evidence or otherwise to substantiate the story. There is no evidence whatsoever that she ever worked in Cleveland Street.

According to Joseph Barnett, on her arrival in London Kelly had worked in a high-class bordello in the West End. He said that she had claimed to have accompanied a gentleman to Paris, but had not liked it there and had returned after about two weeks.

This part of Kelly's story is one which commentators on the Ripper case have had the greatest difficulty in believing, but it is a tale which Kelly seems to have told fairly consistently and for which there is some supporting evidence. On 10 November a Mrs Elizabeth Phoenix called at Leman Street Police Station and said that from the description of Kelly given in the newspapers she felt sure that Kelly was the same woman who had once resided at her brother-in-law's house at Breezer's Hill, off Pennington Street. Mrs Phoenix said the woman had said 'she was Welsh, and that her parents, who had discarded her, still resided in Cardiff, from which place she came. But on occasions she declared that she was Irish'[19]. Mrs Phoenix, who lived at 157 Bow Common Lane, Burdett Road, Bow, said that Kelly was very quarrelsome and abusive when drunk, but 'one of the most decent and nice girls you could meet when sober'[20].

A reporter for the Press Association made inquiries in the area of Breezer's Hill and wrote:

It would appear that on her arrival in London she made the acquaintance of a French woman residing in the neighbourhood of Knightsbridge, who, she informed her friends, led her to pursue the degraded life which had now culminated in her untimely end. She made no secret of the fact that while she was with this woman she drove about in a carriage and made several journeys to the French capital, and, in fact, led a life which is described as that 'of a lady'. By some means, however, at present not exactly clear, she suddenly drifted into the East End, Here fortune failed her and a career which stands out in bold and sad contrast to her earlier experience was commenced. Her experience of the East End appears to have begun with a woman who resided in one of the thoroughfares off Ratcliffe Highway, now known as St George's Street. This person seems to have received Kelly direct from the West End home, for she had not been there very long when, it is stated, both women went to the French 'lady's' residence and demanded the box which contained numerous dresses of a costly description.

Kelly at last indulged in intoxicants, it is stated, to an extent which made her unwelcome. From St George's Street she went to lodge with a Mrs Carthy at Breezer's Hill (off Pennington Street). This place she left about 18 months or two years ago and from that time seems to have left Ratcliffe altogether.

Mrs Carthy said that Kelly had left her house and gone to live with a man who was apparently in the building trade and who Mrs Carthy believed would have married Kelly[21].

Kelly's story is far from impossible. There was a cross-channel traffic in English girls for the brothels of Belgium and France, and Regent Street was particularly noted for apparently independent Frenchwomen, some of whom probably acted as *placeurs,* on the lookout for attractive young women to take abroad. The *placeur* was not seeking virgins or innocent young girls. The 'victim' had to undergo a check for disease and, once abroad, make a formal declaration that they wished to enter a brothel, both of which would have alerted anyone to the job before them. The *placeur*'s trick, apparently, was to misrepresent the income the girl could expect to receive and the conditions in which she was supposed to live[22].

Kelly's story fits the activities of the *placeurs*; approached by a French woman, treated well and her suspicions lulled in a West End brothel, then lured by a 'gentleman' to Paris. By this time the *placeur* would have made a considerable financial investment and Kelly would certainly have been threatened if she had announced her intention of returning to London. Fear may thus account for her not returning to the West End brothel, but seeking sanctuary with the women in St George Street among the teeming population of the East End and for her gradual reliance on alcohol. Of course, this can only be conjecture.

As stated, Kelly left Mrs Carthy's house and went to live with a man who had a connection with the building trade and who Mrs Carthy thought would have married Kelly. It is not certain who this man could have been. Joseph Barnett said that Kelly had for a time lived with a man named Morganstone opposite or in the vicinity of Stepney gasworks. She had then taken up with a man named Joseph Fleming and lived somewhere in Bethnal Green. Fleming was a stonemason or mason's plasterer. He used to visit Kelly, according to Barnett, and Kelly seemed very fond of him. A neighbour of Kelly's in Miller's Court, Julia Venturney, said that Kelly was fond of a man other than Barnett whose name was also Joe. He was, she thought, a costermonger and sometimes visited and gave money to Kelly[23]. Perhaps Barnett confused the order of Kelly's liaisons and she left Mrs Carthy to live with Joseph Fleming, then went to live with Morganstone.

By 1886 Mary Jane Kelly was living at Cooley's Lodging House in Thrawl Street, Spitalfields, and according to an unnamed prostitute, was living there when she met Joseph Barnett[24].

Joseph Barnett first met Mary Jane Kelly in Commercial Street on Friday 8 April 1887, Good Friday. Barnett, a porter at Billingsgate Market and sometime fruit hawker, took Kelly for a drink and they arranged to meet the following day. It was at this second meeting that they decided to live together[25].

Mary Kelly moved out of Cooley's Lodging House in Thrawl Street and took lodgings with Barnett in George Street, off Commercial Street. Later they moved to 'Paternoster Court', Dorset Street. This is presumably Little Paternoster Row, since there is no Paternoster Court off Dorset Street. They were evicted for not paying the rent and for getting drunk. They moved to Brick Lane, one of the most notorious areas of the East End – between Shoreditch High Street and Brick Lane was an area called the Jago in which operated the Old Nichol mob, a gang at one time thought to be responsible for the Whitechapel murders. From Brick Lane they moved to Miller's Court off Dorset Street, to a single room, designated 13 Miller's Court.

Between 26 and 27 Dorset Street there was a three-foot wide arched passage which led into Miller's Court. There were six houses in the court, three on either side, each neatly whitewashed up to the first floor windows.

Kelly's room was the back room of 26 Dorset Street, a false partition having been erected to cut it off from the rest of the house, and it was entered by a door at the end of the arched passage. Anyone entering or leaving Miller's Court would have to pass it.

Kelly's room was about twelve feet square. Opposite the door was a fireplace; on the left of the door were two windows, one of which was near enough for someone to reach through and bolt or unbolt the door. To the right of the door there was a bedside table, so close that the door would bang against it when swung open. Next to the table there was a bed, its head against the door-wall, its side against the right-hand wall. Some sources mention a table and a chair, and a cheap print titled 'The Fisherman's Widow' hanging over the fireplace[26].

Opposite Miller's Court there was Crossingham's common lodging house which catered for upwards of 300 men and women and was described as of a somewhat superior character. Another well-frequented establishment was two doors away at 28 Dorset Street. At 30 Dorset Street was the lodging house where Annie Chapman had lived with Jack Sivvey. It was also reported that Catharine Eddowes had at one time lived in Dorset Street[27]. The lamps in the windows and over the doors of these various establishments meant that Dorset Street was fairly well lit at night, but there was no lighting in Miller's Court, though a wall-light two or three yards from the Court almost illuminated the entrance to the passage. Affixed to the wall two doors away was a large placard advertising a reward of £100 offered by the *Illustrated Police News* for the discovery of the murderer of Mary Ann Nichols.

Kelly had taken the room in her own name at a weekly rent of 4/6. At the time of her death she was 30/- in arrears. This was a very large sum of money and it is surprising that McCarthy had allowed Kelly to accumulate such a debt.

Joseph Barnett lost his job, possibly in late August or early September if the arrears coincided with his loss of employment. On the day of Kelly's murder (9 November), in an interview with Inspector Abberline, Joseph Barnett said that as a result of his losing his job, Kelly had returned to prostitution, for which reason he decided to leave her[28]. The couple had an argument and split up, and Barnett left Kelly between 5 p.m. and 6 p.m. on 30 October. It may have been on this date that they had a fight during which one of the panes of glass in the window nearest the door was broken[29]. Barnett went to live at Mr Buller's Boarding House[30] at 24-25 New Street, Bishopsgate. Following the murder of Kelly, Barnett lived with his sister at 21 Portpool Lane, off Gray's Inn Road[31].

At the inquest and to various journalists Barnett gave a different explanation of his reasons for splitting up with Kelly. He said that she had allowed prostitutes to stay in the room, to which he had objected, and this had caused the rift.

'She would never have gone wrong again,' he told a reporter, 'and I shouldn't have left her if it had not been for the prostitutes stopping at the house. She only let them because she was good hearted and did not like to refuse them shelter on cold bitter nights[32].'

There is some confusion about the identity of the prostitute(s) whom Kelly allowed to use the room. In the same interview he said: 'We lived comfortably until Marie allowed a prostitute named Julia to sleep in the same room. I objected; and, as Mr Harvey afterwards came and stayed there, I left her and took lodgings elsewhere.'

We know that a woman named Maria Harvey stayed with Kelly for a few nights shortly before the murder and it might be inferred from Barnett's statement that she was joined by her husband, in which case 'Julia' would be an alias for Mrs Harvey. However, this was not the case because the police located and interviewed Julia, so 'Mr Harvey' is presumably a mistake for Mrs Harvey. We do not know who Julia was.

This is important. Barnett consistently used the plural 'prostitutes' and 'them', so more than one prostitute was allowed to use the room, and we know of 'Julia' and Maria Harvey. Could there have been others? The importance rests on the fact that several people claimed that they had seen Kelly several hours after the medical experts were of the opinion that she was dead. Most commentators are convinced that these sightings were mistakes. However, the body was mutilated beyond recognition, so was it in fact the body of Mary Jane Kelly or the body of a prostitute whom she allowed to stay the night in her room? Is it possible that Kelly could have feared someone, perhaps someone from her days in the West End? Could she have thought that the body in her room would be mistaken for her and that her widely reported death would bring her worries to an end?

It is easy to build complex theories on very slender evidence, and in this case the 'evidence' can hardly be described as such, but a statement by Barnett at the inquest should be considered.

CORONER: Have you heard her speak of being afraid of anyone?

BARNETT: Yes; several times. I bought newspapers, and I read to her everything about the murders,

	which she asked me about.
CORONER:	Did she express fear of any particular individual?
BARNETT:	No, sir.

Who was it that Mary Kelly was afraid of – the other 'Joe' in her life? The friends of the French woman in Knightsbridge? Could she have been so afraid that she saw the dead body in her room as an advantage to herself? Barnett's testimony shows that Kelly was interested in and informed about the Whitechapel murders. The *Evening News* had earlier observed: 'As women of this sort are now on the alert in Whitechapel, we may infer that the assassin must appeal to them in some way that disarms suspicion. In other words, he cannot suggest by his appearance that he is a bloodthirsty miscreant.'[33] This reasoning must surely apply to Mary Jane Kelly, a young woman reputedly blessed with far greater physical attractions than the earlier victims and therefore not likely to have been so desperate for clients that she needed to take risks with men who may have raised her suspicions. Her killer must therefore have appeared normal and harmless. He may even have been known to her, a view which possibly gains some support from the medical opinion that she could have been asleep when murdered.

Maria Harvey, who had stayed with Kelly on the nights of Monday and Tuesday, 5 and 6 November, moved to a new lodging at 3 New Court, another of the alleys running off Dorset Street on the Wednesday. Later in the day Kelly bought a halfpenny candle from John McCarthy's shop and was later seen in Miller's Court by Thomas Bowyer, a pensioned soldier nicknamed 'Indian Harry'[34], who was employed by McCarthy. His testimony on this sighting could have considerable importance and I give the report in full:

> Harry Bowyer [sic] states that on Wednesday night he saw a man speaking to Kelly who resembled the description given by the fruiterer of the supposed Berner Street murderer. He was, perhaps, 27 or 28 and had a dark moustache and very peculiar eyes. His appearance was rather smart and attention was drawn to him by

showing very white cuffs and a rather long white collar, the ends of which came down in front over a black coat. He did not carry a bag.[35]

There is no particular reason why a reasonably well-dressed man should not have been in the neighbourhood, but it is unlikely that one would have ventured up Miller's Court, a cul-de-sac, without a reason for doing so. Was he a client of Kelly's, somebody who she would therefore have known and had no reason to distrust at a subsequent meeting?

At 8.00 p.m. on Wednesday 7 November Sarah Lewis[36], a laundress living at 24 Great Pearl Street, was in the vicinity of Bethnal Green Road with her sister when they were accosted by a man who asked them to accompany him to a lonely spot. They refused, became alarmed and ran off. The man was of average height, a pale face, and with a black moustache. He was wearing a long brown overcoat over a short black jacket, pepper-and-salt trousers and an unusually high round hat. The black bag he carried was about 9 inches long. Lewis saw the same man in Commercial Street on the night Kelly was murdered.

Maria Harvey claimed at the inquest that she had spent all Thursday afternoon in Kelly's company and was in Kelly's room when Joseph Barnett arrived, at which time she left, leaving 'two men's dirty shirts, a little boy's shirt, a black overcoat, a black crêpe bonnet with black satin strings, a pawn ticket for a grey shawl, upon which 2/- had been lent, and a little girl's white petticoat'[37]. However, The Times and the Daily Telegraph on 10 November 1888, both reported Maria Harvey as saying that Kelly had visited her in New Court and that they had parted company about 7.30 p.m., Kelly going off in the direction of Leman Street. The curious thing is that neither story appears to be true.

Joseph Barnett, who had been in the habit of calling on Kelly most days since their break-up and giving her money when he had any, said that he called on Kelly between 7.30 p.m. and 7.45 p.m. that Thursday night. When asked if anybody was with Kelly when he called, Barnett said, 'Yes. A female who lives in the same court.' The woman referred to was not Maria Harvey, but 20 year old Lizzie Albrook, who lived in Miller's

Court and worked at a lodging house in Dorset Street. Albrook was not called to testify at the inquest, but there can be little doubt that she, not Maria Harvey, was the woman with Kelly when Barnett arrived.

Albrook's evidence is valuable for the insight it provides into Kelly's character. 'About the last thing she said was, "Whatever you do don't you do wrong and turn out as I have." She had often spoken to me in this way and warned me against going on the streets as she had done. She told me, too, that she was heartily sick of the life she was leading and wished she had money enough to go back to Ireland where her people lived. I do not believe she would have gone out as she did if she had not been obliged to do so to keep herself from starvation.'

Lizzie Albrook's evidence inevitably makes Maria Harvey's testimony suspect. Albrook said she left Barnett and Kelly together at 8.00 p.m. Barnett left a short time later. He returned to Mr Buller's boarding house and remained there playing whist until 12.30 a.m., at which time he went to bed.

Sometime during the night – the time is unstated – 20 year old Sarah Roney and a friend met a man in Brushfield Street, the next street along from Dorset Street. He was wearing a black coat and a tall hat and he carried a black bag. The man asked, 'Will you come with me?' The girls refused and inquired about the contents of his bag. 'Something the girls don't like,' he replied, then walked away[38]. This same man may have been seen by a Mrs Paumier on the day following the murder of Kelly.

At 8.00 p.m. Julia Venturney, who lived at 1 Miller's Court, returned to her room and went to bed. She maintained that she had not slept at all that night and that she did not hear any sounds from either Mary Kelly's room or Miller's Court. Her testimony is contradicted by a weight of other evidence; she said that although Kelly often sang Irish songs, she had heard no singing that night, yet other witnesses maintained that Kelly had been singing for some considerable length of time. It must be assumed that Julia Venturney did in fact sleep[39].

Mary Jane Kelly's movements from the time when Joseph Barnett left her in the room in Miller's Court until 11.45 p.m. are unknown. A Press Association reporter interviewed a young woman named Margaret who said that she had spoken to Kelly

151

in Dorset Street and that Kelly had told her that 'she had no money and intended to make away with herself'. A short time later Margaret had seen Kelly go off with a man of shabby appearance.[40]

A source whose name is not given, but who was described as 'an associate of the deceased' and who told the same story about Kelly intending to 'make away with herself', from which it might be safe to assume that it was Margaret, was reported to have seen Kelly at 10.30 p.m. Kelly went off with a respectably dressed man, from whom she had taken some money, and took him to her lodgings 'which are on the second floor'. Kelly, it was said, had a little boy who was taken to a neighbour's house. When he returned to his mother's rooms that morning, a man who was with her mother sent him on an errand.[41]

This woman cannot have been Kelly, who did not live on the second floor and did not have a child. The woman referred to was probably named Lizzie Fisher[42].

There was also a story circulating that the police were looking for a woman named Elizabeth Foster who, it was said, had been drinking with Kelly that night[43]. And it was also said that at 11.00 p.m. she was seen in the Britannia public house (commonly known as 'the Ringers') with a young man with a dark moustache (the man earlier seen by Bowyer?) who appeared very respectable and well dressed. She was then intoxicated[44].

The first reliable report of Mary Kelly after 8.00 p.m. comes from a widow named Mary Ann Cox who lived at 5 Miller's Court. She was a prostitute. At 11.45 p.m. she entered Dorset Street from Commercial Street. Walking just ahead of her was Kelly, accompanied by a man. Kelly, said Cox, was wearing a linsey frock and a red knitted crossover (a shawl) pulled around her shoulders. She was bare-headed and drunk. The man was aged about 35 or 36, was stout, and was dressed in shabby clothes – a long overcoat and a round billycock hat. He had a blotchy face and a full carroty moustache. He was carrying a pail of beer.

Mrs Cox followed them into Miller's Court. They were standing outside number 13 and Mrs Cox said 'Goodnight' as she passed. 'Goodnight,' Kelly replied, and added, 'I am going to sing.' Mrs Cox hurried towards her own room and a minute or two later heard Kelly begin to sing *Only a Violet I Plucked from my Mother's Grave*. At midnight Mary Ann Cox returned to the streets. Kelly was still singing the same refrain.[45]

At 12.30 a.m. a flower-seller named Catherine Picket, having become irritated by Kelly's singing, decided to complain, but was stopped by her husband. 'If it hadn't been for my Dave I should have come out of my room and caught the whitelivered villain,' she said. 'But Dave just says to me, "You leave the woman alone." So I stopped where I was and goes to bed.'[14] We may imagine that the hapless Dave spent the rest of his life being told that but for him Jack the Ripper would have been caught.

By 1.00 a.m. it was starting to rain and Mary Ann Cox returned to her room to warm herself by her fire for a few minutes before returning to the streets. Kelly was still – or had resumed – singing.

About this time Elizabeth Prater, the wife of William Prater, a boot machinist who had deserted her about 5 years earlier, returned to her room (room 20), which was located directly above Kelly's. A prostitute, she stood at the entrance to Miller's Court for about half an hour, waiting for the man with whom she now lived. He did not turn up, so Prater went into Mr McCarthy's shop, where she chatted for about ten minutes before going up to her room. During that time she had not seen anyone enter or leave Miller's Court and there was no sound of singing. Prater went to her room, put two chairs in front of her door, and without bothering to undress, just lay on her bed and went to sleep. She had been drinking that night and slept soundly[46].

At 2.00 a.m. George Hutchinson[47], of the Victoria Home, Commercial Street, had just returned from Romford and was walking along Commercial Street. At the corner of Thrawl Street he passed a man, but paid him scant attention. By Flower and Dean Street he met Mary Kelly, whom he claimed to know very well. Kelly approached him.

'Mr Hutchinson,' she said, 'can you lend me sixpence?'

'I can't,' said Hutchinson. 'I've spent all my money going down to Romford.'

'I must go and look for some money,' said Kelly, who walked in the direction of Thrawl Street. Hutchinson watched

153

her go. As she reached the man whom Hutchinson had earlier passed, the man placed his hand on Kelly's shoulder and said something which Hutchinson did not hear. Kelly and the man laughed. Kelly said, 'All right.' The man said, 'You will be all right for what I have told you.' He then put his arm around Kelly's shoulders and they began to walk back towards Dorset Street.

Hutchinson, standing beneath the lamp outside the Queen's Head public house at the corner of Fashion Street, saw the man distinctly as he and Kelly passed him. He had a soft felt hat drawn down over his eyes, had a dark complexion – Jewish appearance – and a heavy moustache turned up at the ends, dark eyes and bushy eyebrows. He was wearing a long dark coat trimmed with astrakhan, a white collar with a black necktie, in which was fixed a horseshoe pin. He wore dark spats and light button-over boots. A massive gold chain was displayed in his waistcoat. His watch chain had a large seal with a red stone hanging from it. He carried a pair of kid gloves in his right hand and in his left there was a small package. He was about 5 ft 6 ins. tall, aged about 35 or 36.

Kelly and the man crossed Commercial Street and turned down Dorset Street. Hutchinson trailed behind. He watched as they stood talking outside the passage leading to Miller's Court. They stood there for about three minutes. Kelly was heard to say, 'All right, my dear. Come along. You will be comfortable.'

The man put his arm around Kelly, who kissed him and said – incongruously – 'I've lost my handkerchief!' The man pulled a red handkerchief out of his pocket and gave it to her. The couple then went down Miller's Court. Hutchinson waited. He waited until 3.00 a.m. wandering off as a clock struck the hour[48].

Hutchinson did not give this information until 6.00 p.m. on 12 November 1888, by which time the inquest into Kelly's death had been concluded. He later told his story to a representative of the Press Agency and supplied the additional details. He said that he had been out until 3.00 a.m. on 13 November looking for the man and thought, but was not certain, that he had seen him in Petticoat Lane on the morning of 11 November[49].

A young woman named Sarah Lewis made a statement to Inspector Abberline on 9 November and later gave testimony at the inquest. She said that in consequence of having had an argument with her husband, she had gone to stay 'with the Keylers' who lived opposite Kelly in Miller's Court. She said that she arrived in Dorset Street 'between 2.00 a.m. and 3.00 a.m.' and saw a man leaning against the wall of the lodging house opposite the passage leading into Miller's Court. At the inquest her testimony was more precise. She said that the time was shortly after 2.30 a.m., which she knew because she had looked at Spitalfields' Church clock as she passed. She mentioned a man who was leaning against the lodging house wall, but also commented that a young man and woman had passed along the street ahead of her and that she had seen outside 'the Ringers' public house a woman in company with a man who she was sure was the same man who had earlier accosted her[36].

However, several newspapers on 12 November carried interviews with a woman called Mrs Kennedy who told a story which in all essential details was the same as that told by Sarah Lewis. It is beyond question that they were one and the same woman. The differences in times and details in the various reports given by Kennedy/Lewis make it impossible to accept her as a reliable witness. At best she saw and therefore confirms the story of George Hutchinson.

At 3.00 a.m. Mary Cox returned to her room. It was raining hard. There was no noise or light coming from Kelly's room. Mrs Cox went to bed and tried to get some sleep.

Elizabeth Prater, in the room above Kelly's, was woken by her pet kitten Diddles walking across her neck. She thought that the time was after 4.00 a.m. because the lodging house light was off. At the inquest she said: 'I heard a cry of "Oh! Murder!" as the cat came on me and I pushed her down, the voice was a faint voice – the noise seemed to come from close by – it is nothing uncommon to hear cries of murder, so I took no notice. I did not hear it a second time. I heard nothing else whatever.'[46]

Mrs Kennedy/Sarah Lewis also claimed to have heard a cry, which she described as a loud shout. 'The sound seemed to come from the direction of the deceased's room; there was only one scream – I took no notice of it.'[50]

Dr Bond, who examined the body of Mary Kelly, gave it as his opinion that Kelly's face was covered with a sheet at the time of the attack[51], from which it might be assumed that she was asleep. In any event, with no illumination from the interior of the room or from the court and with a sheet obscuring her vision, Kelly is unlikely to have had any intimation of what was about to happen and consequently had no time to cry out. But even if she did have time, is it likely that she would have cried out 'Oh! Murder!' rather than yell for help or simply scream? It must be regarded as doubtful that the cry came from Kelly's room. On the other hand, the cry would be more indicative of the discovery of a murder than an actual attack. But if somebody discovered the body between 3.30 a.m. and sometime after 4.00 a.m., why didn't they report it? This is a question which returns us again to the possibility that the victim was not Kelly, but that Kelly discovered the body.

From the foregoing testimony, Mrs Cox heard Kelly singing at 1.00 a.m., but when Elizabeth Prater returned to the Court a few minutes later there was no noise or light coming from her room. Mrs Kennedy/Sarah Lewis's testimony is too unreliable to be considered – at best she saw Hutchinson and therefore confirms his story, but Hutchinson's evidence has to be regarded as suspect, for not only was his description of the man seen with Kelly exceptionally detailed, he also failed to give his evidence until after the conclusion of the inquest. Having said this, Inspector Abberline regarded Hutchinson's as 'an important statement' and gave it as his opinion that 'the statement is true'. Abberline said that Hutchinson claimed to have known Kelly for three years and to have occasionally given her a few shillings.[52]

Mary Jane Kelly was alive at 1.00 a.m., probably alive at 2.00 a.m, and, if the man seen by Hutchinson was not the murderer, she was possibly alive at and for some time after 3.00 a.m. The medical testimony was that Kelly was murdered between 2.00 a.m. and 3.00 a.m., possibly, but not significantly, later.

At 5.00 a.m. Elizabeth Prater left her room and went to the Ten Bells for a glass of rum. At that time there were two or three men harnessing some horses in Dorset Street, and at

156

5.45 a.m. Mrs Cox heard what she thought to be a man's footsteps leaving Miller's Court.

Catherine Picket woke up at 7.30 a.m. and left her room half an hour later to go to the market to buy some flowers. It was chilly and raining and she thought she would borrow Kelly's shawl. She went to Kelly's room and knocked on the door, but there was no reply. Thinking that Kelly was asleep, she went off to market.

At 8.00 a.m. a tailor named Maurice Lewis who lived in Dorset Street was reported by *The Times,* 10 November 1888, to have seen Kelly leave her room, then return to it a few moments later.

At 8.30 a.m. Caroline Maxwell, the wife of Henry Maxwell, the deputy of the lodging house at 14 Dorset Street, opposite Miller's Court, set off for the milk shop in Bishopsgate Street to get some milk for her husband's breakfast. She claimed to have seen Mary Kelly at the entrance to Miller's Court. Surprised at seeing Kelly up so early, she called across the street, 'Mary, what brings you up so early?'

'Oh! I do feel so bad. I have the horrors of drink on me.'

'Why don't you go to the Ringer's and have half a pint?'

'I've been there and had it,' said Kelly, 'But I've brought it all up again.' Kelly indicated some vomit on the pavement. (This is what Mrs Maxwell told Inspector Abberline, but at the inquest she said that Kelly motioned with her head, from which she assumed that Kelly had been to the pub at the corner).

'I pity the feeling,' said Mrs Maxwell and went off on her trip to the milk shop.

Mrs Maxwell was sternly questioned at the inquest. She admitted that she had only spoken to Kelly twice, but that she had seen her regularly over a period of about four months. She was certain of the time of day, she said, because she had been going to the milk shop in Bishopsgate Street, where she had not been for some time. Inquiries at the milk shop apparently confirmed the day and time of her visit.[53] Furthermore, a young woman whose name was not revealed was reported to have informed the police that she was positive that she had seen Kelly between 8.00 a.m. and 8.45 a.m.[54].

At 9.00 a.m. Mrs Maxwell again saw Mary Jane Kelly. This time she was standing outside the Britannia ('the Ringers') talking to a man. Mrs Maxwell told Inspector Abberline that he looked like a market porter. Kelly, she said, was dressed in a dark skirt, black velvet bodice and maroon shawl (note the description of Kelly's dress given by Mary Ann Cox).

At 10.00 a.m. Maurice Lewis said that he was playing pitch and toss in 'McCarthy's Court'. He and his companions then went to 'the Ringers'. He was positive that on going in he saw Kelly drinking with some other people. He was not sure whether there was a man among them.[55].

These claims are very strange. The witnesses seem to have been sincere, but it is difficult to accept that they saw Mary Jane Kelly. However, if Barnett's identification of Kelly was a lie or a mistake, and if Kelly, on discovering a mutilated corpse in her room, had the presence of mind to use the discovery to arrange her own disappearance, then the possibility, remote though it is, does exist that the victim of room 13 was not Mary Jane Kelly.

At 10.45 a.m. John McCarthy called for his assistant, Thomas 'Indian Harry' Bowyer. 'Go to number 13 and try and get some rent,' he instructed. Bowyer hurried from the shop and went down the passage to Kelly's room. He knocked at the door, but did not get a reply. He tried the door, but it was locked. He knocked again. He looked through the keyhole, but could not see Kelly. He went into the court, reached through the broken pane of glass in the window of room 13 and plucked back the muslin curtain. The first thing he saw was two lumps of flesh on the bedside table. These were Mary Kelly's breasts. He then looked at the bed – the horribly butchered mess that lay there was barely recognizable as a human being.

Boyer rushed back to McCarthy. 'Guv'nor! I knocked at the door and could not make anyone answer. I looked through the window and saw a lot of blood . . .'

'Good God! Harry, you don't mean to say that . . .' McCarthy, with Bowyer following, rushed round to room 13 and looked through the window. 'The sight we saw I cannot drive away from my mind,' he said later. 'It looked more like the work of a devil than of a man. I had heard a great deal about the Whitechapel murders, but I declare to God I had never expected to see such a sight as this. The whole scene is more

158

than I can describe. I hope I may never see such a sight as this again.'[56]

McCarthy told Bowyer not to tell anyone, but to go to the police station and fetch someone. Bowyer hurried off. McCarthy followed. They went to the Commercial Street Police Station and asked for either Inspector Reid or Inspector Abberline. Neither was available. They spoke instead to Inspector Beck who, accompanied by Sergeant Betham, hurried to Miller's Court. Beck took one look and immediately sent for police assistance and the Divisional Surgeon, Dr George Bagster Phillips. The time was now about 11.00 a.m., Friday 9 November 1888.

The precise sequence of events now becomes hazy. The police seem to have maintained a silence on the subject and the newspaper reporters were forced to gather snippets of information from wherever they could. Much of it was wrong. Some of it was wildly inaccurate. The initial report of the murder in the *Eastern Post* (10 November) was almost entirely wrong. Statements were confused or wrongly attributed, and times and names were often incorrect.

The news of the murder soon spread through the neighbourhood. The Press Association reported that 'Women rushed about the streets telling their neighbours the news and shouting their rage and indignation.' A large crowd gathered in Dorset Street. Fortunately, the anticipation of Socialist disturbances in connection with the Lord Mayor's Show had resulted in forty extra constables being sent to the Commercial Street Police Station and Inspector Beck was able to employ these men in crowd control. He cordoned off each end of Dorset Street, cleared idlers away and closed Miller's Court, posting two burly constables at the entrance with orders to let nobody enter or leave. Beck had telegraphed the news of the murder to other police officials and requested bloodhounds[57].

Dr George Bagster Phillips arrived at 11.15 a.m. He viewed the body through the window and satisfied himself that there was nobody in the room in need of his immediate assistance. At 11.30 Inspector Abberline arrived, received a general report from Inspector Beck, and had a hurried conference with Dr Phillips, who advised against entering the room as doing so might obscure the scent for the bloodhounds.

159

At midday Mrs Paumier, a roasted chestnut seller on the corner of Widegate Street, about 2 minutes' walk from Miller's Court, was approached by a man who said, 'I suppose you have heard about the murder in Dorset Street?' Mrs Paumier replied that she had. The man grinned. 'I know more about it than you,' he said and walked off. He was dressed like a gentleman, wore a black coat, speckled trousers and a black silk hat. He was about 5 ft 6 ins. tall, had a black moustache and carried a black shiny bag. Mrs Paumier thought that he was the same man who had accosted Sarah Roney and her friend[58].

After considerable delay and difficulty a photographer was brought to the scene and took photographs through the window. A slight drizzling rain was falling and it was so overcast that it was almost dark in Miller's Court. In the conditions and with the equipment available, the photographer did a remarkable job. The photographs still exist. They convey far better than words ever could the sheer barbarity of Jack the Ripper. More than this, they are a testimony to the nightmare which must have been the murderer's sick and perverted mind.

Inspector Arnold arrived with the news that the order for the bloodhounds had been countermanded and that the door to Kelly's room was to be forced open. McCarthy forced open the door with a pick-axe. The door swung open and hit against the bedside table.

The locked door is a mystery in itself. Barnett said that the key to the door had been lost some time before and that he and Kelly effected entry by reaching through the broken window to bolt or unbolt the door. At the inquest Inspector Abberline referred to 'an impression' that the murderer had taken away the key to the room. On 10 November *The Times* reported a correspondent who had seen the interior of the room and who described 'the lock of the door as a spring one.'

Whatever the means by which the door was locked, it could easily be opened by reaching through the broken window. Surely during the time the police had been waiting in the Court one of them would have assessed that this was the easiest means of effecting entry and would have used it when the time came. Why, then, did the police break open the door with a pick-axe? Had Kelly found the key and neglected to tell Barnett? Did the killer have the key?

Mary Jane Kelly was lying on her back on the bed, dressed only in a chemise. Her throat had been cut from ear to ear down to the spinal column. According to the description of the body given by John McCarthy – a very vivid account which fully conveys the horror of the sight which greeted him when he accompanied the police into the room: 'She had been completely disembowelled, and her entrails had been taken out and placed on the table . . . The woman's nose had been cut off, and her face gashed and mutilated so that it was quite beyond recognition. Both her breasts, too, had been cut clean away and placed by the side of her liver and other entrails on the table[59].'

Although many newspapers stated that no part of the viscera was missing, the *Daily Telegraph* reported, 'We are enabled to state, on good authority, that notwithstanding all that has been said to the contrary, a portion of the body organs was missing.'[60] The Central News also reported 'that the uterus, as in the case of the Mitre Square victim, has been removed.'[61]

A post-mortem was conducted and a report by Dr Bond[62] was submitted to the police and the Home Office on 10 November. It read in part:

> The body was laying on the bed at the time of my visit at two o'clock quite naked and mutilated . . . Rigor Mortis had set in but increased during the progress of the examination. From this it is difficult to say with any certainty the exact time that had elapsed since death as the period varies from six to twelve hours before rigidity sets in. The body was comparatively cold at two o'clock and the remains of a recently taken meal were found in the stomach and scattered about over the intestines. It was therefore pretty certain that the woman must have been dead about twelve hours and the partly digested food would indicate that death took place about three or four hours after food was taken, so one or two o'clock in the morning would be the probable time of the murder . . .
>
> The corner of the sheet to the right of the woman's head was much cut and saturated with blood, indicating that the face may have been covered with the sheet at the time

of the attack . . .

In each case [i.e. all five murders from Nichols to Kelly] the mutilation was inflicted by a person who had no scientific or anatomical knowledge. In my opinion he does not even possess the technical knowledge of a butcher or horse slaughterer or any person accustomed to cut up dead animals . . .

The murderer in external appearance is quite likely to be a quiet inoffensive looking man probably middle-aged and neatly and respectably dressed . . .

Assuming the murderer to be such a person as I have just described, he would be solitary and eccentric in his habits, also he is most likely to be a man without regular occupation, but with some small income or pension. He is probably living among respectable persons who have some knowledge of his character and habits and who may have grounds for suspicion that he isn't quite right in his mind at times. Such persons would probably be unwilling to communicate suspicions to the Police for fear of trouble or notoriety, whereas if there were prospect of a reward it might overcome their scruples[63].

Bond's report is highly speculative, his deductions befitting Sherlock Holmes, and it contains one basic error: Mary Kelly's body was not naked, but dressed in a chemise, this garment being clearly visible in the photographs. Further, although Dr Bond did not examine the previous victims, he felt able, after a reading of the medical notes, to assert confidently that the murderer had no anatomical skill or knowledge whatsoever. Other doctors, Dr Phillips, for example, positively, and Dr Brown tentatively, asserted the opposite.

What is possibly a significant point is that Kelly had undressed. The cuts in the sheet suggested that it had been pulled up around her neck, wholly or partly covering her face. The inference seems to be that Kelly had gone to sleep. The question is, had she permitted a client to spend the night with her, or had she gone to bed alone? If the former, was her client somebody she knew and trusted; if the latter, had she been singled out by her murderer, who had waited until Kelly had retired for the night?

The murder of Mary Jane Kelly was followed by a repeat of the procedures following each of the previous murders – a search of common lodging houses, the questioning of lodgers, a series of arrests and subsequent releases after questioning and investigation.

On 10 November 1888, the Cabinet decided to offer a pardon to any accomplice 'not being the person who contrived or actually committed the murder'. On that same day Sir Charles Warren's resignation was accepted by Home Secretary Henry Matthews – Warren had written an article defending the police for the November issue of *Murray's Magazine*. According to a Home Office circular of 27 May 1879, of which Warren claimed ignorance, the article contravened policy. Warren felt that the policy prevented him from defending the police and that he could not continue as Commissioner if bound by such a restriction. He was replaced by James Monro.

On 11 November the East End was shrouded in a carboniferous fog[64]. At 10.00 p.m. a woman named Humphreys was passing George Yard, where Martha Tabram was murdered, when a man with a blackened face and wearing large spectacles appeared out of the darkness. 'What do you want?' she asked. The man merely laughed and beat a hasty retreat. The woman cried out 'Murder!' and people descended on the spot. The man was caught at the corner of Wentworth Street, among his captors being a well-known pugilist named Bendoff. The police arrived and amid cries of 'Lynch him!' from a rapidly gathered crowd, they took him to the police station.

This black-faced man – the large spectacles becoming large white-painted circles around the eyes, plus a white-painted nose, moustache and mouth – features in a book by Edwin T Woodhall, who claims that the man savagely attacked two government officials and made his escape from custody, later being found drowned in the Thames. Woodhall goes on to say that the story was confirmed by Sir Melville Macnaghten in his autobiography. Macnaghten does in fact express his belief that Jack the Ripper committed suicide in the Thames 'after he had knocked out a Commissioner of Police and very nearly settled the hash of one of Her Majesty's principal Secretaries of State (p. 62). But Macnaghten is actually referring to the resignation of Warren and the press condemnation of Henry Matthews. The suicide victim was not the black-faced man, but a barrister named Druitt.

In fact the black-faced man was a Dr Holt of Willesden who for some days passed had been dressing in various disguises and wandering the streets in the hope of discovering Jack the Ripper. He was released at 1.45 a.m. on 12 November, his foolishness recorded for posterity[65].

The inquest was opened – and closed – on 12 November at the Shoreditch Town Hall under the direction of Dr Roderick Macdonald[66], Coroner for North-East Middlesex. There was some initial dispute between Macdonald and a juryman, the latter maintaining that the body of Kelly had been found in Whitechapel and that the responsibility for conducting the inquest fell to Wynne E Baxter, not to Macdonald and the parish of Shoreditch. Macdonald responded that the body had been taken to the mortuary within his district and that legally he was responsible for conducting the inquest. In fact, as far as I can make out, Macdonald was wrong.

The *Pall Mall Gazette* on 27 December 1889 carried a story about a man who had died in a common lodging house in Heneage Street, Spitalfields, whose body was left for three days perched on the side of a kitchen table because there was at that time no mortuary to which he could be taken 'and as the law stood it would not allow a body to be removed' to a mortuary in a neighbouring district. It is therefore difficult to understand the cause of the dispute and Macdonald's explanation if Dorset Street lay within Macdonald's jurisdiction. But if it did not, Macdonald was wrong in saying that he had jurisdiction over the inquest because the body had been taken to a mortuary within his district. To have taken the body into a neighbouring district was illegal.

Macdonald proceeded to hear the testimony of a handful of witnesses before offering his opinion that enough had been heard for the jury to determine the cause of death and that a verdict should be brought in. The jury returned a verdict of 'wilful murder against some person or persons unknown'.

As Rowland Adams Williams, the former Deputy Coroner of Crickhowell, had written in a letter to *The Times* on 26 September 1888, the object of the inquest was not merely to establish the cause of death, but to give a full description of the injuries – which in the case of Kelly was not done – to establish the identity of the deceased, and to establish as far as was possible the time of death. It was with regard to the latter that Baxter had repeatedly adjourned the inquests which he conducted, so that the police could locate and bring forward witnesses. Had Macdonald done as it seems he should have done then Hutchinson could have been examined under oath and his testimony would have been admissible in a court of law in the event that he was unavailable if somebody stood trial at a later date.

The press expressed much surprise at the sudden termination of the inquest and it must be said that the entire event does seem extraordinary.

The press reported attempts to locate Kelly's family, their anticipated arrival in London, their failure to turn up and the consequent postponement of the funeral. They never did turn up and Kelly was finally buried on Monday 19 November 1888. It was reported that John McCarthy, who was said to have been losing tenants every day since the murder, had offered to defray part of the cost of the funeral, but that the offer was declined, sufficient funds having been subscribed.

Mary Jane Kelly was buried at the exclusively Roman Catholic Leytonstone Cemetery in a French-polished elm and oak coffin with brass handles. The service was conducted by Revd C Ellison[67].

In 1910, in his autobiography, Sir Robert Anderson confidently asserted that Jack the Ripper was a certain low-class Polish Jew. In view of this an event which occurred on Thursday 6 December 1888 might be of considerable importance.

During the house-to-house inquiry following Kelly's murder, Mary Cusins, the deputy of a lodging house in Paternoster Row, told the police about a Polish Jew named Joseph Isaacs, a 30 year old cigar maker, who had lodged at her house for three or four days before the murder, behaving strangely during that time, and had disappeared soon after. On Wednesday 5 December, Isaacs returned to the lodging for a violin bow which he had left there. Cusins followed Isaacs and saw him enter a pawn shop run by a man named

Levenson. Isaacs asked Levenson to repair the bow, but whilst Levenson was engaged, Isaacs grabbed a watch and bolted from the shop, later pawning the watch elsewhere. This information was given to the police, who kept a lookout for the man.

On Thursday 6 December, Isaacs was arrested near Drury Lane and taken to Bow Street Police Station. Inspector Abberline was summoned 'and subsequently brought away the prisoner in a cab, which was strongly escorted . . . Great reticence is observed regarding the affair, and at Commercial Street Station the officials deny any knowledge of the arrest, although the man is understood to be detained there.' Isaacs was charged on Friday 7 December, at Worship Street Police Court, Detective Record asking for a remand, which was granted.

It is obvious that Isaacs was suspected of being Jack the Ripper – and strongly suspected if his being taken off in a 'strongly escorted' cab and the subsequent reticence of the police is to be taken as a guide. It also seems probable that he was able to establish his innocence. But why did the police take such extraordinary precautions with a man whose only crime was to have stolen a watch?[68]

CHAPTER ELEVEN

The Macnaghten Papers

THERE WERE OTHER murders, attempted murders and alleged attempted murders attributed to but not, as far as is known, the work of Jack the Ripper. (see Appendix B). As for the murderer, he was never brought to trial, possibly never identified. It has been suggested that the killing of Mary Kelly fulfilled his purpose and he simply stopped. Alternatively, it is thought that he may have killed himself, been killed by others, or been locked away in an asylum by his family. He may even have suffered a heart attack and died in a common lodging house, his name and antecedents unknown to anyone, his secret never suspected.

On the other hand, there is a body of evidence which suggests that the police at least had a shortlist of probable suspects. Indeed, in his autobiography, Sir Robert Anderson who, as head of the CID, must have been in the best position to know, stated that Jack the Ripper's identity was a 'definitely ascertained fact'. If his statement is true, and I know of no evidence to the contrary, the first and most obvious question is, when was this fact 'definitely ascertained'? The only clue we have is the closure of the police files on the case in 1892.

Two years later a very important document was added to the files by Sir Melville Macnaghten, the Chief Constable CID, who joined the Metropolitan Police in June 1889.

In February 1894 Macnaghten wrote a report which was intended to refute claims being made in a series of articles in the *Sun* newspaper that a young man named Thomas Cutbush was Jack the Ripper. Cutbush had been arrested in March 1891 and arraigned in April of that year on a charge of maliciously wounding Florence Grace Johnson and attempting to wound Isabella Fraser Anderson – he had in fact stabbed the girls in the bottom (imitating an earlier series of attacks in which no more than the women's dresses were ripped with a knife). Cutbush need not detain us. He was not Jack the Ripper.

It is not known if the report was intended for anyone in particular, though it seems likely that it was meant as a guide for the Home Secretary in the event of questions being asked in Parliament. The report is headed 'confidential' and dated '23 February 1894'.

We possess two versions of the report. One, henceforth referred to as the 'Macnaghten Report', is preserved in the Scotland Yard files on the Whitechapel murders[1]. The other is in the possession of Sir Melville Macnaghten's descendants and will be distinguished as the 'Aberconway Papers'[2]. To these there must be added two further 'editions' of the report, one of which certainly existed and the other of which may have done. These need to be explained.

The existence of the 'Aberconway Papers' became known when in 1959 Daniel Farson visited Sir Melville Macnaghten's daughter, Lady Aberconway. These papers are not the originals, but copies (typewritten – by Lady Aberconway's secretary – except for two pages naming three suspects which were handwritten by Lady Aberconway herself). The original document had passed to Lady Aberconway's elder sister, Julia Donner, on their mother's death. From Julia Donner the originals passed to her son, Gerald Melville Donner, and are believed to have gone with him when he went to India, where he died in November 1968. The papers disappeared on his death. Attempts to trace them have failed. However, this third set of papers is of academic interest only, since there is no reason to suppose that they differed in any way from the copy made by Lady Aberconway.

The problem is that in the early 1950s Philip Loftus, an old friend of Gerald Donner's from Harrow, spent Christmas with him and was shown Sir Melville's papers. Loftus's memory of the content of what he saw differs from either of the extant versions.

In a letter to Lady Aberconway in August 1972, Philip Loftus described the suspects as 'Michael John Druitt', 'a feeble-minded man [probably Thomas Cutbush]', and 'a

Polish-Jew cobbler nicknamed Leather Apron.' In a review of Daniel Farson's book *Jack the Ripper* which Loftus wrote for the *Guardian* in October of that same year, he omitted the names of Cutbush and the nickname 'Leather Apron', but added that the material he had seen was 'in Sir Melville's handwriting on official paper, rather untidy and in the nature of rough jottings.'[3]

The 'Polish-Jew cobbler nicknamed Leather Apron' seems to be a reference to one of the three men named in the Macnaghten Report and the Aberconway Papers as 'Kosminski', but nowhere in the extent versions is it stated that 'Kosminski' was a cobbler or that he was nicknamed 'Leather Apron'. This difference suggests that the papers seen by Loftus, henceforth called the 'Donner Papers', either differed from the Aberconway Papers, perhaps being an early draft, or that Lady Aberconway did not make a faithful transcription of the original.

I know of no reason to suppose that the Aberconway Papers are not a faithful copy of the original papers inherited by Julia Donner. Therefore, it is possible that Philip Loftus saw Macnaghten's rough notes. However, the fact that Loftus remembered one of the suspects as being Thomas Cutbush, the very person whom Macnaghten wrote the report to exonerate, indicates that his memory was at fault. The fact is that Loftus had read Tom Cullen's book *Autumn of Terror* in which there is an account of the arrest of John Pizer, so he may have made an erroneous connection between the Polish Jew Kosminski, and the Polish Jew cobbler Pizer. Whilst the 'Donner Papers' cannot be dismissed, I cannot accept their existence without further evidence.

To sum up, we possess two copies of Macnaghten's report, the official copy preserved in the Scotland Yard files and a copy made by Lady Aberconway from Macnaghten's own copy inherited by Julia Donner. The question over which there is some dispute is whether the Aberconway Papers pre- or post-dated the official report.

My own view is that the Aberconway Papers were Macnaghten's draft of the offical report.

Finally, analysis of the two sets of papers makes it abundantly clear that Macnaghten was not working from written sources such as police reports, but was relying on his memory. He probably prided himself on having a good memory; in the preface to his autobiography he wrote: 'I never kept a diary, nor even possessed a notebook, so that, in what I write, I trust to memory alone.' I think he trusted to memory alone when he wrote his report – his memory, however, was beyond question at fault.

For example, on page five of the Aberconway Papers he stated that Elizabeth Stride's murderer had been disturbed when 'three Jews drove up to an Anarchist Club in Berners [sic] Street.' It will be recalled that the murderer was disturbed – if, indeed, he was disturbed – by the arrival of only one man, Louis Diemschutz, in his pony and cart.

This is not merely a simple error. It has further ramifications. It will be recalled that a man was seen with a woman believed to have been Catharine Eddowes by three Jews – Lawende, Levy, and Harris – who had just left the Imperial Club near Mitre Square. There is a possibility, perhaps a probability, that Macnaghten confused these men with Diemschutz.

Macnaghten later refers to a suspect bearing a resemblance to a man seen by a City PC in the vicinity of Mitre Square, where Eddowes was murdered. Whilst it is not impossible that a City PC could have seen the suspect, the possibility has to be considered that Macnaghten again confused the two incidents and that the PC in question was PC William Smith of the Metropolitan Police, who saw in Berner Street a man in the company of a woman whom he later identified as Elizabeth Stride.

There are other examples in which Macnaghten shows some confusion about the facts. For example – and this also illustrates one of the differences between the draft and the report – he states in the report that Stride's murderer 'was disturbed by some Jews who drove up to a Club (close to which the body of Elizabeth Stride was found)'.

Macnaghten here displays an imprecision which has nothing to do with the structure of the sentence. The murderer was disturbed because Diemschutz drove his pony and cart into the passage where the murder was committed. He did not, as is the inference of Macnaghten's statement, drive up to a Club

170

'close to' the place where Stride's body was found.

This may seem insignificant, but it is an error in inference which is of crucial importance, particularly when coupled with the plurality of Jews ('some Jews'), in that it shows that Macnaghten was relying upon memory, not working from a written source.

There are many other examples, but these should serve to demonstrate that Macnaghten cannot be regarded as a reliable source. To turn now to what he has to say specifically about the Jack the Ripper murders. It is here necessary to compare the differences between the draft and the report.

The most obvious difference is that Macnaghten deleted from the report almost every personal comment. The result is that the report reads like informed police opinion, whereas from the notes it is clear that much was Macnaghten's own. Possibly the most important deletion is the claim in the notes that against the three named men 'the police held very strong suspicion'. In the report Macnaghten merely says that any one of the three men was 'more likely than Cutbush to be the killer'. This deletion poses the question whether or not the police did have strong suspicions – or any suspicions at all – about the three men.

A related argument suggests that Macnaghten did not intend that any special significance should be attached to the three men; that they were merely three names randomly selected from a list of any number of supects intended to do no more than illustrate the characteristics of the type of man – a type 'more likely than Cutbush' – to have copmmitted the Whitechapel murders. It must be understood that there is no apparent foundation for this conjecture. In the first place, if they had been randomly selected, there would have been no need for Macnaghten to exonerate two of them in favour of Druitt. Secondly, if, as seems probable, Sir Robert Anderson's unnamed Polish Jew was Kosminiski and that – at least as far as Anderson was concerned – Kosminski's guilt was a 'definitely ascertained fact', it is clear that Kosmenski was also a primary candidate. Two of those named were therefore regarded as likely to have committed the murders. The available evidence certainly suggests that Macnaghten did not simply select the names from a much longer list of suspects. Until evidence can be shown to the contrary, the balance of probability is that if the police ever did know the identity of Jack the Ripper, he was one of these three men.

One might also question whether or not Macnaghten was altogether certain about what he put in his report. In the draft he wrote of Montague John Druitt that 'it was alleged that he was sexually insane'. In the report this allegation became a statement of fact. Similarly, in the draft he stated it as his opinion that Druitt's family suspected him of having been the killer, whereas in the report they are said to have believed that he was the killer. It calls for caution when allegations can become statements of fact and suspicions become beliefs between the writing of a draft and the final copy.

We must now turn to what is known about the three named men and what Macnaghten has to say of them.

CHAPTER TWELVE

Montague John Druitt

1854, June: William Druitt, 34, married Ann Harvey, aged 24.

1857, 15 August: Montague John Druitt (henceforth abbreviated to MJD) was born at Westfield, an imposing house in Wimborne, Dorset.

1870: MJD won a scholarship to Winchester. In that same year the last of the Druitts' seven children was born and Ann Druitt's health began to fail.

1876: William Druitt was forced to retire through ill health. He was 56. MJD won a scholarship to New College, Oxford.

1880: MJD graduated with a 3rd Class Honours degree in Classics.

1881: MJD took a teaching job at a school at 9 Eliot Place, Blackheath. The headmaster was George Valentine.[1] He had purchased the establishment in 1873 from Revd Thomas Jackson Nunns, who had bought a school in Maidenhead called St Piran's, which still exists. Valentine's school, which was a completely new establishment, probably opened in September 1873.

It has been stated that the school was a 'cramming shop'[2], but I know of no evidence that this was the case. It was not a second-rate establishment, but a boarding school preparing boys for the universities, the army and the professions, and many of its pupils achieved distinction in later life. Valentine appears to have been widely respected and the school was well staffed with graduate teachers and servants. In a report of Mr Valentine's death[3], the school was described as 'a highly successful educational establishment'.

1881: MJD began playing for the Morden Cricket Club, Blackheath, and was soon appointed Treasurer of the Club. The records of the Blackheath Hockey Club[4] show that at this

173

time George Valentine proposed and Assistant Master Frederick Henry Lacey seconded MJD for membership. He continued to pay his 10/6 annual dues until his death.

1882, 17 May: MJD was admitted to the Inner Temple, the certificate being signed by J B Maule, presumably a member of the Treasurer's Office Staff. MJD paid his fee of £10 2s. 8d. and the stamp duty of £25[5].

1883, 14 July: MJD was nominated for membership of the MCC He was elected on 26 May 1884.

1885: Morden Cricket Club merged with the Blackheath Cricket, Football and Lawn Tennis Company Ltd, and MJD became a Director, being appointed Treasurer and Company Secretary. On 29 April he was called to the Bar of the Inner Temple[6]. The Law Lists of 1886-7 record that he had chambers at 9 Kings Bench Walk. Several writers have argued that he was resident at this address, but this is highly unlikely. Mr Neil Rhind, to whose expertise and prodigious knowledge about Blackheath I willingly defer, has suggested that MJD was probably Senior Resident Master at Eliot Place.

The Law List entry for 1886 records MJD was of the Western Circuit and of the Winchester Sessions. The entry for 1887 records that he was a special pleader for the Western Circuit and Hampshire, Portsmouth and Southampton Assizes.

A special pleader was a legal practitioner who devoted his attention to the drawing of common-law pleadings. The term was generally used to describe a class of lawyers who were students at the Inns of Court and who were enlisted to practise as counsel under the Bar by virtue of stamped certificates issued by the Inland Revenue. These pleaders confined themselves to what is known as chamber practice, namely pleading in civil proceedings, advising in cases, attending summonses in judges' chambers and teaching pupils. Not having been called to the Bar they had no right of audience in court but could conduct cases referred to arbitration, and otherwise act as counsel.

It is unanimously declared among Ripper writers that MJD's legal career did not flourish – he is generally described as a 'failed barrister'. I know of no evidence to support this allegation. Druitt's failure seems to be an assumption based on the erroneous belief that he took the teaching job *after* he had been admitted to the Inner Temple. It was thus reasonable to conclude that he resorted to teaching because his legal career had proved unsuccessful.

It has been suggested by representatives of the Inner Temple that if MJD's career had indeed failed to get off the ground – if, as some writers have asserted, he never obtained a single brief – he would have been politely but firmly 'advised' to vacate his chambers.

Further, there is the fact that when Druitt died he left an estate valued at £2,600. He did not own property, so the bulk of his estate was cash[7]. Druitt had borrowed money from his father in the form of an advance deducted from a legacy of £500 contained in a codicil of his father's will. This money had been used to finance his legal education. He did not further inherit from his father's estate. He evidently had no money of his own at that time. £1,083 of MJD's estate was posthumously inherited from his mother, leaving a balance of £1,517. Even if the whole £500 of his father's bequest is deducted from this sum, leaving £1,017, MJD left more money than he could have earned as a teacher. Teaching salaries were begining to increase – a certified principal and assistant teacher could earn £119 (men) and £72 (women), on average in 1883[8]. Even if Druitt had been earning above this figure, say £200 per annum, almost double the average, his total earnings would only have been £1,400. In view of the quite considerable expenses that he would have had to meet – chambers fees, travelling costs, moving with the Blackheath social elite – it is clear that MJD's estate far exceeded his earnings as a teacher and that he had a secondary income, presumably the law.

It is of course unusual that MJD should have been a special pleader after he had been called to the Bar, but rules at the Inns of Court were less strict in the 1880s than they are today. It is possible that MJD, like barristers before and since, discovered that he did not have a flair in the courtroom and consequently took on chambers practice, offering legal advice to barristers, clients and others. This work was and is lucrative, and cannot be interpreted as a sign of a failed career.

1885, 27 September: MJD's father died of a heart attack aged 65. Ann Druitt's mental state began to deteriorate. She

175

developed delusions and became melancholic (defined at the time as a form of clinical depression accompanied by strong suicidal urges). She attempted to take her life with an overdose of laudanum (tincture of opium). In July 1888 she was sent to the Brook Asylum in Clapton, London, where she was placed under care of Dr Frederick William Pavy. Two months later she was sent on leave of absence to an establishment in Brighton, where she was looked after by Dr Joseph Raymond Gasquet. She remained there until 31 May 1890, when she was sent to the Manor House Asylum, Chiswick. She died there from heart failure on 15 December 1890.

It has been suggested by some 'Druittists' – supporters of the theory that MJD was Jack the Ripper – that Ann Druitt's condition might have had some bearing on the mental state of her son, thus explaining his motive for murdering and mutilating Whitechapel prostitutes. Mrs Druitt's mental condition took the form of delusions – that she was being electrified, for example – an unreasonable refusal to spend money, and the rejection of food. However, it is clear that mental instability was an inherited trait in her family: her mother committed suicide whilst insane and Ann's sister also suffered a bout of mental illness. If MJD inherited this trait he could have become depressed and suicidal as a result of any significant disappointment (such as the loss of his job). His suicide is therefore explicable without recourse to other theories[9].

1888, 8 September: At 11.00 a.m. MJD was playing cricket at Blackheath. On 19 November he was present at a Board meeting of the Cricket Club, where he 'proposed that an acre of land be taken behind the Grand Stand at a similar proportionate rent to that paid for the present land. The proposal to be referred to a Committee to report.' It is evident that ten days after the murder of Mary Jane Kelly, he was continuing to carry out his responsibilities. His brain had not, as yet, given way completely, as Macnaghten was to assert. MJD was dismissed from Eliot Place for 'a serious offence', probably on 30 November.[10] It is to be assumed, but is by no means certain, that he was summarily dismissed, but it is significant that 30 November seems to have been the end of term. The offence might have been committed weeks before, and Druitt could have been working out his employment under notice of dismissal. We do not know what the offence was, but it is best to bear in mind that 'seriousness' is relative – an offence which George Valentine considered 'serious' may not have been so regarded elsewhere.

1888, 3 December: MJD was last seen alive[11]. On 11 December, William Harvey Druitt, MJD's eldest brother, who lived in Bournemouth and was part of the firm of J and W H Druitt, solicitors of Borough Chambers in that town, learned from a friend that MJD had not been seen at his chambers for over a week[11]. William investigated, learned that MJD had been dismissed from Eliot Place, and found a suicide note among his effects. On 21 December the Minutes of the Blackheath Cricket, Football and Lawn Tennis Co. record: 'The Honorary Secretary and Treasurer, Mr M J Druitt, having gone abroad, it was resolved that he be and he is hereby removed from the post of Honorary Secretary and Treasurer.' Among those present at the meeting was Frederick Henry Lacey – had MJD actually expressed his intention of leaving the country, or was 'gone abroad' a euphemism? On 31 December MJD's body was pulled from the Thames near Chiswick.

1889, 2 January: The inquest into MJD's death was held at the Lamb Tap, Chiswick, under the direction of Dr Thomas Diplock.[12] The inquest papers do not appear to have survived. Accounts of the discovery of the body were given in several newspapers (see Appendix C), but the fullest is to be found in the *Acton, Chiswick and Turnham Green Gazette,* 5 January 1889.

FOUND DROWNED. – Shortly after midday on Monday, a waterman named Winslade, of Chiswick, found the body of a man, well-dressed, floating in the Thames off Thorneycroft's. He at once informed a constable, and without delay the body was at once conveyed to the mortuary. On Wednesday afternoon, Dr Diplock, coroner, held the inquest at the Lamb Tap, when the following evidence was adduced:- William H Druitt said he lived at Bournemouth, and that he was a solicitor. The deceased was his brother, who was 31 last birthday. He was a barrister-at-law, and an assistant

177

master at a school in Blackheath. He had stayed with witness at Bournemouth for a night towards the end of October. Witness heard from a friend on 11 December that deceased had not been heard of at his chambers for more than a week. Witness then went to London to make inquiries, and at Blackheath he found that deceased had got into serious trouble at the school, and had been dismissed. That was on 30 December. Witness had deceased's things searched where he resided, and found a paper addressed to him (produced). The coroner read this letter, which was to the effect:- 'Since Friday I felt that I was going to be like mother, and the best thing for me was to die.' Witness continuing, said deceased had never made any attempt on his life before. His mother became insane in July last. He had no other relative. Henry Winslade was the next witness. He said that he lived at No. 4, Shore Street, Paxton Road, and that he was a waterman. About one o'clock on Monday he was on the river in a boat, when he saw the body floating. The tide was at half flood running up. He brought the body ashore and gave information to the police. PC George Moulson, 216 T [13]', said he searched the body, which was fully dressed, excepting the hat and collar. He found four large stones in each pocket in the top coat; £2.10s. in gold, 7s. in silver, 2d. in bronze, two cheques on the London and Provincial Bank (one for £50 and the other for £16), a first-class season ticket from Blackheath to London (South Western Railway), a second-half return Hammersmith to Charing Cross (dated 1 December), a silver watch, gold chain with silver guinea attached, a pair of kid gloves, and a white hankerchief. There were no papers or letters of any kind. There were no marks of injury on the body, but it was rather decomposed. A verdict of suicide whilst in unsound mind was returned.

On 7 Februry at a Board meeting of the Blackheath Cricket Club 'It was resolved that the Directors had heard with much regret of the death of Mr M J Druitt who had zealously fulfilled the duties of Honorary Secretary and Treasurer for three years.' Ann Druitt died on 15 December 1890, and on 24 July

1891, William Druitt inherited MJD's estate.

The last reference to MJD that I have been able to locate – other than Macnaghten's report and speculation resulting therefrom – is an article by Malcolm Christopherson entitled 'The Blackheath Cricket Club'[14]. This article indicates that Druitt possessed considerable ability as a cricketer.

The report in the *Acton, Chiswick and Turnham Green Gazette* is the most detailed account of the inquest that we possess, but it also has the appearance of having been written by an inexperienced journalist – it does not even mention the name of the subject of the inquest, nor does it refer to any medical testimony which, I understand, should have been given! It also includes several mistakes. It says that 'there were no papers or letters of any kind found on the body', whereas both the *County of Middlesex Independent* of 2 January 1889 and the *West London Observer* of 5 January 1889 refer to the authorities having contacted Bournemouth as a consequence of papers being found on the body, as indeed they must have been for the police to have contacted William Harvey Druitt.

The report also states that on MJD's body there was found 'a first-class season ticket from Blackheath to London (South Western Railway)'. The direct line from Blackheath to London would have been from Blackheath to Charing Cross – which was the nearest main line railway station to the Inner Temple – and was by the South Eastern Railway, not by the South Western Railway.

A far more important mistake, if it is a mistake, is contained in the line referring to William Harvey Druitt's visit to London in consequence of learning that his brother had not been seen at chambers for over a week. The newspaper reports that at Blackheath he learned that MJD 'had got into serious trouble at the school and had been dismissed'. *That was on 30 December*.

This statement is open to interpretation. It could refer to the date when MJD was dismissed from the school, in which case the date would be wrong because MJD was unquestionably dead by 30 December. Or it could refer to when William Harvey Druitt visited the school and learned that his brother had been dismissed.

The interpretation we choose largely depends on whether or not MJD's week-long absence from chambers had caused alarm. If it was so unusual as to occasion concern then one must doubt that William Harvey Druitt would have let three weeks (and the Christmas festivities) pass without making any inquiries. On the other hand, William Harvey's informant on 11 December may merely have commented on MJD's absence from chambers in passing ('Where's Montague? I haven't seen him in chambers for over a week.') and it may not have been until MJD failed to contact his brother at Christmas that William Harvey Druitt became alarmed.

On the whole I feel that it is unlikely that William Harvey Druitt would have allowed the two weeks approaching Christmas to pass without making inquiries about his brother. I am inclined to believe that the date in the report is wrong, that it should be 30 November and that it refers to the date of MJD's dismissal from Eliot Place.

There are other differences between the various newspaper reports. One states that papers found on the body indicated that MJD 'was a resident of Bournemouth'; another states that 'friends' in Bournemouth had been contacted, whereas the reality was that MJD's brother was informed; a further difference is that MJD's suicide note was addressed to George Valentine.

On the subject of the suicide note, several writers have said that MJD actually wrote: 'Since Friday I felt I was going to be like mother, and the best thing for me was to die.' In fact, as the *Acton, Chiswick, and Turnham Green Gazette* makes clear, these words were *not* a direct quote, but merely indicated gist of the letter as a whole. This view is supported by the description of the letter's content in the *Richmond and Twickenham Gazette*, 5 January 1889, where it was described as 'to the effect that "what he intended to do was best for all parties".'

Druitt's decision to commit suicide might not, therefore, have had any direct bearing on his mother's mental state. He might simply have meant that he feared that he would be an embarrassment or disgrace to his family.

Stephen Knight observes:

> Would a man who had committed five brutal murders accompanied by horrific mutilations over a period of ten weeks sit down and write, several weeks after the final

180

murder, that he had been feeling apprehensive about his state of mind *since Friday*? The idea that he had not become just a little worried about his behaviour between 31 August and 9 November is almost comic.[15]

Of course, there is absolutely no reason why the letter could not have been written weeks before MJD killed himself, written long before his homicidal urges – assuming that he ever had any – had taken control. But if the letter *was* written shortly before his suicide, and if MJD was dismissed on Friday 30 November, it would seem that his doubts about his mental condition had a direct relationship with his dismissal from Eliot Place. Since the school seems to have been connected with the most enjoyable and perhaps important aspects of MJD's social life, perhaps the loss of his job and any shame about the cause may have depressed him to the extent that he realized that he was suffering from the same symptoms of melancholia as had reduced his mother to a deluded and pitiful woman. This alone could explain why MJD killed himself.

To return to Sir Melville Macnaghten, almost everything he has to say about Druitt is wrong. In the Aberconway Papers – his draft report – he says:

Mr M J Druitt, a doctor of about 41 years of age and of good family, who disappeared at the time of the Miller's Court murder, and whose body was found floating in the Thames on 31 Dec: i.e. 7 weeks after the said murder. The body was said to have been in the water for a month, *or more* – on it was found a season ticket between Blackheath and London. From private information I have little doubt but that his own family suspected this man of being the Whitechapel murderer; it was *alleged* that he was sexually insane.

In the final report he says:

A Mr M J Druitt, said to be a doctor and of good family, who disappeared at the time of the Miller's Court murder, and whose body (which was said to have been upwards of a month in the water) was found in the

Thames on 31 Dec. – or about 7 weeks after that murder. He was sexually insane and from private info. I have little doubt but that his own family believed him to have been the murderer.

In his autobiography he says:

> Although, as I shall endeavour to show in this chapter, the Whitechapel murderer, in all probability, put an end to himself soon after the Dorset Street affair in November 1888, certain facts, pointing to the conclusion, were not in possession of the police until some years after I became a detective officer. (p. 54)

> There can be no doubt that in the room at Miller's Court the madman found ample scope for the opportunities he had all along been seeking, and the probability is that, after his awful glut on this occasion, his brain gave way altogether and he committed suicide; otherwise the murders would not have ceased. (p. 61)

> I do not think there was anything of religious mania about the real 'Simon Pure' nor do I believe that he had ever been detained in an asylum, nor lived in lodgings. I incline to the belief that the individual who held up London in terror resided with his own people; that he absented himself from home at certain times, and that he committed suicide on or about the 10 November 1888, after he had knocked out a Commissioner of Police and very nearly settled the hash of one of Her Majesty's principal Secretaries of State. (p. 62)

We must now examine in detail what Macnaghten says.

He says that Druitt was 'said to be a doctor'. Setting aside the question of who it was that said this, Druitt was in fact a barrister/teacher. It has been suggested that Druitt may have had a brief flirtation with medicine between graduation and his application to the Inns of Court, but this would not have made him a doctor nor given anyone any cause to refer to him as one. Whatever the source of this information, it was wrong. But the highly significant point is that the mistake shows that neither

Macnaghten nor his source could have been acquainted with the evidence given at the inquest into Druitt's death, where Druitt's occupation was clearly stated.

Further evidence for this conclusion is contained in a statement in Macnaghten's autobiography in which he states his belief that Druitt 'resided with his own people' and 'absented himself at certain times'. Neither is true, as would have been perfectly clear from the evidence given at the inquest. However, the *West London Observer* (see Appendix C) reported that papers found on Druitt's body 'indicated that he was a resident of Bournemouth'. Druitt's brother, William Harvey, lived in Bournemouth, of course, but the point is that the papers found on Druitt's body indicated that Druitt lived there too.

The important fact is that Macnaghten knew about the season ticket from Blackheath to London which was found on Druitt's body. This proves that the source of Macnaghten's information post-dated Druitt's suicide. But the inaccurate biographical information shows that he had no knowledge of the evidence given at the inquest, so his source must be dated before the inquest took place. It therefore seems highly probable that he drew his information from a report of the discovery of Druitt's body, possibly the report submitted by PC Moulson, the policeman summoned when Druitt's body was pulled from the Thames.

In the Aberconway Papers Macnaghten stated that Druitt was 'about 41 years of age'. Druitt was 31 years old. However, both the *County of Middlesex Independent* and the *West London Observer* reported that the body when pulled from the Thames looked to be that of a man aged about 40.

The precision of the age given by Macnaghten suggests that he did not base it upon the estimated age of a decomposing corpse – nobody would be so pedantic as to estimate the age of a corpse as 41 years. A more reasonable explanation is that Macnaghten wrote '41' when he meant '31', but there is *no* evidence to show that he was in possession of any accurate biographical information about Druitt, so he is not likely to have known Druitt's true age. An alternative and more probable explanation is that something among the papers found on Druitt's body suggested that he was 41.

Macnaghten says that 'Druitt disappeared at the time of the

Miller's Court murder'. In his autobiography he is even more precise, saying that Druitt 'committed suicide on or about 10 of November 1888'. The former statement carries an unwarranted inference, whilst the latter is wrong. There seems to be no question but that Macnaghten assumed that Druitt's mental stability completely collapsed after the murder of Mary Jane Kelly and that he committed suicide within days. Neither assumption is true. Druitt continued to teach at the school in Blackheath until perhaps as late as 30 November; he evidently regularly visited his chambers until about the same date, otherwise his week-long absence would not have warranted comment; and he continued to fulfil his responsibilities with the Cricket Club. He would seem to have conducted his life in the way to which he was accustomed until at least the end of November.

Macnaghten says that Druitt was 'alleged' to be sexually insane. It is clear from page 109 of his autobiography, where he refers to the murderer Neill Cream as a 'sexual maniac', that Macnaghten defined this term as a person who derived pleasure from killing. However, the point is that Macnaghten *did not know* that Druitt was sexually insane.

Macnaghten is unlikely to have obtained this information from a member of Druitt's family because the person concerned would surely have provided Macnaghten with accurate biographical information. It was therefore obtained at second hand, but from a source who again failed to provide Macnaghten with accurate biographical information. Whoever or whatever Macnaghten's source was, the information was not known to be true. At best it has to be regarded as hearsay and of dubious reliability.

The most damning evidence against Druitt must be the suspicion or belief of the family that he was responsible for the Whitechapel murders. However, this statement is subject to the same questions as the allegation that Druitt was sexually insane. Moreover, even if it was true, the Scotland Yard and Home Office files provided ample testimony that many people were suspected by their family and friends.

Finally there is what might be called 'negative' evidence – that is inferences drawn from what was not said. In contrast to what he had to say about Kosminski and Ostrog – they were homicidal and had a great hatred of women, which are very good reasons for suspicion having fallen on them – Macnaghten has nothing of this kind to say about Druitt beyond unsubstantiated allegations about Druitt's mental state and the opinion of his family.

From Macnaghten's writings it is abundantly clear that *he did not know for certain* that Montague John Druitt was Jack the Ripper. From the foregoing analysis it is difficult to avoid the conclusion that Macnaghten in fact knew nothing whatsoever about Druitt (other than hearsay about his mental state and the opinion of his family) except what was contained in PC Moulson's report concerning the discovery of Druitt's body in the Thames. The important and perhaps unanswerable questions are therefore, when and why did suspicion ever fall on Druitt and why was Macnaghten inclined to favour Druitt above any other suspect (especially when his superior, Robert Anderson, seems to have believed that the Ripper was a Polish Jew)?

I believe that part of the answer is provided by a sentence in Macnaghten's autobiography, the significance of which seems to have been generally overlooked. He wrote:

> Although, as I shall endeavour to show in this chapter, the Whitechapel Murderer, in all probability, put an end to himself soon after the Dorset Street affair in November 1888, certain facts, pointing to this conclusion, were not in possession of the police till some years after I became a detective officer.

The words 'in all probability' indicate an uncertainty as to whether the Whitechapel murderer 'put an end to himself' shortly after the murder of Kelly; whether he did commit suicide, or was perhaps murdered; whether the suspect did in fact die at all soon after the murder of Kelly; or whether the suspect was Jack the Ripper.

The suspect was unquestionably Montague John Druitt. There is no question that he died in December 1888 and little or no question that he committed suicide. There is, however, ample proof that Macnaghten did not know for certain that Druitt was the Whitechapel murderer. I suggest that this lack

185

of proof is the uncertainty revealed by the words 'in all probability'.

The next revealing phrase is 'certain facts pointing to this conclusion'. To what conclusion is he referring? Whatever it was, it was *indicated* by the 'certain facts' received. Without wishing to labour the point, since the 'certain facts' indicated, rather than proved, something, they did not indicate that Druitt was dead. This was an established, incontrovertible fact. The 'certain facts' must therefore have indicated that Druitt was the murderer.

In other words, Macnaghten is saying that some years after June 1889, when he became a detective officer, information was received which implicated Druitt in the murders. Therefore Druitt was *not* a suspect until 'some years' *after* June 1889, though obviously before February 1894, when Macnaghten wrote his report.

This information was therefore received at a time when Macnaghten held the rank of Chief Constable CID. It seems reasonable to suppose that allegations against Druitt, if taken seriously, would have been investigated and reported on. Such a report would certainly have been available and have been of considerable interest to Macnaghten. However, a report would have contained accurate biographical details about Druitt – information which Macnaghten clearly did not possess.

If allegations against Druitt were officially investigated then a report would have been produced. Macnaghten obviously did not have access to this report, therefore the inference is that the allegations were investigated at a very senior level, the report being withheld from even the Chief Constable CID (and also, presumably, from Anderson, Assistant Commissioner CID, who even as late as 1910, believed the Ripper to have been a Polish Jew). This inference takes us into the realms of the 'cover-up', what in espionage circles is known as the 'wilderness of mirrors' where nothing is as it appears.

Supposing that there was a very senior-level cover-up, it follows that Macnaghten would have been made party to the information in confidence. Macnaghten must have then betrayed the trust of his informant when he put the 'secret' information in a report which was probably destined for the very people, as far as we can tell, who wanted the information kept secret. On receiving Macnaghten's report the Home Office officials did – nothing! They made no attempt to silence Macnaghten or to retrieve his copy of the report from the Scotland Yard files and destroy it. Instead, in 1903, they promoted Macnaghten, the betrayer of trusts, to Assistant Commissioner CID, and put him in a position to learn and talk about even more sensitive information. No, I cannot accept that there was a cover-up.

The 'certain facts' recieved by the authorities present a conundrum. If taken seriously they would have been investigated and a report containing accurate biographical information would have been produced. Macnaghten clearly did not possess any accurate biographical information about Druitt, therefore the report was either withheld from him, which seems improbably, or no report was produced, in which case the allegations against Druitt could not have been taken seriously. Why, then, did Macnaghten favour Druitt! Indeed, why did he receive information about Druitt in the first place?

From Macnaghten's writing it appears that the only reason he had for suspecting Druitt was that Druitt killed himself within a matter of weeks of the murder of Mary Jane Kelly. Macnaghten also gave it as his opinion that the suicide of the murderer was the most reasonable explanation for the cessation of the murders.

This conclusion is perhaps confirmed by Inspector Abberline. In an interview given in 1903 to the *Pall Mall Gazette,* Abberline, having been asked his opinion on a suggestion made in a Sunday newspaper (probably an article by George Sims, a friend of Macnaghten's who wrote under the name of 'Dragonet' in the *Referee*) that the Whitechapel murderer 'was a young medical student who was found drowned in the Thames', Abberline is reported to have replied: 'I know all about that story. But what does it amount to? Simply this. Soon after the last murder in Whitechapel the body of a young doctor was found in the Thames, but there is absolutely nothing beyond the fact that he was found at that time to incriminate him.'[16]

Abberline's pronouncement seems to confirm the foregoing analysis of Macnaghten's writings and it is therefore difficult not to conclude that suspicion fell on Druitt simply because he killed himself at the beginning of December 1888. But mental instability and suicidal urges would seem to have run through Druitt's mother's side of the family. Anything – the loss of his job, for example – could have pushed Druitt over the edge.

However, it seems impossible to accept that Sir Melville Macnaghten was so irresponsible as to base an accusation on such a flimsy connection as the mere fact that Druitt committed suicide several weeks after the murder of Mary Jane Kelly. I can only suppose that he had other reasons which caused suspicion to fall on Druitt.

A possibility is that during 1888 suspicion did fall on a young medical student or doctor whose name and whereabouts were unknown. If this person bore a superficial likeness to the description of Druitt in PC Moulson's report then Macnaghten may have assumed that the suspect and Druitt were one and the same person.

Who the medical student or doctor in this hypothesis might have been is of course not known, but the name of John Sanders springs to mind. It will be recalled that at the time of the murders of Nichols and Chapman, the police attempted to trace the whereabouts of three insane medical students who had studied at the London Hospital. They found two, but the third, John Sanders, proved impossible to locate. According to Abberline, inquiries had been made at 20 Aberdeen Place, St John's Wood, where it was learned that a Mrs Sanders had lived until going abroad some years earlier.

In fact Mrs Sanders did not live at this address, but at 20 Abercorn Place, St John's Wood, where, according to street directories, she was living in 1888 and continued to live for several years thereafter. Since inquiries at the London Hospital would have furnished the police with John Sanders's correct address, I can only assume that inquiries were made at Abercorn Place and that Abberline wrote 'Aberdeen Place' by mistake. Further, since Mrs Sanders was still living at that address in 1888, the police investigator must have misunderstood his informant. Perhaps Mrs Sanders had merely gone abroad on holiday and not, as the investigator believed, gone abroad to live.

John Sanders, whose father was an army surgeon, did come from a fairly good family, he may have been sexually insane, his family may have suspected him of having committed the

188

Whitechapel murders, and as far as is known, he did live with his family.

Whether or not Macnaghten confused Sanders with Druitt, it is disturbing to think that he might have named the wrong person. However, this does seem to be the only explanation[17].

Continuing from page 138. after the suspect had been identified at the Seaside Home where he had been sent by us with difficulty in order to identify him to identification, and he knew he was identified. On suspect's return to his brother's house in Whitechapel he was watched by police (city CID) by day & night. In a very short time the suspect with his hands tied behind his back, he was sent to Stepney Workhouse and then to Colney Hatch and died shortly afterwards ——— Kosminski was the suspect ———

D.S.S.

For a long time, Druitt has been regarded as the primary suspect but, according to this Swanson marginalia, the suspect is named as Kosminski (see p. 193)

CHAPTER THIRTEEN

Michael Ostrog and
Other Russian Suspects

NOTHING BEYOND WHAT Macnaghten tells us is known about Michael Ostrog. We are told that he was 'a mad Russian doctor and a convict and unquestionably a homicidal maniac'. He was said to have been habitually cruel to women and to have carried surgical knives and instruments about with him. He was 'subsequently detained in a lunatic asylum' – meaning, I think, that he had been detained in an asylum subsequent to the Whitechapel murders – and he was 'still alive' when Macnaghten wrote in February 1894.

An important statement is that 'his whereabouts at the time of the Whitchapel murders could never be satisfactorily accounted for'. The impression is that at some date between the beginning of 1889 and the end of 1893, Michael Ostrog was put in an asylum. He obviously came to the attention of the police, who must have considered that he was possibly the Whitechapel murderer – presumably because of his state of mind, but possibly because he committed or attempted to commit a Ripper-like crime. The police, however, were unable to show that he had ever been in the Whitechapel area at the time of the murders.

I, and other researchers, have checked medical directories, death registers and assorted workhouse and asylum records, but have failed to turn up any reference to Michael Ostrog. This may mean that he was committed to an asylum somewhere outside London, perhaps in Scotland, thus accounting for the absence of his name from the death registers.

Michael Ostrog does feature in a theory proposed by Donald McCormick[1]. His theory need not concern us in detail. He claimed to have once been shown a lithograph copy of a

January 1909 issue of the *Ochrana Gazette,* a bulletin issued by the Tzarist Secret Police, which reported the death of a man named Vasilly Konovalov. The report stated that Konovalov, who had been born at Torshok, Tver, in 1857, was wanted for several murders, among them the murder of five women in the East End of London in 1888 – an obvious reference to the Whitechapel murders. It was also reported that Konovalov used the aliases of Alexey Pedachenko and Andrey Luiskovo.

Donald McCormick's book was originally published in 1959 – before the Aberconway Papers and the name of Ostrog had come to light. In the revised edition of his book published in 1970 McCormick speculated about whether or not 'Ostrog' could have been among the aliases used by Konovalov. By 1987, in the revised and updated edition of his book *A History of the Russian Secret Service* (written under the pseudonym of Richard Deacon), McCormick's memory of the *Ochrana Gazette* article was that it declared dead 'a man known under the names of Pedachenko, Luiskovo, Konovalov and Ostrog'![2]

McCormick has not produced the *Ochrana Gazette* report, though one assumes that he has sought to locate such an important reference to the Whitechapel murders – at the Okhrana Archive at the Hoover Institution, for example. To the best of my knowledge, nobody else has ever seen it.

One curious element is that McCormick says the edition containing the report was dated January 1909, yet it twice refers to Petrograd. This city was not known by the name of Petrograd in 1909. It was known as St Petersburg until the Revolution of 1914.

McCormick's information cannot possibly be considered until such time as he can produce the *Ochrana Gazette* article.

Suspicion did in fact fall on a Russian in 1888. A story about a Russian named Nicholas Wassili was widely reported in December 1888, but I have traced it back to a newspaper dated 13 November[3] in which the tale was ascribed to 'a correspondent telegraphing from Berne' and citing an unnamed Lucerne journal as the source. A slightly later report[4] credits the story to 'a correspondent of *Independence Belge* at Berne'. The story was that Wassili – born at Tiraspol in 1847 and educated at the University of Odessa – went to Paris in the early 1870s. In 1872 he was arrested for the murder of one or more prostitutes and was sent to an asylum. He was released as cured at the begining of 1888 and it was suggested – but not known – that he may have come to London.

I have tried to obtain further information about Wassili, but the authorities – the Ministère de la Culture et de la Communication[5] and the Prefecture de Police – have no information on Wassili.

Considerable efforts to find out information about Ostrog, Konovalov and Wassili have also been made in the Soviet Union, library records, reference books and specialists on the history of Russian crime and criminal law having been consulted. Nothing, as yet, has been found about any of them.

CHAPTER FOURTEEN

Kosminski

THE REMAINING candidate named by Macnaghten was a Polish Jew named Kosminski. In his draft Macnaghten wrote:

> Kosminski, a Polish Jew, who lived in the very heart of the district where the murders were committed. He had become insane owing to many years indulgence in solitary vices. He had a great hatred of women, with strong homicidal tendencies. He was (and I believe still is) detained in a lunatic asylum about March 1889. This man in appearance strongly resembled the individual seen by the City PC near Mitre Square.

In his report Macnaghten wrote:

> Kosminski, a Polish Jew, residing in Whitechapel. This man became insane owing to many years of indulgence in solitary vices. He had a great hatred of women, specially of the prostitute class, and had strong homicidal tendencies; he was removed to a lunatic asylum about March 1889. There were many circs. connected which made him a strong 'suspect'.

We must now turn to Sir Robert Anderson's autobiography published in 1910, in which he says:

> During my absence abroad the Police had made a house-to-house search for him, investigating the case of every man in the district whose circumstances were such that he could go and come and get rid of his bloodstains in secret. And the conclusion we came to was that he and his people

were certain low-class Polish Jews; for it is a remarkable fact that people of that class in the East End will not give up one of their number to Gentile justice.

And the result proved that our diagnosis was right on every point . . . I will merely add that the only person who had ever had a good view of the murderer unhesitatingly identified the suspect the instant he was confronted with him; but he refused to give evidence against him.

In saying that he was a Polish Jew I am merely stating a definitely ascertained fact. And my words are meant to specify race, not religion. For it would outrage all religious sentiment to talk of the religion of a loathsome creature whose utterly unmentionable vices reduced him to a lower level than those of the brute.

Reference should be made to an observation advanced by Donald Rumbelow[1], which has been uncritically accepted and repeated by others. Rumbelow seems to have misunderstood what Anderson actually wrote. Thinking that Anderson was saying that the murderer had been identified as a direct result of the house-to-house searches undertaken whilst he, Anderson, was abroad, Rumbelow concluded that 'it seems abundantly clear that Anderson was accusing John Pizer (Leather Apron) of being the Ripper.' Rumbelow proceeds to identify the witness who refused to testify as Emanuel Delbast Violenia.

In fact Anderson said nothing of the sort. He wrote that as a result of the house-to-house search it was concluded that the murderer was a low-class Polish Jew and that when the killer was eventually identified this conclusion was proved to be correct in every particular. There is nothing in what Anderson says to justify the inference that the murderer was identified upon Anderson's return from abroad. Rumbelow also presumably forgot the reference to the suspect being 'caged in an asylum'[2], which of course John Pizer never was.

Until recently nobody seemed to have connected Anderson's Polish Jew with the Polish Jew named Kosminski in Macnaghten's report. Of course, there was no certainty that they were one and the same person, but any doubts on that

194

score were removed at the end of 1987 when what is potentially the most important piece of evidence came to light.

The last surviving daughter of Chief Inspector Donald Swanson died in 1981, and some of his possessions passed to her nephew, Swanson's grandson. Among them was a copy of Sir Robert Anderson's autobiography in which Chief Inspector Swanson had pencilled some comments on what Anderson wrote about the Polish Jew. On reading about Martin Fido's book, Swanson's grandson revealed the existence of the marginalia to a journalist working on the *Daily Telegraph* and a report duly appeared[3]. The marginalia is reproduced below in full for the first time.

On page 144 Anderson wrote: 'And Mr Herbert Gladstone added that, in some of the cases where no one was made amenable, the criminals were known to the Police, but evidence to justify an arrest was not obtainable.' In the margin Swanson wrote: 'such was every case of murder where the murderer was not charged because evidence was not obtainable.'

On page 138 Anderson wrote: '. . . I will merely add that the only person who had ever had a good view of the murderer unhesitatingly identified the suspect the instant he was confronted with him; but he refused to give evidence against him.' Swanson added at the bottom of the page: 'because the suspect was *also a Jew* and also because his evidence would convict the suspect, and witness would be the means of murderer being hanged which he did not wish to be left on his mind.' In the margin Swanson wrote: 'And after this identification which suspect knew, no other murder of this kind took place in London.'

On the endpaper Swanson wrote: 'Continuing from page 138 after the suspect had been identified at the Seaside Home[4] where he had been sent by us with difficulty in order to subject him to identification, and he knew he was identified. On suspect's return to his brother's house in Whitechapel he was watched by police (City CID) by day and night. In a very short time the suspect with his hands

195

tied behind his back, he was sent to Stepney Workhouse[5] and then to Colney Hatch and died shortly afterwards – Kosminski was the suspect – DSS.'

Before looking more closely at the implications of the Swanson marginalia it is necessary to outline and examine a theory advanced by Martin Fido[6].

Before the Swanson marginalia came to public attention through the feature in the *Daily Telegraph,* Martin Fido had made the connectioin between Anderson's unnamed Polish Jew and the Polish Jew named Kosminski referred to by Macnaghten. Both sources referred to Kosminski having been committed to an asylum[2], so Fido set himself the task of gaining access to and searching through all the asylum records. His exhaustive search produced three names of interest.

NATHAN KAMINSKY. The Whitechapel Infirmary Admissions and Discharge Book for 1888 recorded that on 24 March an unmarried Polish Jew named Nathan Kaminsky was admitted for the treatment of syphilis. He was discharged as cured six weeks later. The similarity of the name 'Kaminsky' to 'Kosminski'; the proximity of Kaminsky's address, 25 Black Lion Yard, to the area where 'Leather Apron' was sought and John Pizer was found; the syphilis indicating use of the local prostitutes – all these elements suggested that Nathan Kaminsky could have been the man meant by Anderson. Significantly, there was no record of Nathan Kaminsky's death in the records of St Catherine's House. Of course, he could have died outside England and Wales or he may have Anglicised his name, but it was also possible that, if he was the suspect, he was entered in the asylum records under a different name.

DAVID COHEN. In early December 1888 the Metropolitan Police found a Jew wandering the streets of Whitechapel. He was clearly unable to take care of himself, so they took him to the Whitechapel Infirmary. The records give his name as David Cohen, aged 23, a tailor. His address was given as 86 Leman Street. Fido checked this address and found that it was a Protestant Boys' Club and obviously a mistake; the correct address, Fido suggested, was possibly 84 Leman Street, a temporary shelter for poor homeless Jews. Cohen proved to be highly dangerous to himself and to others. He was sent to Colney Hatch Asylum on 12 December 1888, where he was kept under restraint and where he died on 20 October 1889. He had no known next of kin.

AARON KOSMINSKI. In the admissions and discharge book at Colney Hatch Martin Fido found an entry for Aaron Kosminski – *the only Kosminski in the Colney Hatch records*. He was admitted on 7 January 1891 and had been treated at the Mile End Old Town Workhouse in July 1890. He believed that he was guided and his movements controlled by 'an instinct that informs his mind'. This 'instinct' told him the movements of all mankind; told him not to accept food from other people, for which reason he lived off food which he could scavenge from the gutters. According to a statement made by a man named Jacob Cohen of 51 Carter Lane, St Pauls, Aaron Kosminski practised 'self-abuse'[7], refused to wash, and had not attempted work for many years[8]. He said that Aaron had once threatened his sister with a knife, but the records report that he was not violent or dangerous.

According to the records consulted by Fido, Aaron Kosminski's address was given as Lion Square. Fido rightly points out that this is 'a definite error, as no such place existed', but the records he consulted were wrong, as we shall see.

Aaron Kosminski had a brother, Woolf. Aaron was transferred from Colney Hatch to the Leavesden Asylum – an asylum for imbeciles – in 1894 and he died there on 24 March 1919.

At first Martin Fido suspected that Nathan Kaminski and David Cohen were one and the same person and that somehow they/he became confused with Aaron Kosminski. However, there was and is no suggestion that Nathan Kaminski was anything other than a sufferer from syphilis. Nor should any significance be attached to the disease itself. The incidence of venereal disease in the 1880s was high and accounted for 0.5% of all deaths from natural causes in England and Wales between 1881 and 1884 – greater than smallpox (0.382%),

197

typhus (0.135%) and cholera (0.094%)[9].

Setting aside Nathan Kaminsky, Martin Fido concluded that of all the people mentioned in the asylum records David Cohen was the most likely to have been Jack the Ripper. Indeed, he went further and catagorically stated: 'Jack the Ripper has been found.'

Martin Fido's theory is not as complex or as improbable as it seems from his book. Essentially it is quite simple. It is that the Metropolitan Police found a Jew wandering the streets of Whitechapel at the beginning of December 1888. He was incapable of taking care of himself, so the police took him to the Whitechapel Workhouse. Because the police and/or the workhouse officials could not learn (or could not pronouce) his name, they registered him under the name of 'David Cohen', apparently a sort of 'John Doa' name commonly given to Jews. At some point 'David Cohen' was positively identified as Jack the Ripper.

Some time later the Metropolitan Police learned that the City Police had kept surveillance on Aaron Kosminski. Certain similarities between 'Cohen' and Aaron Kosminski – they were the same age, for example – led the Metropolitan Police to think that Aaron Kosminski was the Jew whom they had picked up and sent to the workhouse. They consequently cited information applicable only to Kosminski in their report on 'Cohen'.

Fido's theory neatly explains why Major Smith of the City Police, who knew nothing about 'Cohen' and thought that the Met's suspect was Aaron Kosminski, was so vitriolic in his autobiography towards Anderson's claim that the Ripper's identity was 'a definitely ascertained fact'.[10] Of course, it does not explain why Smith should have assumed that Anderson meant Aaron Kosminski; in 1887 Charles Booth, in a paper read to the Royal Statistical Society, estimated that there were approximately 45,000 Jews in the East End of London. It was probably an overestimate, but there is no question but that there was a large Jewish population. Why, then, should Major Smith have automatically assumed that Anderson's Polish Jew was Aaron Kosminski?

Fido's theory is neat and appealing. The murders stopped at the same time as 'David Cohen' was picked up; 'Cohen' is apparently the only Jew in the records of Colney Hatch who was violent enough to have been Jack the Ripper; and 'Cohen' died within a year of being admitted to the asylum, just as Swanson asserts. But having said this, there are several objections.

By far the most important is Swanson's statement that the suspect was identified at the 'Seaside Home'. This was the name by which the Convalescent Police Seaside Home in Brighton was commonly known and referred to. It seems an unusual place for an identification to have taken place and not one likely to have been frequently used for this purpose. Swanson is not liable to have made a mistake about it. The Seaside Home did not exist until March 1890 and the property was not even acquired until November 1889. 'David Cohen', of course, was dead by this time. He could not have been identified there.

Another objection is raised by Swanson's assertion that following the identification the suspect returned to his brother's house, where he was watched day and night by the City CID. In one respect this reference to the City Police seems to support Martin Fido's theory because, whilst Aaron Kosminski did have a brother, Woolf[11], the Colney Hatch records state that 'David Cohen' had no known next of kin. The City CID therefore could not have kept watch on 'Cohen' and consequently must have been keeping watch on someone else, presumably Aaron Kosminski.

The problem is this: I cannot believe that the Metropolitan Police would have released the suspect after a positive identification without keeping him under very close observation. The officers in charge of the investigation – among whom Swanson must be numbered – would therefore have known precisely what happened to him after the identification. If the suspect was 'David Cohen', Swanson would have known that he did not and could not have returned to the house of a brother he did not have. Swanson would never have written that this was what happened. That he did write that this was the case means that it did take place and that the suspect cannot have been 'David Cohen'.

One can only add that if the suspect was 'Cohen' and if he did have a brother, the police would have known the suspect's real name and would not have registered him under a 'John Doa'; ergo, his name was David Cohen and cannot be the suspect whom Swanson called Kosminski.

Thirdly, on 17 July 1889, James Monro reported to the Home Office regarding the murder of Alice McKenzie: 'I need not say that every effort will be made by the police to discover the murderer, who, I am inclined to believe, is identical with the notorious Jack the Ripper of last year.[12]' Medical evidence later showed that McKenzie was not a victim of Jack the Ripper, but Monro's initial thoughts show that he thought that the Ripper was still at liberty. Similarly, on 11 September 1889, Monro speculated whether a murder victim found in Pinchin Street had been killed by Jack the Ripper. He concluded that she was not[13], but his thoughts show that he believed Jack the Ripper to be at large. 'David Cohen', of course, was already in Colney Hatch and, according to Fido, already identified as the Ripper. If he had in fact been the Whitechapel murderer then Monro's speculation would have been pointless.[14]

Martin Fido has countered this objection by arguing that the Metropolitan Police did not decide that 'Cohen' was indeed the Ripper until several years after 1888 – 9, when they reviewed the files and concluded that the identification was 'unquestionably reliable'. This is plausible, of course, but it raises questions which seriously weaken the force of Anderson's statement.

If Martin Fido's argument is true then the identity of Jack the Ripper was not and could not have been the 'definitely ascertained fact' claimed by Anderson. Had Jack the Ripper been positively identified then the files would have been closed. The fact that they remained open until 1892 means there must have been an element of doubt about the identification.

This raises the question of whether Robert Anderson's statement was an exaggeration. Strangely enough a remark by Swanson raises certain doubts. In the marginalia he wrote: 'And after identification, which the suspect knew, no other murder of this kind took place in London.'[7] If the suspect was indeed Jack the Ripper then this statement is so blindingly obvious that one wonders why Swanson ever bothered to make it; but it would be a valid comment if the cessation of the murders was interpreted as meaning that the suspect was indeed Jack the Ripper.

If the cessation of the murders was the basis for Anderson's catagoric pronouncement then it devalues it to a considerable extent, since the cessation of the crimes could have been purely coincidental with the suspect's identification. This is particularly true if the suspect was indeed identified at the Seaside Home in or after March 1890, 16 months after the murder of Mary Jane Kelly.

Anderson's writings need to be fully examined to see if he was regularly in the habit of exaggeration and over-statement before one could assert with any authority that he is likely to have been anything less than strictly accurate when he said that the Ripper's identity was a 'definitely ascertained fact'. This is such a precise statement that I feel that it has to be accepted until very good evidence can be produced – if ever it can be produced – to show that he was wrong or otherwise imprecise.

But to return to Martin Fido's theory: Fido is unquestionably one of the best-informed writers on the subject and his theory is neat and appealing, but there are serious objections for which Fido has offered no explanation, not the least of which is Swanson's reference to the identification of the suspect having taken place at the 'Seaside Home'. These objections need to be resolved before his hypothesis can be accepted.

Chief Inspector Swanson wrote that the suspect was named Kosminski and that he was sent to Colney Hatch. Martin Fido's search through the Colney Hatch records produced only one man named Kosminski – Aaron Kosminski. Despite the fact that nothing in the records shows that Aaron could have been Jack the Ripper, he must remain the strongest candidate.

According to the Religious Creed Register[15] of the Mile End Old Town Workhouse, Aaron Kosminski was first treated there on 12 July 1890. At this time he was living at 3 Sion Square (not 'Lion Square' as Martin Fido thought from an error in a different set of records), which was at the top end of Mulberry Street (where John Pizer, the man arrested as 'Leather Apron', lived). Three days later, Aaron was discharged into the care of his brother, Woolf, who was living at 16 Greenfield Street, two streets away from Mulberry Street.

Aaron seems to have lived with his brother until 4 February 1891, when he was readmitted to the Mile End Old Town Workhouse. Three days later he was sent from the Workhouse to Colney Hatch Asylum. He was discharged to Leavesden, an asylum for imbeciles, on 19 April 1894, where he died on 24 March 1919, from gangrene of the left leg.

These dates tie in remarkably well with what Swanson has to say in the marginalia. Aaron Kosminski could have been identified at the Seaside Home some time in January 1891, and been returned to his brother's home, where he remained under surveillance (by the City Police – though why the City Police would have been involved is a mystery) until taken to the Mile End Old Town Workhouse on 4 February.

Of course, the major objection to Aaron Kosminski being the suspect is that he did not die a short time after admission to Colney Hatch, but lived until 1919. However, he was discharged to Leavesden in April 1894, which raises the possibility that news of his discharge somehow became garbled in transmission, leading to the erroneous assumption that Kosminski was dead.

Another objection is that Aaron Kosminski was not identified until about January 1891, over two years after the murder of Mary Jane Kelly. It is generally believed that a Ripper-type killer does not suddenly stop killing, but continues until caught or until his brain gives way completely and he commits suicide.

I can claim no expertise on this aspect of the case, though I understand much depends on the murderer's mental condition and the motivation for committing the crimes. However, there are precedents for intervals of over a year between murders. There were two intervals of thirteen months and one of fifteen months between murders committed by Peter Sutcliffe, the Yorkshire Ripper. And between June 1962 and January 1964 thirteen women were murdered by the Boston Strangler. There was then a gap of nine months before an abortive attempt led to the arrest of Albert De Salvo.

In the case of Aaron Kosminski, his mental illness took the form of instructions from what he called his 'instinct' to the effect that he should not work, should not accept food from anyone, and should not wash. He does not sound like a man who had committed five horrific murders.

The Colney Hatch records are not clear about the duration of Kosminski's illness. There are three lines on which is supposed to be given the patient's age at the time of the first attack, the supposed cause of the illness, and the duration of the existing attack. In Aaron's case his age at the time of the first attack is given as 25 years, the supposed cause is said to have been unknown, and the duration of the existing attack is given as six months. Against these entries someone has written in red that the existing attack had lasted six years and that the supposed cause was self-abuse. However, the existing information was not ruled out, from which one could conclude that it remained valid.

In other words, although Aaron Kosminski may have practised self-abuse for six years, this being thought to have caused his insanity, the illness did not make itself obvious until he was 25 years old. Since he was 54 years old when he died in 1919, he would have been 25 in 1890, which coincides with his admission to the workhouse in July of that year. The second attack would therefore have been in or about August 1890, six months before his admission to Colney Hatch.

Aaron Kosminski's bodily state was described in the records as 'fair', which suggests that he had not been living off food found in the gutters for very long, certainly not as long as six years. Indeed, had he been scavenging and hearing his voices (or 'instincts') for six years, or since 1884, would he have been released from the Mile End Old Town Workhouse after his admission in July 1890? Was Aaron Kosminski obviously insane in 1888?

This has a certain relevance: on 1 October 1888, the *Evening News* observed of the East End prostitutes: 'As women of this sort are now on the alert in Whitechapel, we may infer that the assassin must appeal to them in some way that disarms suspicion. In other words, he cannot suggest by his appearance that he is the bloodthirsty miscreant.' There is merit in this observation and it is difficult to imagine that Kosminski, unwashed, scavenging from the streets, deluded and rambling about what his 'instincts' told him to do, would have disarmed anyone; and where would he have got the money which his intended victims would have required to see before going to work? However, if these aspects of his condition did not manifest themselves until 1890, perhaps he could have been disarming in 1888.

In spite of this, there is no evidence in the Colney Hatch records that Aaron Kosminski was Jack the Ripper. He is described as dangerous neither to himself nor to others. Whether or not he was violent in 1891, surely somebody would have warned the administrators of the asylum if there was any suspicion that Aaron had committed the Whitechapel murders. It does not look as if Aaron Kosminski was Jack the Ripper, but at present he must be regarded as the strongest candidate – or the Swanson marginalia is so badly in error as to be seriously devalued as a source.

One question to which no one seems to have fully addressed themselves is that of the identity of the witness who, according to Anderson, was 'the only person who ever had a good view' of the Whitechapel murderer and who 'unhesitatingly identified the suspect the instant he was confronted with him'. This man was a Jew (which seems to rule out George Hutchinson, who gave a detailed description of a man seen to enter Miller's Court with Mary Kelly), and he refused to testify because he knew that his testimony would result in the conviction and execution of the suspect, which he did not want to have on his conscience.

First, if Swanson's 'Seaside Home' was the Convalescent Police Seaside Home in Brighton then the obvious candidate for the witness would be a policeman, possibly the policeman referred to by Sir Melville Macnaghten in the Aberconway Papers (he said that Kosminski 'in appearance strongly resembled the individual seen by the City PC near Mitre Square'); although, as suggested earlier, it is possible that Macnaghten confused and transposed the details of the Stride and Eddowes murders and that the policeman meant by Macnaghten was PC William Smith, who saw a woman he later identified as Elizabeth Stride with a man in Berner Street.

However, I believe that there were few if any Jewish policemen at that time. Moreover, a policeman is unlikely to have refused to testify. So who could the witness have been and what was it that he saw?

Of the witnesses that we know about (and there may be

dozens about whom we know nothing), only two, possibly three, men are likely to have been the witness.

One was Israel Schwartz, who saw a man assault Elizabeth Stride outside the gates to the passage in which her body was found some fifteen minutes later. The others are Joseph Lawende and Joseph Hyam Levy, who saw a man talking with a woman identified from clothing as being Catharine Eddowes.

Lawende stated that he could not recognize the man again. Levy declared his inability to even describe the man. But even if the man they had seen was indeed 'Kosminski', he need only have said that he had been accosted by Eddowes, had turned her down and had gone about his business. The onus of proof would have been on the police and it is difficult to see how they could have proved anything, merely on the testimony of Lawende and Levy. This leaves Schwartz.

The conflicting details between the report in the *Star* and the report by Inspector Abberline in documents in the police files make it very difficult to be sure exactly what Schwartz saw; perhaps Schwartz was himself uncertain about the details of what he had seen. But it seems that he witnessed an unprovoked attack on Elizabeth Stride at the very place where her body was later found. If he had identified the suspect as the man he had seen then the police could probably have at least got a conviction for assault.

I must admit to being bothered by Swanson's assertion that the witness refused to testify 'because his evidence would convict the suspect, and witness would be the means of the murderer being hanged, which he did not wish to be left on his mind'. Again this is a very precise statement. Moreover, Swanson does not say that the witness's refusal to testify was based on his own assessment of the value of his evidence. The witness knew, and Swanson says nothing to suggest that he personally did not share the view, that his evidence was so strong that it would with absolute certainty bring about the conviction and execution of the suspect. What could the witness have seen that made him – and, presumably, the police – so certain that it would gain a conviction?

Apart from seeing the suspect in the act of committing one of the murders or reeking of blood in the vicinity of one of the crimes, it is difficult to know what Schwartz, Lawende or Levy could have seen. Indeed, could they have seen anything that was unquestionably bound to gain a conviction?

This leads to a piece of pure speculation. I wonder if the police possessed other evidence against the suspect which the witness's testimony served to support or confirm. If so, what could this 'other' evidence have been?

Accepting that the suspect was identified at the Seaside Home in or after March 1890, the length of time that had passed since the murder of Mary Kelly would suggest that the evidence was not something like a possible murder weapon, bloodstained clothing, strange behaviour or having been absent from home when the murders took place. It must have been something of greater importance, such as the suspect having been seen with one of the victims shortly before her murder.

The possibility I am thinking of is if two witnesses saw the suspect at different times with two of the Ripper's victims. With, say, both Stride and Eddowes, who were both seen with men fitting the same general description. If one of the witnesses – possibly the witness who refused to testify – was Schwartz, his evidence, that he had actually seen the suspect assault Elizabeth Stride, would indeed have been crucial. But who could the other witness have been?

Preserved at the Public Record Office are papers[16] relating to an application for naturalization made in December 1877 by a Polish Jew named Martin Kosminski. Among those who stood as his referee was Joseph Hyam Levy, the same Joseph Hyam Levy who saw a man with Catharine Eddowes – his name, address, occupation and signature put it beyond question that he was the same man.

It will be recalled that on 9 October 1888 the *Evening News* reported: 'Mr Joseph Levy is absolutely obstinate and refuses to give the slightest information. He leaves one to infer that he knows something, but that he is afraid to be called on the inquest.' Also, although he denied at the inquest that he could identify either the man or the woman he had seen at Church Passage, he was strangely evasive when the City Solicitor, Mr Crawford, tried to get him to explain why he had apparently been alarmed by the couple. One explanation, of course, is that he knew or was known to Eddowes. On the other hand, perhaps he knew or was known to the man in Eddowes's company.

Martin Kosminski was born in Kalisch, Poland, on 12 July 1845, the son of a furrier named Mark. He is known to have had at least one brother, Samuel[17]. On 8 May 1872, he married Augusta Barnett at the Great Synagogue. Augusta was a dressmaker, the daughter of a burial ground keeper named Moritz. They had three children: Charles[18], Jessie[19] and Katie[20]. In December 1877 he was granted British naturalization.

The trade directories show that Martin Kosminski conducted business as a furrier from a variety of addresses from 1878 until 1922, when the business took his son's name. The business continued to operate under Charles Kosminski's name until 1934, although Charles died in 1925, possibly by his own hand.

Curiously, Martin Kosminski's death is not registered at St Catherine's House. Such absences are not rare – his death would not be registered there if he were resident outside England and Wales – but they are sufficiently uncommon to raise a query, especially since in this case the death of his wife, brother and son are all on record.[21]

Martin Kosminski's name also features in the electoral registers until his wife's death in 1921. Electoral registers are not conclusive proof that a person was still alive, for someone could have continued to fill in the various forms in Martin's name, because he was the householder. That assumes that the person filling in the forms did not know that the person in question was dead.

Another mildly curious fact is that in a codicil to her will dated 15 August 1916 Augusta stated that monies advanced by her to Martin for the purpose of running his business need not be repaid by him providing that he continued to run the business. However, when Augusta died in 1921 the business was immediately taken over by and traded under the name of Charles Kosminski. Martin could have paid the monies or the debt could have been waived by the estate. However, it is odd that Martin's name should vanish from all the records at the same time as Augusta died.

Having said all this, the evidence strongly indicates – but

does not conclusively prove – that Martin Kosminski was alive and conducting his business affairs in 1916 and probably until 1921. He was not, or certainly does not appear to have been, the 'Kosminski' named by Swanson and Macnaghten. However, Martin need not have been the suspect. It could have been a brother or a cousin about whom nothing is at present known. It would be interesting if future research could produce a family link between Martin and Aaron Kosminski.

It has to be said that the Levy-Kosminski connection could be a huge coincidence, but Kosminski was not a particularly common name, so the odds against such a coincidence must be considerable.

Setting aside the identity of the suspect and the witness, the most important question is whether the sources allow us to infer the probable dates for the suspect's admission to the Workhouse and his death.

We can be reasonably certain that the suspect had not been identified before September 1889, because at that time James Monro speculated in a report to the Home Office that the Pinchin Street murder was possibly, but from the medical evidence unlikely to have been, the work of Jack the Ripper. Such speculation would have been pointless if at that time Jack the Ripper had been positively identified as 'Kosminski'. Moreover, there is the additional evidence from the Swanson marginalia that 'Kosminski' was identified at the Seaside Home, which, as I have said, did not open until March 1890.

However, since Macnaghten names 'Kosminski' in his report dated 23 February 1894, it is clear that the suspect had been identified by that time. Macnaghten, of course, states that 'Kosminski' was detained in a lunatic asylum 'about March 1889', but Macnaghten has been shown to be an unreliable source and the inference drawn from Monro's Home Office reports and Swanson's assertion that the identification took place at the Seaside Home must be preferred.

'Kosminski' was therefore identified between March 1890, when the Seaside Home opened, and February 1894, when Macnaghten wrote his report.

A further clue is afforded by a document among Chief Inspector Swanson's private papers. This document, referred to earlier, is a list of the victims of the Whitechapel murders.

Added to the list in a hurried hand – indicating that it was appended after the list had been drawn up – is the name of Francis Coles, who was murdered on 13 February 1891. Why should Swanson have included the name of Coles if 'Kosminski' had at that time been identified and committed?

The Coles murder is also the last to feature in the Metropolitan Police 'Whitechapel Murders' file, which was officially closed in 1892. The implication seems to me to be that the Coles murder was the last in a series of crimes which were for some reason thought to be connected, and whilst the last murder certainly attributed to Jack the Ripper was that of Mary Kelly in November 1888, it is hard to escape the conclusion that all the murders in the file were somehow linked to the search for Jack the Ripper. Something therefore happened after the Coles murder which led the police to close the file. Was it the identification of 'Kosminski'?

This is not to say that 'Kosminski' had anything to do with the murder of Frances Coles, merely that for some reason 'Kosminski' came to the attention of the police during their investigation of this crime.

This possibility leads me to wonder whether a reference in the first annual report of the Convalescent Police Seaside Home could indeed have a bearing on what Swanson wrote about this establishment having been used for the identification. The report refers to two guests taken by 'special request'. If these guests were 'Kosminski' and the witness or witnesses, it would be possible to narrow the date of identification to between 13 February 1891 and 1 March 1891. The commital to Colney Hatch would therefore have been during or very soon after this time.

This is complete speculation, of course, but it is attractive in view of the fact that the files were closed in 1892. Sadly, if the theory is correct, it takes Aaron Kosminski out of the frame. He was sent to Colney Hatch on 7 February 1891, a week before the murder of Coles. The police would hardly have taken him from Colney Hatch to be identified at the Seaside Home, then returned him to his brother's house before carting him off to the workhouse again.

As for when Kosminski died or was thought to have died, the following was reported in the *Pall Mall Gazette* on 7 May 1895:

The theory entitled to the most respect, because it was presumably based upon the best knowledge, was that of Chief Inspector Swanson, the officer who was associated with the investigation of all the murders, and Mr Swanson believed the crimes to have been the work of a man who is now dead.

If Swanson meant 'Kosminski', as must surely be the case, then 'Kosminski' was believed to be dead by 7 May 1895.

Another clue is contained in the Aberconway Papers. Macnaghten wrote of Kosminski: 'He was (and I believe still is) detained in a lunatic asylum . . .' This statement is for some reason omitted from the report and it is difficult to know what, if any, credence should be given to it. Since we obviously cannot ignore it, we should perhaps accept it with caution.

'Kosminski' may therefore have died between 23 February 1894 and 7 May 1895. Nobody surnamed 'Kosminski' is recorded in the registers of St Catherine's House as having died during that period. Aaron Kosminski, if he can still be regarded as a suspect, was transferred to Leavesden in April 1894.

Aaron Kosminski could fit most of what Swanson says about the suspect. He is also the only 'Kosminski' to have died in an asylum anywhere in England and Wales between 1888 and 1924. His mental state does not preclude the possibility that he was the man identified by the witness and whom Anderson believed to be the murderer. That he was Jack the Ripper remains to be seen but the opinion of Anderson and Swanson must weigh heavily in the balance of any assessment of the evidence.

The Welsh Connection

FOR A WHILE this story seemed to provide the best clue to Mary Kelly's background. The story is a very confused one, the facts of which are not entirely clear, and which, since it ultimately seems to have no bearing on Mary Jane Kelly, I would dismiss. However, from my own researches I know that up to a point my inquiries had been preceded. For those in whose footsteps I followed, and for those who may embark on the tortuous trail in the future, I shall relate the story as briefly as possible.

On 12 and 13 November 1888, the Swansea reporter of the *Western Mail* published a statement by a Mr John Rees to the effect that when married to his first wife he had employed Mary Jane Kelly as a servant. Kelly's father, a marine store dealer, said Rees, had been very friendly with a Carmarthen doctor named John Morgan Hopkins whose daughter, Mary Jane Florence, had become John Rees's second wife.

To complicate the story, in June 1888 Mary Jane Florence Rees had been charged with attempting to perform an illegal abortion. In December she was found guilty and sent to prison for ten years. John Rees was also charged and tried that December for the same crime, but was found innocent. However, reports of his arrest confused him with a man named James Roger Rees, who lived at 45 Trafalgar Terrace, Swansea, whereas John Rees lived at 18 Trafalgar Street. None of this is relevant but it can seem so from certain sources.

To return to John Rees's alleged employment of Mary Jane Kelly: Rees claimed to have employed her at Llanelli, where Rees was locally known as 'John Rees the Stepney'. The Stepney was a local hotel near the board school, and it was somewhere near the school that Rees claimed that Kelly was born. Rees said that on leaving his employment, Kelly had gone to Swansea, where she frequented the Unity Inn. From Swansea she had gone to Cardiff and thence to London.

On 15 November, the *Western Mail* published a letter from Mrs Jane Williams, the landlady of the Unity Inn in Swansea, stating that nobody named Mary Jane Kelly had frequented her establishment, although an occasional patron was an Abigail Kelly who had subsequently married a Scottish stonemason named Muir at Llanelli and emigrated with her husband and two children to Kansas City.

On that same date, 15 November, *The Llanelly and County Guardian* reported:

> It has been stated that Kelly was a Llanelli woman and that she left here a few years ago. This however does not appear to be correct, as an investigation failed to associate her with the town. No doubt the statement was made with reference to the Kelly family on the Wern, but all the girls are accountable for, two having left for America while the other lives with her husband near Cardiff.

The 1861 census shows that at 42 Wern Road, Llanelli, which was about a quarter of a mile from the National School, there lived a family named Kelly – Dennis Kelly, a marine store dealer, with his wife Julia and his daughters, one of whom was named Abigail, who at that time was two years old. In April 1881 Abigail married William Muir at St Mary's Catholic Church, Llanelli.

There is little room for doubt that John Rees employed Abigail Kelly, not Mary Jane Kelly. The only question arises from a statement by Mr Rees published in the *Western Mail* on 13 November, that some six months earlier Rees had met Kelly in London. 'She ran across the street to him and addressed him in Welsh.' According to other information, Abigail Kelly was living with William Muir in Kansas City, so, if Rees was telling the truth, whom did he meet in London? Was it Abigail or Mary Jane, or could Abigail and Mary Jane have been one and the same? I did not pursue inquiries in Kansas City, but I would be interested in knowing the results if anybody does[1].

Other Ripper Murders?

IN HIS AUTOBIOGRAPHY Sir Melville Macnaghten says that the press at one time or another ascribed as many as fourteen murders to Jack the Ripper[1]. The police would seem at one time to have thought that there were possibly six, but it would seem that Anderson, Macnaghten and Swanson[2] only credited Jack with five: Nichols, Chapman, Stride, Eddowes and Kelly. However, some other murders were widely credited to the Whitechapel murderer of 1888, though only one, that of Alice McKenzie, on 17 July 1889, has any merit.

On 21 November 1888, Annie Farmer claimed to have been attacked. This attack took place at Satchell's Lodging House, 19 George Street. Her throat was only slightly cut. The *New York Times* reported: 'The police place no credit in her story of an attack. They believe she inflicted the injury herself . . .[3]' There is little doubt that this was the case. Rumbelow has suggested that this woman was the same as Amelia Farmer, the friend of Annie Chapman who gave evidence at Chapman's inquest. I know of no supporting evidence for this opinion[4].

On 3 December 1888 (the day Druitt was last seen alive), Harriet North was attacked. She was stabbed, but received only superficial injuries, in Belgrave Road near King's Cross. She has, however, never been suspected of being a Ripper victim.

On 20 December 1888, Rose Mylett (also known as 'Fair Alice' Downey; 'Drunken Liz' Davis or Millett or Mellett) was found in Clarke's Yard between 184 and 186 High Street, Poplar. At first the police believed that she had died from natural causes, but medical testimony indicated that she had been strangled[5]. Robert Anderson continued to maintain the former view in his autobiography, wherein he wrote that Mylett's 'was a death from natural causes, and but for the 'Jack the Ripper' scare, no one would ever have thought of suggesting that it was a homicide'.[6]

On 17 July 1889, Alice McKenzie (also known as 'Clay-Pipe Alice') was found murdered and mutilated in Castle Alley. Monro reported to the Home Office that he was inclined to believe the murderer to be 'identical with the notorious Jack the Ripper of last year'[7], but Dr Phillips concluded 'that the wounds had not been inflicted by the same hand as in the previous cases'.[8] However, in a letter to Anderson Dr Thomas Bond stated:

> I see in this murder evidence of similar design to the former Whitechapel murders viz. sudden onslaught on the prostrate woman, the throat skilfully and resolutely cut with subsequent mutilation. Each mutilation indicating sexual thoughts and a desire to mutilate the abdomen and sexual regions. I am of the opinion that the murder was performed by the same person who committed the former series of Whitechapel murders.[9]

One cannot help but wonder whether Bond and Phillips would have agreed on the time of day. It is particularly interesting to note that here Bond admits that the woman's throat had been cut skilfully – *as in the previous murders*; hence he seems now to admit some skill on behalf of Jack the Ripper!

Anderson, defending his assertion that the last Ripper murder was that of Mary Kelly, wrote:

> I am here assuming that the murder of Alice McKenzie on the 17th of July, 1889, was by another hand. I was absent from London when it occurred, but the Chief Commissioner investigated the case on the spot and decided that it was an ordinary murder, and not the work of a sexual maniac.[10]

Whether or not this is what Monro came to believe, he certainly did not believe it when he reported to the Home Office.

On 10 September 1889 a body, minus head and legs, was found in a railway arch in Pinchin Street. The woman was not murdered on the spot, the body having been dumped there, and she had been dead between 24 and 36 hours[11]. Monro again speculated that it was 'a fresh outrage by the Whitechapel murderer known by the horribly familiar nickname of Jack the Ripper', but he concluded that this was not the case, there being no evidence of sexual frenzy[12]. It may be that this was the report which Anderson confused with that pertaining to Alice McKenzie.

On 13 February 1891, Frances Coles (also known as Frances Colman, Frances Hawkings, 'Carrotty Nell') was found murdered in Swallows Gardens. Blood was still flowing from her neck when she was found by a police constable, who heard the footsteps of a man, possibly the murderer, receding from the scene. Dr Phillips gave it as his opinion that he did 'not connect this with the series of previous murders'.[13]

Newspaper Accounts of the Death and Inquest of Montague John Druitt

'FOUND IN THE RIVER: The body of a well dressed man was discovered on Monday off Thorneycroft's torpedo works, by a waterman named Winslow. The police were communicated with and the deceased was conveyed to the mortuary. The body which is that of a man about 40 years of age, had been in the water about a month. From certain papers found on the body friends at Bournemouth have been telegraphed to. An inquest will be held today.' *County of Middlesex Independent*, 2 January 1889.

'SAD DEATH OF A LOCAL BARRISTER: An inquiry was on Wednesday held by Dr Diplock, at Chiswick, respecting the death of Montague John Druitt, 31 years of age, who was found drowned in the Thames. The deceased was identified by his brother, a solicitor residing at Bournemouth, who stated that the deceased was a barrister-at-law, but had recently been an assistant at a school in Blackheath. The deceased left a letter, addressed to Mr Valentine, of the school, in which he alluded to suicide. Evidence having been given as to discovering the deceased in the Thames — upon his body were found a cheque for £50 and £16 in gold – the Jury returned a verdict of "suicide whilst of unsound mind".

'The deceased gentleman was well known and much respected in the neighbourhood. He was a barrister of bright talent, he had a promising future before him, and his untimely end is deeply deplored. The funeral took place in Wimborne cemetery on Thursday afternoon, and the body was followed to the grave by the deceased's relatives and a few friends.' *Southern Guardian*, 5 January 1889.

'FOUND DROWNED – a man named Winslow discovered the body of a respectably dressed man in the river opposite Thorneycroft's works. The body was conveyed to the mortuary. It appears to be that of a man 40 years of age, and was in an advanced state of decomposition, showing that it had been in the water for some considerable time. Papers found in his possession indicated that he was a resident of Bournemouth. An inquest was held by Dr Diplock on Wednesday, and a verdict of 'Found drowned' was returned.' *West London Observer*, 5 January 1889.

'DR DIPLOCK ON WEDNESDAY held an inquest at the Lamb Tap on the body of Montague John Druitt aged 31, whose body was recovered from the Thames off Thorneycroft's Wharf on Monday by a waterman named Henry Winslade. The pockets of the deceased, who was a stranger to the district, were found filled with stones, and after a letter had been read in which he wrote to the effect that "what he intended to do would be best for all concerned", the jury returned a verdict of suicide by drowning whilst temporarily insane.' *Richmond and Twickenham Times*, 5 January 1889.

'SUICIDE IN THE THAMES: Dr Diplock held an inquiry at the Lamb Tap, Chiswick, on Wednesday of the body of a gentleman named Montague John Druit [sic], 31 years of age, which was found by a waterman floating in the Thames off Thorneycroft's on Monday. The pockets of the deceased were found to contain stones. The jury returned a verdict of "suicide during temporary insanity".' *County of Middlesex Independent*, 5 January 1889.

Notes and References

Chapter One

1. **B R Mitchell:** *European Historical Statistics 1750-1970,* 1975, pp. 128-9. Central Statistical Office, *1976 Abstract,* p. 48. Census Returns, *Parliamentary Papers* 1883 LXXX (C.3722), p.x.

2. M Greenwood and others: 'Deaths by Violence 1837-1937', *Journal of the Royal Statistical Society,* Vol. 104, 1941, p. 154.

3. B R Mitchell and P Deane: *Abstract of British Historical Statistics,* Cambridge, 1962, p. 12.

4. F W S Craig: *British Parliamentary Election Results 1885-1918,* 1974. p. 587.

5. Hamilton Fyfe: *Northcliffe,* 1930, p. 29.

6. Sir Robert Ensor. *England 1870-1914,* Oxford: Oxford University Press. pp. 310-16. Gives a good account of Victorian journalism. Also see Colin Ford and Brian Harrison: *A Hundred Years Ago, Britain in the 1880s in Words and Photographs.* Harmondsworth, Middlesex: Penguin Books, 1983, to which I am indebted for providing an overview of the period. pp. 54-8.

7. *Bath and Cheltenham Gazette,* 10 October 1888.

8. Quoted by Harris, p. 61.

9. Robert Anderson: *The Lighter Side of My Official Life,* p. 25.

10. Letter from Harcourt to Howard Vincent dated 23 January 1881, quoted by S H Jeyes and F D How in *The Life of Sir Howard Vincent,* 1912.

11. Anderson: *op. cit.,* pp. 123-4.

12. Troup memorandum, 8 April 1910. HO 144/926/A49962, sub. 7.

13. 'Condition of the Working Classes. Report and Tabulation of Statements made by men living in certain selected districts of London in March 1887', *Parliamentary Papers, 1887, LXXI.*

14. M J Cullen, 'The 1887 Survey of the London Working Class', *International Review of Social History,* 1975, I. pp. 53, 55.

15. G E Buckle ed.: *Queen Victoria, Letters, Third Series, Vol.* I, London: Murray, 1930, pp. 52-3.

16. *The Times,* 20 March 1886.

17. *Pall Mall Gazette* quoted by Watkin W Williams: *The Life of General Sir Charles Warren,* Oxford: Basil Blackwell, 1941, p. 196. Also supplied most of the biographical detail.

18. Belton Cobb: *Critical Years at the Yard.* London: Faber and Faber, 1956, p. 226.

19. *Morning Post,* 24 December 1888.

20. Williams: *op. cit.,* p. 220.

21. Anderson: *op. cit.,* p. 128.

22. Williams: *op. cit.,* p. 225.

23. Matthews minutes of 17 and 28 March 1888. HO/144/190/A46472B, subs. 4 and 6.

24. Macnaghten, p. 52.

25. *ibid,* p. 53.

26. Correspondence between Warren and Monro in late April and May in HO/144/190/A4672B sub.9 and MEPO 4/487.

27. Document by Monro in private hands quoted by Martin Howells and Keith Skinner: *The Ripper Legacy.* p. 94.

28. Anderson: *op. cit.,* pp. 134-5.

29. Detective Chief Inspector Swanson is not mentioned by Farson, McCormick or Underwood, for example.

30. Macnaghten: *op. cit.,* pp. 273-4.

31. Rumbelow, p. 138 gives the name as Bella Harding and says 'We don't know who she was or the relationship between them.' Abberline's death certificate at the Bournemouth Registrar's office, which is more reliable than that at St Catherine's House, certainly reads 'Huslling'. She gave her residence as 195 Holdenhurst Road, which was the Abberline home, but as yet nothing more is known about her.

32. *Ordinary Lives.* London: Virago Press, 1982.

33. Ford and Harrison: *op. cit.,* p. 227.

34. Leonard Woolf: *Sowing. An Autobiography of the Years 1880-1904,* 1960, p. 57.

35. Draft Letter, 25 October 1888, MEPO 3/141 fol. 158-63.

36. Samuel Smith: *My Life and Work,* 1903, p. 107.

37. Arthur Brinckman: *Notes on Rescue Work,* 1885, p. 87.

38. Draft letter, MEPO 3/141 (see note 35).

Chapter Two

1. Cullen, p. 32.

2. *Reynolds News,* 29 October 1950.

3. *East London Observer,* 31 March 1888.

4. *East London Advertiser,* 14 April 1888.

5. Information about the murder of Martha Tabram, unless otherwise stated has been taken from the *East London Advertiser,* 11 August, 18 August, 25 August 1888; *East London Observer,* same dates; *Eastern Post,* same dates. MEPO 3/140 fol. 34-60.

6. MEPO 3/140 fol. 44.

7. HO 144/221/A49301C 8a. Also Report dated 8 September 1888 by Chief Inspector Donald Swanson, MEPO 3/140 fol. 38.

8. Most writers refer to him as 'Albert' Crow, but Swanson's report, MEPO 3/140 fol. 38, confirms his name as Alfred.

9. MEPO 3/140 fol. 54.

10. MEPO 3/140 fol. 48.

11. *East London Advertiser,* 18 August 1888.

Chapter Three

1. Rumbelow p. 41, refers to a statement by Nichols made on 13 February 1888 at the Mitcham Workhouse, in which she claimed to have been born in August 1851 and to have been married to William Nichols on 16 January 1864 when aged only twelve. This was certainly the date when she got married, but at the inquest her father said that 'she was nearly forty-four years of age' (*East London Observer,* 8 September 1888) when she died. This would date her birth in 1845, six years earlier than the year she gave at the Mitcham Workhouse.

2. Edward Walker was living at 16 Maidswood Road, Camberwell, at the time of his daughter's death.

3. William Nichols was a resident of Coburg Road off the Old Kent Road at the time of his wife's death and was employed by Messrs Perkins, Bacon and Co. of Whitefriars Road.

4. Marriage Certificate.

5. *East London Observer,* 8 September 1888.

6. *East London Observer,* ibid.

7. Rumbelow, p. 41.

8. *East London Observer,* 1 September 1888.

9. *East London Observer,* 8 September 1888.

10. Matters, pp. 37-8.

11. *The Times,* 1 September 1888.

12. Harry Tomkins, whose Christian name is sometimes given in the press as 'Henry', lived at 12 Coventry Street, Bethnal Green.

13. Certain newspapers gave Emily Holland's name as 'Jane Oram'

and Inspector Abberline (MEPO 3/140 fol. 246) calls her 'Ellen Holland'.

14. PC John Neil was born on 1 August 1850 at Macroom, County Cork, Ireland. He had joined the Metropolitan Police on 26 July 1875 (Warrant No. 59168) and served wholly in J Division (Bethnal Green). He resigned on 22 April 1897 subsequent to receiving wounds whilst on duty.

15. MEPO 3/140 fol. 242.

16. Our sources, newspaper accounts and the Ripper books frequently contradict one another. Some also contain wholly fictional material which is not easily explained away as 'poetic licence'. Charles Cross is given this name in a report by Inspector Abberline (report dated 19 September 1888, MEPO 3/140 fol. 242) and in the *Manchester Guardian* (4 September 1888), the *East London Observer* and the *Eastern Argus* (8 September 1888), among others. *The Times* erroneously calls him 'George Cross', as do Cullen (p. 25), Rumbelow (p. 37), Underwood (pp. 91-2), and Wilson/Odell (pp. 17-18). He is called 'William Cross' by Odell (p. 29), McCormick (p. 31), and Farson (index). Matters only refers to him by his surname; Fido, Harris and Knight get it right.

Both Cullen (p. 23) and Rumbelow (pp. 38-9) say that Cross and Paul were porters at Spitalfields market; Farson (p. 23) and Odell (p. 29) say that Cross was a carter.

Matters (p. 32) and McCormick (p. 31) both give accounts which are completely at odds with the story given by Cross and Paul in Farson (p. 23), Matters (p. 32), McCormick (p. 31) and Odell (p. 29 – the error is corrected in his collaborative effort with Colin Wilson): all say that Cross and Paul saw blood, which, of course, they did not; and all say that the two men ran to fetch a constable, literally bumping into 'PC' Haine at the corner of Brady Street. They say that Cross and Paul took him to where Nichols' body lay, where they found PC Neil and another officer. The three officers are then described as exchanging notes about the time. McCormick describes the conversation among the men, 'PC' Haine speculating that Nichols had been murdered by a gang of thugs, Cross suggesting that she may have been murdered by a Jew, and Neil being pompous and overbearing.

Since Cross and Paul did not return to the scene of the murder subsequent to their discovery of the body, the conversation reported by McCormick cannot have taken place. It is therefore curious that in the introduction to his book Donald McCormick wrote that 'The first person narratives which are recorded are based on (and in most cases literally transcribed from) statements actually made by the persons concerned either to the police at inquests on the victims, in cross-examination, or in diaries and newspaper reports.'

17. So said PC Thain. PC Neil said during the inquest that his words were: 'Here's a woman has cut her throat. Run at once for Doctor Llewellyn.'

18. Dr Rees Ralph Llewellyn (1851-1921), a local physician, died aged 70 at Toxteth Lodge, 108 Stamford Hill, Middlesex, on 17 June 1921.

19. *The Times* (18 September 1888), which gives PC Thain the name of 'Phail', said that 'he did not take his cape to the slaughterer's but sent it by a brother constable. When he was sent for the doctor he did not first go to the horse-slaughterer's and say that as a murder had been committed he had better fetch his cape.' However, *The Illustrated London News* (22 September 1888) stated that at the inquest PC Thain said that 'he went to fetch his cape because he did not know where he would be sent by his inspector'.

Here we have two reports of the testimony given by the same man in the same place, yet one report completely contradicts the other. *The Times* reporter had clearly misunderstood the testimony. This is a good example of the value of cross-checking source material.

20. Report by Inspector Abberline dated 19 September 1888, MEPO 3/140 fol. 249.

21. Inspector John Spratling, J Division, (Warrant No. 53457), joined the Metroplitan Police on 27 December 1870, retired on 8 March 1897.

22. For Knight's theory see *Jack the Ripper: The Final Solution*; Inspector Helson's report dated 7 September 1888 is in MEPO 3/140 fol. 237.

23. HO 144/220/A49301.

Chapter Four

1. *Brighton Gazette, Hove Post and Surrey Telegraph,* 9 October 1920. *Sussex Express,* 9 October 1920. *The Times* 16 September, 2, 7 October, 4 December 1920. Also see Fido p. 26.

2. *New York Times,* 4 September 1888.

3. *The Times* 7 September 1888, *Eastern Argus, Eastern Post* 8 September 1888.

4. Anderson: *op. cit.,* pp. 134-5.

5. This document is preserved in private hands.

6. Biographical details and other material either comes from papers preserved by Inspector Swanson's family or from their memories of many visits to him in their childhood.

Chapter Five

1. A police report (see note 3) calls him John Donovan.

2. *Yorkshire Post,* 11 September 1888. It was at first stated that Annie Chapman's husband was named Frederick Chapman and that he was veterinary surgeon at Windsor. This has been repeated by several writers. I cannot state that Chapman had never been a veterinary surgeon, but I have found no evidence that he was.

3. HO 144/221/A49301C sub.8a and MEPO 3/140 fol. 16, 18-20.

4. *Manchester Guardian,* 10 September 1888. I do not know whether Sivvey was his surname or merely a nickname. Either way, it was certainly bestowed upon Annie Chapman.

5. The fight between Chapman and Cooper is not important, beyond establishing that the blacked eye and bruised breast were not caused by her murderer. However, it provides a good example of the extent to which testimony could differ. According to Amelia Farmer, Chapman had told her that the fight took place on 1 September, that Chapman had been in 'the Ringers' with Ted Stanley when the row with Cooper broke out, but that the blows had been made in the lodging house that evening. Cooper said the fight took place on 2 September and that she had struck Chapman in 'the Ringers' itself. John Evans, the night watchman at 35 Dorset Street said that the fight had taken place on 6 September in the kitchen of the lodging house. The probability is that the date given by Farmer is correct, since Donovan stated that Chapman had been away from the lodging house throughout that week.

6. Again the testimony is confused. On 10 September the *Manchester Guardian* published a statement by Donovan to the effect that Chapman had come to the lodging house at about 3.00 p.m. and asked to use the kitchen, which he permitted her to do, and that he had not seen her again until 1.45 a.m. when he asked her for her bed money. She had not got it and he turned her out. At that time she had been drunk and he had castigated her, saying, 'You can find money for beer but not for your bed.' However, another report states that she had asked for use of the kitchen at 11.00 p.m. and had left at 2.00 a.m. In a third version Donovan reportedly said that at 11.00 p.m. Chapman had passed the doorway to the lodging and spoken to

Donovan. She had returned at about 1.40 a.m. She was drunk and eating a baked potato. He had asked her for her money and she had replied 'I haven't enough now, but keep my bed for me. I shan't be long.'

I gain the impression that Donovan gradually changed his story in order to portray himself in a better light, rather than as a wicked landlord who turned a sick woman onto the streets and into the arms of the Whitechapel murderer for the sake of 4d.

These different versions of the story are interesting insofar as they show Donovan's character and reliability as a witness. He later maintained that he knew and could identify the man known as 'Leather Apron' and expressed surprise that he was not called to identify a man who was arrested on suspicion of being this individual. If the value of his testimony was suspect, this would explain why the police did not contact him.

7. Donovan, Evans and Stevens all described Chapman as being drunk, yet Dr George Bagster Phillips, who conducted the post-mortem, testified at the inquest that Chapman's stomach had contained a little food – probably the baked potato – but no fluid. There was no appearance of alcohol and he was convinced that she had taken no strong alcohol for some hours before her death.

At most Chapman had a pint of beer at 'the Ringers' some time before 1.45 a.m., three hours before she met her death. It seems highly unlikely that she was therefore drunk when seen by the above witnesses. She was very ill, however, and this, coupled with fatigue and physical deprivation may have given her the appearance of being drunk.

8. The *Evening Post*, 15 September 1888, gives her the Christian name 'Harriet'.

9. Mrs Long's address is taken from sources shown in note 3. Some newspapers gave her address as 198 Church Row, Whitechapel.

10. Dr George Bagster Phillips (1834-97) was the Metropolitan Police Divisional Surgeon. He died on 27 October 1897 at the age of 63.

11. *The Lancet* 29 September 1888, p. 637.

12. Report by Chief Inspector Swanson to Home Office, dated 19 October 1888. HO 144/221/A49301C.

13. Inspector Joseph Lunniss Chandler, (Warrant No. 56638) joined the Metropolitan Police on 17 March 1873 and retired 4 April 1898.

14. An error perpetuated by almost every writer on the subject of Jack the Ripper – and expanded on by some – Cullen (p. 51), Matters (p. 44), McCormick (p. 43), Odell (p. 36), Rumbelow

(p. 48), Underwood (p. 9) and Wilson and Odell (p. 23), is that laid out at Chapman's feet were two brass rings together with a few pennies and two farthings. 'The apparent ritualistic significance,' write Wilson and Odell, 'would be mulled over in great detail in the years to come.' The mulling could have been more profitably spent in acquiring accurate information, for there were *no* coins or rings.

Dr Phillips commented that the piece of muslin and the pocket comb had the appearance of having been placed or arranged there, but the press and the police report make it abundantly clear that there were no coins and certainly no rings.

Chapman had in fact been wearing three brass rings on the middle finger of her left hand. According to Eliza Cooper, the woman with whom Chapman had the fight, Chapman had bought these rings from 'a black man'. The rings were missing when the body was found and there was an abrasion over the ring finger which looked to have been caused by the rings being wrenched off, presumably but not certainly by the murderer. The rings were patently brass, but the murderer might have mistaken them for gold in the dark – though why anyone should have thought that a woman of Annie Chapman's obvious poverty should have possessed gold rings is a mystery. The police did try to find the rings, inquiries being 'made at all pawnbrokers, jewellers, dealers'.

Among the writers who have realised that the story of the rings is a fiction is Richard Whittington-Egan. He says (p. 46) that the story of the rings can be traced back to the *Pall Mall Gazette*. Despite a fairly determined search no trace of this article has been found.

15.   William Thicke (The name is usually spelt 'Thicke', but in various sources the 'e' is absent. I have spelt the name with the 'e') was nicknamed 'Johnny Upright'. Born 20 November 1845 in Salisbury, Wiltshire, the son of Charles and Mary Thicke, he joined the Metropolitan Police, H Division, on 6 March 1868.

I would love to know more about Sgt. Thicke. Frederick Porter Wensley in his book *Detective Days* (London: Cassell, 1931; published as *Forty Years of Scotland Yard,* New York: Garden City Publishing Company, 1930) stated that the nickname 'Johnny Upright' was a tribute to his character and bearing, but Arthur Harding 'a Bethnal Green villain of the next generation, believed that the name was a sarcastic tribute to his willingness to "fit up" a suspect' (Fido p. 214).

On 10 September 1889, Mr J Haslewood of White Cottage, High Road, Tottenham, wrote to the Home Secretary saying that he had 'very good grounds to believe that the Whitechapel murderer is a member of the police force' and offering to reveal the man's identity on receipt of assurances that his (Haslewood's) identity would not be made known to the police. Despite reservations, E. Leigh Pemberton wrote back on Henry Matthews's behalf and offered strict confidentiality. Haslewood replied on 14 October 1889 naming Sergeant Thicke and recommending that it be ascertained 'what disease he is troubled with'. The Home Office Minutes record: 'I think this plainly rubbish – perhaps prompted by spite,' – see HO 144/220/49301A subs. 177.

Chapter Six

1. HO 144/221/A49301C sub. 8a (report 3).
2. HO 144/221/A49301C sub. 8a.
3. Major Henry Smith (d. 2 March 1921) became Commissioner of the City of London Police in 1890. Retired Lt. Col. Sir Henry Smith on 25 December 1901. He died in Edinburgh.
4. *The Times*, 10 September 1888.
5. MEPO 3/140 fol. 11.
6. *East London Observer*, 15 September 1888.
7. *Jewish Chronical*, 14 September 1888.
8. *New York Times*, 9 September 1888.
9. *Eastern Argus*, 8 September 1888.
10. Letter from ETA in *The Times*, 22 September 1888.
11. *The Yorkshire Post*, 10 September 1888.
12. *The Times, Manchester Guardian, Yorkshire Post*, 11 September. *The Times*, 12, 14 September 1888.
13. MEPO 3/140 fol. 12-13, report by Det. Insp. Styles dated 11 September; fol. 21-3, report by Sgt. Thicke dated 17 September; fol. 24-5, report by Inspector Abberline dated 18 September 1888; fol. 26-8, statement by Mrs Issenschmidt dated 19 September; fol. 29-32, report by Insp. Helson dated 19 September; fol. 254-6, report by Insp. Abberline dated 19 September. Also *The Times* 13, 14 September, *The Guardian* 13, 17 September, *East London Advertiser*, 22 September.
14. Charles Ludwig was also called Ludwig Wetzel and Charles Ludwig Wetzel in the press. See *The Times* 19, 26 September, *Manchester Guardian* 19 September (which is also the source of the information that Elizabeth Burns had only one arm), *Yorkshire Post* 19 September 1888.
15. *East London Advertiser*, 15 September 1888.

16. *Manchester Guardian,* 12 September 1888.

17. *Manchester Guardian,* 10 September 1888.

18. John Pizer (c.1850-97) lived at home with his 70 year old stepmother and married brother. He worked for Mr Nicholson, his sister-in-law's father as a boot maker. Pizer, who claimed at the time of his arrest on suspicion of being 'Leather Apron' to be of weak constitution, may have been telling the truth for he died on 5 July 1897 aged 47, from 'Gastro Enteritis Collapse' at the London Hospital.

On 11 October 1888, John Pizer appeared at the Thames Police Court. On the previous Thursday morning he had left his home and gone to get some cheese for breakfast. A woman named Emily Patzwold insulted him and called him 'Leather Apron'. He ignored her and walked on. Returning with his purchase, the same woman struck him three times in the face, knocking off his hat, which, as he bent to pick it up, gave the woman the opportunity to further assault him. Neighbours then came to his assistance and Pizer's brother informed the police of the incident. Emily Patzwold was fined 10s. and 2s. costs. (*Daily Telegraph,* 12 October 1888).

19. *Manchester Guardian,* 13 September 1888.

20. This unattractive portrait of John Pizer appeared in the frequently anti-semitic *East London Observer,* 15 September 1888. Anti-semitism appears to have been rife and reached disgusting levels in print in the general press.

21. *East London Advertiser,* 13 October 1888.

22. Martin Fido (p. 211) says, 'It would be very useful to know just who J43 and J173 brought in. It certainly was not John Pizer, who had stayed indoors in his stepmother's house for the week preceding his arrest, well out of the way of Bethnal Green.' My understanding, however, is that John Pizer returned home at 10.45 p.m. on Thursday, 6 September, that he chatted with his sister's boyfriend, then went to bed. The following morning his brother advised him to stay indoors, which he did until his arrest on the following Monday, 10 September. He could therefore have been the man in police custody on Sunday, 2 September.

Martin Fido believed that Pizer had stayed indoors because of the general animosity towards the Jews in consequence of the murder of Annie Chapman, but it would seem that he acted on his brother's advice on the night of 6 or the morning of 7 September, that is *before* Chapman's murder.

23. MEPO 3/140 fol. 238. Report dated 7 September 1888 by Inspector Helson.

24. Fido, pp. 212, 214.
25. MEPO 3/140 fol. 248-9.
26. Report by Robert Anderson to Home Office dated 23 October 1883. HO 144/221/A49301C.
27. Alexander C Bruce, Ass. Comm. December 1884-March 1914.
28. HO A49301B sub. 2.
29. *East London Observer,* 24 November 1888.
30. *The Times,* 11 September 1888.
31. *East London Observer,* 22 September 1888.
32. Letter from JP to *The Times,* 19 September 1888.
33. Letter from Roland Adams Williams, former Deputy Coroner for Crickhowell, Breconshire, to *The Times,* 26 September 1888.
34. *The Times,* 26 September 1888.
35. *British Medical Journal,* 29 September 1888.
36. *The Lancet,* 29 September 1888.
37. The *Law Journal* quoted by the *Eastern Post,* 29 September 1888.
38. *British Medical Journal,* 6 October 1888.
39. Anderson: *op. cit.,* p. 138.
40. Swanson's copy of Anderson's autobiography is in private hands.
41. Anderson: *op. cit.,* p. 135.

Chapter Seven

1. This information is supplied in Rumbelow, pp. 74-5, who credits Klas Lithner, listed in Rumbelow's bibliography as the author of an article in a journal *Bra om Deckare* No.60, 1982, pp. 14-15. Published by Bra Deckare, Södra vägen, Högänas, Sweden.
2. Charles Preston. Inquest testimony. *The Times,* 4 October 1888.
3. Michael Kidney. Inquest testimony. *The Times,* 4 October 1888.
4. Marriage certificate. At the inquest testimony was given by her nephew, PC Walter Frederick Stride (Warrant No. 62349) 436 W. Born on 24 March 1858, he had joined the Metropolitan Police on 11 March 1878 and resigned on 20 October 1902. He was married to Sarah Rebecca Stride and at the time of his retirement they were living at 77 Mitcham Road, Croydon, Surrey.
5. *The Times,* 4 September 1878.
6. The *Daily Telegraph,* 6 October 1888. Sven Olsson was a clerk of the Swedish Church – located in Prince's Square, later renamed Swedenborg Gardens. The Church was demolished in the early 1920s.

Olsson returned to Sweden where he died in the 1930s. I am indebted to the former Rector, Sven Evander, for information relating to Stride.

7. *Manchester Guardian, Evening News,* 8 October 1888.

8. Elizabeth Tanner, inquest testimony. Tanner said that Stride had lodged at 32 Flower and Dean Street on and off for six years.

9. Michael Kidney. Inquest testimony. *The Times,* 4 October 1888.

10. Catherine Lane, a charwoman living at 32 Flower and Dean Street, also said that Stride had told her that she had formerly lived in Devonshire Street.

11. At the inquest Michael Kidney said that he padlocked the door to his and Stride's room and that he had the only key. He knew that Stride was able to get in and out somehow, but did not know how she managed it. However, among the possessions found on her body was a padlock-type key.

12. Catherine Lane. Inquest testimony. *The Times,* 4 October 1888.

13. Ann Mill reported in the *Manchester Guardian,* 2 October 1888.

14. Catherine Lane was married to a dock labourer named Patrick Lane and she had lived at 32 Flower and Dean Street since 11 February, but had known Stride for six or seven years. Charles Preston, a barber, had lived at that address for 18 months – see inquest testimony, *The Times,* 4 October 1888. Preston said that four or five months earlier Stride had been arrested one Saturday night for being drunk and disorderly at the Queen's Head public house and had been released on bail the following day.

15. Thomas B Eyges (known at MOT): *Beyond the Horizon,* Boston: Group Free Society, 1944, pp. 79-83.

16. Philip Kranz (real name Jacob Rombro) was born in Podolia, a region in the SW Ukraine. He left Russia during the pogroms of 1881 and arrived in London by way of Paris, where he had spent some time as a student. He became editor of *Arbeter Fraint* on the recommendation of its founder, Morris Winchesvsky, and remained so until May 1889, when he emigrated to the United States, becoming editor of *Arbeter Zeitung* in New York.

17. See J H Mackay: *The Anarchists,* Boston, 1891 p. 183-7 for a full description of the Berner Street Club. It is quoted in William J Fishman, *East End 1888,* London: Duckworth, 1988. I must express my appreciation of William J Fishman and Duckworth for an advance copy of this book. I feel sure that it will become essential reading for anyone interested in the social history of the period in general and the locality in particular.

18. *Evening News,* 1 October 1888.

19. Louis Deimschutz. Interview with the *Evening News*, 1 October 1888.

20. Abraham Heabury, quoted in the *Yorkshire Post*, 1 October 1888.

21. Edward Spooner. *The Times*, 3 October 1888.

22. Dr Phillips, *Daily Telegraph*, 6 October 1888.

23. Report by Sgt. White MEPO 3/140, fol. 212.

24. Report by Chief Inspector Swanson to Home Office HO 144/221/A49301C.

25. William Marshall. Inquest testimony, 6 October. The Census Records show that William Marshall, bootmaker, lived at this address with his wife, May, a laundress, and their children, William and Janine. It is not clear whether the father or the son was the witness.

26. PC William Smith: born 14 September 1862, at Milton, Oxford. Joined the Metropolitan Police on 19 March 1883, P Division (Camberwell).

27. PC William Smith. Inquest testimony. *The Times*, 6 October 1888. Also HO 144/A49301C 8a.

28. *Evening News*, 1 October 1888.

29. Charles Letchford, quoted *Manchester Guardian*, 1 October 1888.

30. William West. Inquest testimony. *The Times*, 2 October 1888.

31. Joseph Lave, quoted in the *Manchester Guardian*, 1 October 1888.

32. Report by Chief Inspector Donald Swanson dated 19 October 1888 to the Home Office. HO/144/221/A49301C 8a.

33. Report by Inspector Abberline dated 1 November 1888 in reply to a query from Home Secretary Matthews regarding the meaning of the word 'Lipski'. MEPO 3/140 fol. 204-6.

34. The *Star*, 10 October 1888.

35. James Brown. Inquest testimony. *The Times*, 6 October 1888.

36. The identity of the man with the black bag is revealed in the Home Office files. Before the files were made available for public inspection several writers made the not unreasonable connection between him and a man taken into custody on the night of the murder by PC Robert Spicer, 101 H.

In a letter published in the *Daily Express* on 16 March 1931 PC Spicer explained how on the night of Stride's murder he had come upon a man sitting with a prostitute on a brick dustbin in Heneage Street. The man carried a black Gladstone bag and had blood on his shirt-cuffs. Spicer took the man to the police station on suspicion of being Jack the Ripper, but to his horror his superiors immediately released him on his telling them he was a doctor who lived in Brixton, a claim which Spicer's superiors did not even bother to corroborate. Spicer asked 'Then what is a respectable doctor doing sitting on a dustbin in a dark and dirty alley at this hour of the morning with a common prostitute? It doesn't make sense.'

Spicer's question was both naive and self-explanatory. It should have counselled caution before his story was accepted. But some people not only accepted it, they tried and were convinced that they had succeeded in identifying the doctor in question.

In 1972 in *City,* the magazine of the City of London Police, B E Reilly explained how for various reasons he had concluded that the doctor in question was a certain 'Dr Merchant' who died in December 1888.

B E Reilly's article illustrates the necessity of returning whenever possible to primary source material. Spicer wrote in his letter that 'I left the force five months after this suspect had been released. Yet I saw the man several times after this in Liverpool Street Station accosting women.' Obviously, if Spicer saw his Brixton doctor in 1889, the doctor cannot have been 'Dr Merchant' who died in December 1888. B E Reilly's 'research' was in vain.

PC Spicer joined the Metropolitan Police on 11 April 1887. He did not, as some writers have assumed, resign through disgust or disillusionment, but was dismissed on 25 April 1889 for being drunk on duty and unnecessarily interfering with two private persons. I do not know, but I strongly suspect that the two private persons were the Brixton doctor and his prostitute friend, and that the incident described in the *Daily Telegraph* letter was an exaggerated account of an incident which in reality took place long after the murder of Elizabeth Stride.

37. Louis Deimschutz, quoted in the *Manchester Guardian,* 1 October 1888. Inquest testimony. *The Times,* 2 October 1888.

38. Morris Eagle, quoted in the *Manchester Guardian,* 1 October 1888, *The Times,* 2 October 1888.

39. Edward Spooner. Inquest testimony. *The Times,* 3 October 1888.

40. Fido, pp. 62-3.

41. Comment on Stride should mention the initial difficulty of identifying her. An unnamed individual was reported in *The Times,* 1 October 1888, to have identified the body as that of Annie Fitzgerald, who had been charged and convicted a great number of times at the Thames Police Court for drunkenness, and whenever so charged had pleaded that she suffered from fits and had not been drunk.

A woman named 'One-armed Liz' (Elizabeth Burns?) told a reporter she had identified the body as that of Annie Morris (see *Yorkshire Post,* 1 October 1888), whilst somebody else said that the body was that of 'Wally' Warden who lived in Brick Lane (see *Evening News,* 1 October 1888).

The most remarkable claim was made by Mrs Malcolm, the wife of a tailor named Andrew Malcolm, who maintained that the body was that of her sister Elizabeth Watts, whom she had been in the habit of meeting and providing with money every Saturday for the past five years. Mrs Malcolm's sister was later discovered and claimed that she had not seen Mrs Malcolm for years. One is almost convinced that poor Mrs Malcolm had in fact been meeting Stride, masquerading as her sister. (see *Bath Chronicle,* 4 October 1888; *Bath and Cheltenham Gazette,* 10 October 1888; *The Times,* 24 October 1888;)

Chapter Eight

1. The spelling of her Christian name and that of her mother is Catharine not Catherine, on her birth certificate. Catharine is also the spelling used by Smith (p. 159).

2. Birth certificate.

3. *Manchester Guardian,* 5 October 1888.

4. *Wolverhampton Chronicle,* 10 October 1888.

5. *Daily Telegraph,* 4 October 1888.

6. The police had considerable difficulty in locating Conway. Their only clue was that he had belonged to the 18th Royal Irish and drew an army pension, but the only Conway they could find was the wrong man. When Thomas Conway eventually learned about Eddowes's murder and presented himself to the police it was learned that he had enlisted and drawn his pension under the assumed name of Thomas Quinn.

7. Annie Phillips, quoted in the *Wolverhampton Chronicle,* 10 October 1888. At the time of her mother's death Annie Phillips was living at 12 Dilston Grove, Southwark Park Road. She was married to Louis Phillips, a lamp-black packer. Two years earlier Eddowes had nursed her daughter through her confinement, but her over-drinking and appeals for money had led mother and daughter to part on bad terms. At that time Annie had been living in King Street, Bermondsey, but had soon left that address and had moved several times since. She had never left a forwarding address and her mother did not know where to find her.

8. Mrs Elizabeth Fisher, quoted in the *Wolverhampton Chronicle,* 10 October 1888.

9. John Kelly, quoted in the *Evening News,* 10 October, 1888.

10. Frederick William Wilkinson. Inquest testimony. *The Times,* 5 October 1888. Coroner's Inquests (L) 1888. No. 135. Corporation of London Records Office.

11. John Kelly. Inquest testimony. *The Times,* 5 October 1888. Coroner's Inquests (L) 1888. No. 135. Corporation of London Records

Office.

12. Eliza Gold. Inquest testimony. *The Times,* 5 October 1888. Coroner's Inquests (L) 1888. No. 135. Corporation of London Records Office.

13. See Mitchell and Deane; *op. cit.,* p.78. Charles Whitehead, in the *Journal of the Royal Agricultural Society of England,* 3rd Series. I (1890), pp. 323, 336. E T J Collins, 'Migrant Labour in British Agriculture in the Nineteenth Century.' *Economic History Review,* February 1976, pp. 41-5.

14. John Kelly. Interview with the London *Star,* quoted by the *Yorkshire Post,* 4 October 1888.

15. *East London Observer,* 13 October 1888.

16. PC Louis Frederick Robinson (Warrant No. 5921), joined the police force on 9 December 1886, aged 21 years 2 months, and retired (PC 303C, Bishopsgate) on 1 February 1912.

17. Sergeant James George Byfield (Warrant No. 4171), joined the police force on 8 May 1868 aged 19 and retired on 3 January 1895.

18. George Henry Hutt (Warrant No. 5274), joined the police force on 31 January 1879, aged 24 years 11 months. He retired on 7 November 1889.

19. PC Edward Watkins, 881 City, (Warrant No. 4420), joined the police force on 25 May 1871, and retired on 28 May 1896.

20. Coroner's Inquests (L) 1888 No. 135. Corporation of London Records Office.

21. The address is given as 79 Fenchurch Street in a report from Superintendent McWilliam to the Home Office dated 29 October 1888.

22. Report by Chief Inspector Donald Swanson dated 6 November 1888. HO 144/221/A49301C 8c.

23. Coroner's Inquests (L) 1888 No. 135. Corporation of London Records Office. *Daily News,* 12 October 1888.

24. Report dated 19 October 1888, by Chief Inspector Donald Swanson. HO 144/221/A49301C 8c.

25. Smith wrote:

> At the exit leading direct to Goulston Street, opposite the corner where the murder was committed, there was a club, the members of which were nearly all foreigners. One, a sort of hybrid German, was leaving the club – he was unable to fix the hour – when he noticed a man and woman standing close together. The woman had her hand resting on the man's chest. It was bright moonlight, almost as light as day, and he saw them distinctly. This was, without doubt, the murderer and his victim. The inquiries I made at Berner Street, the evidence of

the constable in whose beat the square was, and my own movements, of which I kept careful notes, proved this conclusively. The description of the man given me by the German was as follows: Young, about middle height, with a small fair moustache, dressed in something like navy serge, with a deerstalker's cap – that is, a cap with a peak both for and aft. I think the German spoke the truth, because I could not 'lead' him in any way. 'You will easily recognise him, then,' I said. 'Oh no!' he replied; 'I only had a short look at him.' The German was a strange mixture, honest apparently, and intelligent also. He 'had heard of some murders,' he said, but they didn't seem to concern him.' (Smith: *op. cit.,* pp. 158-9).

Reference might also be made to an earlier remark: 'though within five minutes of the perpetrator one night, and with a very fair description of him besides, he completely beat me . . .' (p. 147), and 'In Dorset Street, with extraordinary audacity, he washed them [his hands] at a sink up a close, not more than six yards from the street. I arrived there in time to see the bloodstained water.' (p. 153).

Some writers seem to have assumed that Smith saw the bloodstained water in the sink in Dorset Street on the night of Eddowes's murder, but on page 161 it is made clear, I think, that he was talking about a later incident, possibly the murder of Mary Jane Kelly. Be this as it may, it is quite clear that Smith was not 'within five minutes' of the murderer on the night of Eddowes's murder. The murderer had long gone by the time Smith arrived on the scene. Furthermore, if the 'very fair description' was the description supplied by Joseph Lawende, it was not available to Smith until several hours later when house-to-house inquiries led to his discovery. Unless Smith is mistaken in all that he says, he must be referring to a murder subsequent to that of Eddowes – presumably Kelly's.

Returning to Smith's account of Lawende, how, one wonders, did inquiries at Berner Street, the evidence of PC Watkins, and particularly Smith's own carefully noted movements 'conclusively' prove that the man seen by Lawende was Eddowes's murderer? There are also several errors – Lawende was reasonably certain of the time, whereas Smith says Lawende 'was unable to fix the hour'; the man's jacket was 'pepper-and-salt', not 'navy serge'; and he wore a cap with a peak which gave him the appearance of a sailor, not a deerstalker.

26. Henry Homewood Crawford (knighted in 1910) represented the City Police at the inquest into the death of Catharine Eddowes. Born

in London on 12 June 1850, he married Louisa Truscott (daughter of Sir Francis Wyatt Truscott, Lord Mayor of London, 1879-80, and sister of Sir George Wyatt Truscott, Lord Mayor of London, 1908-9) in 1874. He died on 17 November 1936. For anyone interested, he was a prominent Freemason, among his many posts being Master of the Grand Master's Lodge No. 1.

27. PC James Harvey (Warrant No. 5045) joined the City Police on 30 November 1876 aged 21 years 8 months. He was dismissed on 1 July 1889.

28. PC James Thomas Holland (Warrant No. 3620) transferred to the City from the Metropolitan Force on 25 August 1865. Retired unfit on 18 February 1892.

29. Dr George William Sequeira, 34 Jewry Street, Aldgate. Died 14 October 1926.

30. Dr William Sedgwick Saunders, Medical Officer of Health and Public Analyst for the City of London.

31. Dr Frederick Gordon Brown. Inquest testimony. *The Times,* 12 October 1888.

32. Report by Chief Inspector Donald Swanson to the Home Office dated 6 November 1888. HO 144/221/A49301C 8c.

33. Inspector Edward Collard (Warrant No. 4157). Joined the City Police on 6 March 1868 aged 22. He died in the Police Hospital, Bishopsgate, on 4 June 1892, having attained the rank of Chief Inspector in the Bishopsgate Division.

34. Dr Frederick Gordon Brown, surgeon to the City of London Police. He retired in 1914 and died at Tailours, Chigwell, Essex, on Sunday, 15 January 1928. See obituary in *The Lancet,* 21 January 1928, p. 161. He was a prominent Freemason and Past Grand Officer of the Grand Lodge of England.

35. Superintendent James McWilliam, City Detective, (Warrant No. 2852). Joined the City Police on 15 March 1858, aged 20 years 11 months. Retired on 31 December 1903.

36. Superintendent Alfred Lawrence Foster (Warrant No. 3636). Joined City Police on 29 September 1864. Retired unfit on 26 May 1892.

37. Smith, pp. 149-50.

38. Detective Daniel Halse (Warrant No. 3429) joined the police force on 16 July 1863 aged 24. He retired unfit on 6 August 1891.

39. Detective Robert Outram (Warrant No. 3771) joined the police force on 18 August 1865, aged 20. He retired on 31 January 1895 having attained the rank of Detective Inspector.

40. Detective Edward Marriot (Warrant No. 5830) joined the police

force on 16 July 1885 and retired on 6 May 1909, unfit as a result of an injury sustained whilst on duty.

41. PC Alfred Long (Warrant No. 69841) 254 A Division, temporarily assigned to assist H Division. Joined on 6 October 1884. Dismissed in July 1889 for being drunk on duty and being considered unfit for the police force.

42. Superintendent Thomas Arnold (Warrant No. 63324). Joined 17 February 1879. Retired 19 January 1903.

43. Report by Superintendent J Arnold dated 6 November 1888. HO 144/221/A49301C 8c.

44. Report from Sir Charles Warren to the Home Office dated 6 November 1888. HO 144/221/A49301C 8c.

45. Knight's theory – which was that the murders were committed by Sir William Gull, a Freemason, with the assistance of others, among them Sir Robert Anderson, for the purpose of silencing those to whom Mary Jane Kelly had imparted the information that the Duke of Clarence had secretly married and had a child by a Catholic shopgirl – has been thoroughly discredited by Melvin Harris and Donald Rumbelow, both of whom have produced books which are required reading.

Chapter Nine

1. *East London Observer,* 6 October 1888.

2. *The Times,* 1 October 1888.

3. *Manchester Guardian, Yorkshire Post,* 1 October 1888.

4. *New York Times,* 1 October 1888.

5. *Yorkshire Post,* 2 October 1888.

6. *The Times,* 2 October 1888.

7. *Manchester Guardian,* 3 October 1888.

8. *The Daily Telegraph* and *The Star* are undated and quoted in Jones and Lloyd pp. 111-12.

9. *Manchester Guardian,* 2 October 1888.

10. Letter from Henry Matthews to Evelyn Ruggles-Brise dated 5 October, 1888. J S Sanders papers, MS. Eng. hist. c.723. Reproduced with the permission of the Bodleian Library, Department of Western Manuscripts, Oxford.

11. Letter from Sir Charles Warren to Henry Matthews dated 6 October 1888. HO 144/220/A49301 B sub. 9. Almost the whole of A49301 B deals with the question of the offer of a reward. It seems clear that the metaphorical knives were out and everyone was

watching their backs.

12. *East London Observer,* 13 October 1888.

13. *The Times,* 4 October 1888.

14. Report by Chief Inspector Swanson to the Home Office dated 19 October 1888. HO/144/221/A49301C 8a.

15. Anderson: *op. cit.,* pp. 135-6.

16. *Yorkshire Post,* 8 October 1888; *The Times,* 9 October 1888; *Wolverhampton Chronicle,* 10 October 1888.

17. William Bull on 2 October (see *Manchester Guardian,* 4 October 1888); Alfred Napier Blanchard on 6 October (see *The Times,* 8 October, 1888); Benjamin Graham, 17 October (see *Eastern Post,* 27 October, 1888).

18. *Yorkshire Post,* 8 October 1888.

19. Lees's diary preserved at Stanstead Hall. Quoted by Harris: *op. cit.,* p. 104.

20. Report from Chief Inspector Swanson to Home Office dated 6 November 1888. HO/221/A49301C 8c.

21. Fido, p. 79.

22. *The Times,* 23 October 1888.

23. Smith, p. 154.

24. Report from Superintendent Arnold dated 22 October 1888. MEPO 3/141 fol. 166.

Chapter Ten

1. She was also known as Marie Jeanette Kelly and it was by this name that Joseph Barnett referred to her (inquest papers and newspaper reports) and her death was registered. However, in the inquest reports and statements taken on the day of her murder (Greater London Archives, Coroner's Papers MJ/SPC/NE 1888, Box 3, No. 19) various neighbours and friends (Thomas Bowyer, Mary Ann Cox, Maria Harvey, John McCarthy, Caroline Maxwell) all stated that they knew and referred to her as Mary Jane. The weight of inference is that Mary Jane was her name and that Marie Jeanette was an affectation.

2. Anderson: *op. cit.,* p. 137. 'The last and most horrible of that maniac's crimes was committed in a house in Miller's Court on the 9 November.'

3. Report from Sir Melville Macnaghten dated 23 February 1894. MEPO 3/141 fol. 178: 'Now the Whitechapel murderer had 5 victims and 5 victims only', the last being Mary Kelly.

4. Macnaghten, p. 60.

5. Lizzie Albrook. Statement to press (probably to the Press Association). *Western Mail* (Cardiff), 12 November 1888.

6. John McCarthy, who was 37 in 1888, was a naturalized British subject, having been born in France. Rumbelow (p. 101) has pointed out that since 26 and 27 Dorset Street were owned by McCarthy and rented out almost entirely to prostitutes, they were 'locally known as McCarthy's Rents, which was probably a local phrase referring to the prostitutes in Miller's Court controlled by McCarthy and not the houses that he owned as has been often assumed'. I cannot recall ever having come across a contemporary reference to 'McCarthy's Rents', although 'X's Rents was a common expression. The nearest such reference that I can call to mind is a description of Miller's Court as 'McCarthy's Court' (in a statement by Maurice Lewis, *Illustrated Police News,* 17 November 1888). The police described McCarthy 'as a most respectable man' who had been 'recently awarded a prize for collecting money for the hospitals' (Central News report quoted by the *Western Mail,* 10 November 1888).

7. McCarthy. Interview with Central News. *The Times,* 10 November 1888. Barnett, in a statement given to Inspector Abberline on 9 November 1888 said: 'She had a brother named Henry serving in 2nd Battalion Scots Guards, and known among his comrades as Johnto, and I believe the Regiment is now in Ireland.' MJ/SPC/NE 1888. Box 3 No. 19. Corporation of London, Greater London Archives, Coroner's Papers.

The *Yorkshire Post* (12 November 1888) reported: 'The authorities have been making inquiries concerning the soldier who, according to Barnett, was in the Second Battalion of the Scots Guards. The Regiment is now in Dublin, and it is understood that inquiries will be immediately promoted there.' The result of any such inquiries was not published in any source that I have seen.

The *Army Lists* records that the 2nd Battalion Scots Guards proceeded from Chelsea Barracks to Dublin in August 1888 – during June 1889 they went to The Curragh, a plain in Co. Kildare, which had been the site of a military camp since 1646; they returned to Chelsea in August 1889. Unless Barnett had a particular interest in troop movements, it seems reasonable to suppose that Mary Jane Kelly must have received a communication from her brother in or shortly before August 1888. It seems that Kelly did have a brother serving in the 2nd Battalion Scots Guards.

The Regimental Records are incomplete. Apparently there were 35 men surnamed Kelly serving with the Scots Guards Regiment as a whole, but only two served in the 2nd Battalion, neither was born in Limerick, Co. Limerick, or Munster, and no man surnamed Kelly who was born in Wales served in the Regiment.

8. Mrs Carthy. Press Association interview. *Western Mail,* 10 November 1888.

9. Maria Harvey, quoted in *The Times,* 10 November 1888.

10. Press Association report. *Western Mail,* 10 November 1888.

11. Cullen; pp. 163, 167.

12. John McCarthy, quoted in *The Times,* 13 November 1888.

13. Caroline Maxwell. Inquest testimony. *Daily Telegraph,* 13 November 1888.

14. Jones and Lloyd, p. 65.

15. A thorough search – triple checked – of the marriage registers of St Catherine's House shows that of the 34 women named Kell(e)y married in England and Wales in the nine years between 1874 and 1883, only three married in Wales. None of them was the Mary Jane Kelly.

16. At that time there was only one infirmary in Cardiff, the now Cardiff Royal Infirmary, and inquiries have indicated that no medical records for that period have survived.

17. *Western Mail,* 12 November 1888.

18. Knight, p. 34.

19. Elizabeth Phoenix, quoted in the *Western Mail,* 12 November 1888.

20. Elizabeth Phoenix quoted in the *Yorkshire Post,* 12 November 1888.

21. Press Association. *Western Mail,* 13 November 1888.

22. Kellow Chesney: *The Victorian Underworld.* London: Maurice Temple Smith, 1970. pp. 343-9.

23. Julia Venturney, quoted in *The Times* and the *Western Mail,* 13 November 1888.

24. Press Association. *Western Mail,* 10 November 1888.

25. Joseph Barnett told a newspaper reporter that he had met Kelly 'last Easter twelve month'. At the inquest he spoke of their having met on a Friday night. Easter Sunday 1887 was 10 April, so Barnett and Kelly would have met on Good Friday, 8 April 1888. (See *Observer,* 11 November 1888; *The Penny Illustrated Paper,* 17 November 1888; and others.)

26. The only reference to 'The Fisherman's Widow' that I have been able to find is in the description of Kelly's room published in the *Pall Mall Gazette,* 12 November 1888, and sources, such as the *Manchester Guardian,* 13 November 1888, which quoted therefrom. A picture is

shown in a drawing of the room in *Reynolds Newspaper*, 18 November 1888, the strict accuracy of which seems questionable.

27. *Daily Telegraph*, 10 November 1888.

28. Statement by Joseph Barnett to Inspector Abberline. MJ/SPC/NE 1888. Box 3 No. 19. Corporation of London, Greater London Archives, Coroner's Papers.

29. Elizabeth Prater, who occupied the room above Kelly's, said that the couple had fought about ten days earlier – *Daily Telegraph*, 10 November 1888.

30. According to McCarthy. *Illustrated Police News*, 17 November 1888.

31. Joseph Barnett. Inquest testimony.

32. Joseph Barnett, quoted in the *Western Mail*, 12 November 1888.

33. *Evening News*, 1 October 1888.

34. *Daily Telegraph*, 10 November 1888. *Penny Illustrated Paper* (which carries a sketch of Bowyer), 17 November 1888.

35. *Western Mail*, 12 November 1888. The fruiterer, of course, is Matthew Packer, whose testimony is somewhat unreliable.

36. Sarah Lewis testified at the inquest, relating how she had been accosted by a man in the vicinity of Bethnal Green Road whom she recognised in Commercial Street on the night of Mary Kelly's murder. Lewis was at the time on her way to the house of Mrs Keyler, 'a friend' who lived at 2 Miller's Court, opposite Kelly's room. Her story was reported in most newspaper accounts of the inquest published on 13 November 1888. However, on 12 November, two newspapers, *The Times* and the *Manchester Guardian*, carried substantially the same story but credited to a woman named Kennedy, both stating that Kennedy's parents occupied 2 Miller's Court. Kennedy and Lewis are clearly the same person. Her statement in the *Manchester Guardian* was more detailed than given elsewhere and, if true, requires that it be accorded greater credence. She said:

> 'He invited us to accompany him into a lonely spot, as he was known about there and there was a policeman looking at him.' She asserts there was no policeman in sight. He made several strange remarks, and appeared to be agitated . . . He avoided walking with them and led the way into a very dark thoroughfare, at the back of the workhouse, inviting them to follow, which they did. He then pulled open a small door in a pair of large gates and requested one of them to follow him, remarking, 'I only want one of you.' Whereupon the women

became suspicious. He acted in a very strange and suspicious manner, and refused to leave his bag in the possession of one of the ladies. Both women became alarmed and escaped . . . A gentleman who was passing is stated to have intercepted the man while the women made their escape.' (*Manchester Guardian*, 12 November 1888).

37. Statement by Maria Harvey at inquest. MJ/SPC/NE 1888. Box 3 No. 19. Corporation of London, Greater London Archives, Coroner's Papers.

38. Sarah Roney. Press Association interview. *The Times*, 10 November 1888.

39. Julia Venturney, quoted in *The Times* (which gives her name as Julia ven Teurney) and the *Western Mail*, 13 November 1888.

40. Press Association. 12 November 1888.

41. Press Association, *The Times* and the *Western Mail*, 10 November 1888.

42. *New York Times*, 10 November 1888.

43. *Yorkshire Post*, 12 November 1888.

44. *Illustrated Police News*, 17 November 1888. The information was apparently given by John McCarthy.

45. Mary Ann Cox. Inquest testimony and statement to Inspector Abberline. MJ/SPC/NE 1888. Box 3, No. 19. Greater London Archives, Coroner's papers.

46. Elizabeth Prater. Inquest testimony.

47. By a curious coincidence, a man of this name featured in an article in the *Pall Mall Gazette*, 12 January 1889, under the heading 'IS HE THE WHITECHAPEL MURDERER?' The article read: 'The Panama "Star and Herald" asks this startling question while recording a telegram from Elgin, Illinois, U.S.A., which runs:-"Seven or eight years ago George Hutchinson, an inmate of the Elgin lunatic asylum, was very handy with his knife. He delighted to visit the hospital slaughter-house, and made many peculiar toys from bones. After escaping from Elgin he was captured at Kankakee. He escaped from that place, and murdered a disreputable woman in Chicago, mutilating her body in a way similar to the Whitechapel cases. He was returned to Kankakee, but afterwards again escaped, and has been at large for three or four years.'

48. George Hutchinson. Statement dated 12 November 1888, signed by Hutchinson, Inspector Abberline, Sergeant E Badham, Inspector C Ellisdon, Superintendent Arnold. MEPO 3/140 fol. 227-9.

49. *The Times*, 14 November 1888.

50. Sarah Lewis. Inquest testimony.

51. Report by Dr Bond. MEPO 3/141 fol. 150-7.

52. Report by Inspector Abberline dated 12 November 1888. MEPO 4/140 fol. 230-2.

53. MJ/SPC/NE 1888. Box 3, No. 19. Corporation of London, Greater London Archives, Coroner's papers.

54. *The Times,* 10 November 1888.

55. *Illustrated Police News,* 17 November 1888.

56. John McCarthy. Interview given to Central News. Reported in various newspapers. *The Times,* 10 November 1888.

57. Sir Charles Warren, on the recommendation of Home Secretary Matthews, had experimented with the use of bloodhounds and conducted trials to see how effective they could be. They were supposed to have been available for use, but were not.

58. Mrs Paumier. Press Association interview. *The Times,* 10 November 1888.

59. McCarthy. Interview with Central News. *The Times,* 10 November 1888.

60. *Daily Telegraph,* 13 November 1888.

61. Central News. *Western Mail,* 10 November 1888.

62. Dr Thomas Bond, surgeon to the Westminster Hospital and to A Division of the Metropolitan Police, killed himself by jumping out of a third-floor window at his home on 6 June 1901 – see *The Times,* 7 June 1901; *The Lancet,* 8 June and 15 June 1901. His health had been poor and he had been in pain for some considerable time, and he had often contemplated suicide. In middle life he had suffered from insomnia which coupled with overwork led him to use drugs. It is not stated, but is possibly inferred by virtue of being mentioned, that he was addicted to the use of narcotics. Presumably this did not impair his faculties, but such a possibility should be borne in mind.

63. Report by Dr Thomas Bond. Various copies in the MEPO and HO files. Original is in MEPO 3/141, fol. 150-7.

64. *Yorkshire Post,* 12 November 1888.

65. *The Times, Western Mail, Manchester Guardian,* 12 November 1888, *Western Mail,* 13 November 1888, *Illustrated Police News,* 17 November 1888.

66. Dr Roderick Mcdonald, Liberal MP and Surgeon to K Division of the Metropolitan Police.

67. *Yorkshire Post,* 15 November 1888, *Eastern Post,* 17 November 1888, *The Times,* 20 November 1888, *Police Chronicle and Guardian,* 24 November 1888.

68. *The Times, Western Mail,* 7 December 1888, *Western Mail,* 8 December 1888.

Chapter Eleven

1. Macnaghten Report. MEPO 3/141 fol. 177-83.
2. Aberconway Papers. Preserved in private collection.
3. Letter from Philip Loftus to Christabel, Lady Aberconway, dated 11 August 1972. Preserved in private collection. Review of Farson, the *Guardian*, 7 October 1972.

Chapter Twelve

1. George Valentine (1842-1912). He retired in 1893 and died on 26 May 1912. *Blackheath Local Guide and District Advertiser*, 30 December 1893; 8 June 1912).
2. Daniel Farson: *Jack the Ripper*, London: Michael Joseph, 1972, p. 115.
3. *Blackheath Local Guide and District Advertiser*, 8 June 1912.
4. Blackheath Hockey Club Records. Held at the Local History Centre, The Manor House, Lee, London SE13 5SX.
5. Admission stamp book, Vol. 1880-4, fol. 639, Library, Inner Temple.
6. Call Book for period 1875-94 (no details are given except the name). Library, Inner Temple.
7. Letters of Administration, 24 May 1891. Principal Registry, Family Division, Somerset House.
8. T H Escott: *England: Its People, Polity, and Pursuits*, 1885 edition, p. 277.
9. Ann Druitt's case papers plus covering letter from Dr Gasquet to Dr T S Tuke of the Manor House Asylum, dated 6 June 1890. The Wellcome Institute for the History of Medicine. Wellcome MS. 6651, pp. 251-9, plus letter, 251* 251**. (The letter does not have a folio number. It is inserted between folio 250 and 251. It is two pages in length and designated as above). It was widely assumed that Ann Druitt had been confined to the Manor House Asylum in Chiswick in June 1888 and that Druitt committed suicide after visiting her, his body having been found in the Thames at Chiswick. Howells and Skinner discovered that Ann Druitt was not at the Manor House in December 1888, but a rare failure in their otherwise dilligent research was their inability to locate her case notes. These show that she was in Brighton at the time of MJD's suicide.
10. It has been argued that a mystery remains in that the inquest was not told the reason why Druitt was sacked, a point which was

important in that his dismissal was an obvious explanation for his suicide. As indicated in the text, the most detailed known account of Druitt's inquest is the report published in the *Acton, Chiswick and Turnham Green Gazette*. This report seems to betray the hand of an inexperienced journalist – it does not name the subject of the inquest, it contains several errors, and it does not record medical testimony, which I am given to understand to have been required. That the reason for Druitt's dismissal was not given in the report should not be taken as meaning that it was not given at the inquest; nor should it be assumed that it was unsavoury for public airing.

11. Seven days before 11 December was Tuesday 4 December. Perhaps Druitt went to his chambers on Monday 3 December, but it may be that, as this was the beginning of the week, it was the first day on which it was certain that he had not been seen thereafter. In other words, Druitt may have 'gone missing' before 3 December.

12. Dr Thomas Bramah Diplock (1830-92). He was married, with five children. He was forced to retire through cancer in September 1891, and died at his residence, Mornington House, Chiswick, on Friday 29 April, 1892. (See obituaries in *West London Observer*, 7 May 1892, and the *Acton, Chiswick and Turnham Green Gazette*, 7 May, 1892. For further details see *The Chiswick Times* 9 April 1912, 10 May 1918.)

13. PC George Moulson. Joined the police force on 9 April 1883. Resigned on 4 November 1905.

14. 'The Blackheath Cricket Club' by Malcolm Christopherson. *The Blackheath Art Club Magazine and West Kent Review*, April/May 1893.

15. Knight, p. 137.

16. Inspector Abberline, quoted in the *Pall Mall Gazette*, 31 March 1903.

17. Before leaving MJD mention should be made of the frequently discussed story which Donald McCormick claimed to have taken from the six-volume handwritten *Chronicles of Crime* by a Dr Thomas Dutton (d. 1935). In this document, which has disappeared, Albert Bachert, a member of the Whitechapel Vigilance Committee, was told by the police in March 1889 that Jack the Ripper was dead and that he had been fished out of the Thames two months earlier. Bachert agreed not to reveal this information providing that there were no further murders attributable to Jack the Ripper (McCormick, p. 194).

In a source which can and has been checked, the *Pall Mall Gazette*, an interview with Bachert was published on the day before the inquest into the murder of Frances Coles. Bachert is quoted as having said: 'If evidence is brought forward which can prove that it was committed by the late Whitechapel fiend, I shall at once re-form the Vigilance Committee, and appeal to the public for aid.'

In the opinion of Howells and Skinner (p. 144): 'That one word "late" proves beyond a shadow of doubt that Albert Bachert knew that Jack the Ripper was dead at a time when this would have been privileged information.' It would seem to confirm Dr Dutton's story.

I do not share Howells and Skinner's opinion. Frances Coles was murdered in February 1891, so in referring back to the Whitechapel murders of 1888, Bachert could have described them as having been committed by the 'late', meaning 'previous' or 'former' Whitechapel fiend.

Secondly, in his autobiography Sir Melville Macnaghten expressly stated that information pointing to the conclusion that MJD was Jack the Ripper was not received by the police until several years after Macnaghten's induction into the police force in June 1889. If the man about whom the police are supposed to have spoken to Bachert was MJD, they cannot have given him the information in March 1889, which was before Macnaghten had joined the police and before the police had received the information implicating Druitt in the murders.

Bachert certainly existed: William Albert Bachert was born on 16 September 1860 at 12 Mountford Street, Whitechapel, the son of John Bachert and his wife Georgine (née Fisher). In 1888 he was living at 13 Newnham Street. He was an engraver. He featured in press reports throughout 1888. On 30 September he gave information about a man he had seen in the Three Nuns Hotel and about whom he entertained suspicions (*The Times,* 1 October); there is a letter from him in the *Evening News* (6 September); and in October it was reported that he had made an application against Mr Bradlaugh, MP, for certain payments which he claimed had not been made. Mr Bradlaugh responded by providing documented evidence that he had paid Bachert. (*The Times,* 12 October).

Chapter Thirteen

1. McCormick, p. 223.
2. Richard Deacon: *A History of the Russian Secret Service,* Revised Edition, London: Grafton Books, 1987, p. 101.
3. *Western Mail,* 13 November 1888.
4. *Manchester Guardian,* 15 November 1888.
5. Series F7 (general police) and BB18 (criminal affairs).

Chapter Fourteen

1. Rumbelow, pp. 225-7.

2. Sir Robert Anderson does not mention that the suspect was sent to an asylum in his autobiography, but in an earlier work, *Criminals and Crime: Some Facts and Suggestions*, he refers to Jack the Ripper being 'safely caged in an asylum'. Also see Anderson's preface to Hargrave Lee Adam's *The Police Encyclopedia* in which he states that 'there was no doubt about the identity of the criminal'.

3. *Daily Telegraph*, 19 October 1987.

4. 'Seaside Home' was the name by which the Convalescent Police Seaside Home was commonly known and referred to. It was first located at 51 Clarendon Villas, West Brighton, this property having been purchased for the purpose in November 1889, and being officially opened by the Countess of Chichester on 17 March 1890. On 21 July 1893, a new home was opened at Hove, Brighton.

5. Stepney Workhouse, located St Leonard Street, Bow.

6. Fido, pp. 207-20, 228-32; I was also kindly given access to and have quoted from a manuscript of Mr Fido's revised chapter which will appear in another edition of his book.

7. It is interesting to note that in both the Aberconway Papers and the report Sir Melville Macnaghten wrote that Kosminski 'became insane owing to many years indulgence in solitary vices', which probably means the same as 'self-abuse', i.e. masturbation.

8. Although Donald Rumbelow incorrectly identified Anderson's Polish Jew as John Pizer, it is possible that the conclusion Anderson reached on his return from abroad was based on the same evidence as that on which the police had acted when they arrested John Pizer. In other words, they may have been looking for 'Leather Apron' in the vicinity of Mulberry Street – at the top end of which lived Aaron Kosminski. With this in mind, it is interesting to note that the description of 'Leather Apron' given in the *Manchester Guardian* on 10 September 1888 said of 'Leather Apron' that he 'does not work'; the same was also said of Aaron Kosminski.

9. R Pinker: *English Hospital Statistics 1861-1938*, 1966.

10. Smith, pp. 159-62. Smith is an unreliable source and also ill-informed, not only about the murders, but also about Sir Robert Anderson. He misinterprets what Anderson wrote, thinking that Anderson was making an attack on the Jews in general. He also advises Anderson to read the Bible – Anderson was a Biblical scholar of distinction.

11. Woolf Kosminski died on 6 April 1930, aged 86 years. He was a

master tailor and was at the time living at 23 Baker Street, Stepney. His death was registered by his son.

12. Report by Monro to Home Office. 144/220/A49301 I, sub.1. dated 11 July 1889.

13. Report by Monro to Home Office. 144/220/A49301 K, sub.1 dated 11 September 1889.

14. There are two further observations regarding 'David Cohen'. With reference to note 8 and the search for 'Leather Apron', John Pizer's mother's name was 'Cohen' – could there have been a family connection? Secondly, a search through the registers for the birth of a 'David Cohen' produced only one person of that approximate age (23; born c.1865). This was a Davis Cohen, born 8 November 1867 at 1 Dawson's Place, Whitechapel, the son of a tailor named Marks.

15. The Religious Creed Register and most of the asylum and workhouse records are preserved at the Greater London Record Office.

16. Martin Kosminski. Naturalization Papers. HO 145 9452/69905.

17. Samuel Kosminski. Naturalization Papers. HO 293/131470. Born Kalisch, 10 November 1857.

18. Charles Kosminski. Born 24 January 1873 at 36 New North Road, Hoxton, Middlesex. He drew up his will on 9 March 1925 and died the following day. An inquest on 13 March 1925 failed to reach a conclusion as to whether his death was accidental or suicide.

19. Jessie Kosminski. Born about 1875.

20. Katie Kosminski. Born 3 February 1877.

21. Only 19 men surnamed Kosminski are listed in the Death Registers at St. Catherine's House for the period 1873-1951. Five were children or were not born in 1888. A further four (Aaron, Charles, Samuel and Woolf) are known to us from other sources.

Appendix A

1. *Cambria Daily Leader,* 12 November 1888.
   The Cambrian, 16 November 1888.
   Carmarthen Journal, 16 November 1888.
   Herald of Wales, 17 November 1888, 15 December 1888, 22 December 1888.
   The Llanelly and County Guardian, 15 November 1888, 6 December 1888.
   South Wales Daily News, 20 December 1888.
   Western Mail, 12, 13, 15 November 1888.

Appendix B

1. Macnaghten, p. 55.
2. Anderson, p. 137; Macnaghten, MEPO 3/141, report dated 23 February 1894; Swanson, report dated 10 November 1889, MEPO 3/140 fol. 140, refers to the Ripper murders having begun in Buck's Row and ended in Miller's Court.
3. *New York Times,* 23 November 1889.
4. Rumbelow, pp. 195-6.
5. Report by Monro to Home Office, HO 144/221/A49301H 1
6. Anderson, footnote p. 137.
7. Report by Monro to Home Office, HO 144/221/A493011 1.
8. Report by Inspector Arnold dated 17 July 1889, HO 144/221/A49301I 1; also see letter from Dr Phillips dated 22 July 1889, MEPO 3/140 fol. 271.
9. Letter by Dr Bond to Robert Anderson dated 18 July 1889, MEPO 3/140 fol. 262.
10. Anderson, footnote p. 137.
11. MEPO 3/140 fol. 169.
12. Report by Monro dated 11 September 1889, MEPO 3/140 fol. 128; also see HO 144/22/A49301K 1.
13. Report by Superintendent Arnold dated 13 February 1891, MEPO 3/140 fol. 117.

Bibliography

Books about Jack the Ripper

The following is not a comprehensive list of books on the subject, merely those books referred to in the text. All have been published in hardback and paperback and some have been revised several times. Page references may differ between hardback and paperback and the revised editions. The edition I have used is marked thus *.

TOM CULLEN
Autumn of Terror
London: The Bodley Head, 1965. (Issued as *The Life and Times of Jack the Ripper,* London: Fontana Books, 1973 *.

DANIEL FARSON
Jack the Ripper
London: Michael Joseph, 1972. London: Sphere Books, 1973 *.

MARTIN FIDO
The Crimes, Detection and Death of Jack the Ripper
London: George Weidenfeld and Nicolson, 1987.

MELVIN HARRIS
Jack the Ripper: The Bloody Truth
London: Columbus Books, 1987.

MICHAEL HARRISON
Clarence: The Life of the Duke of Clarence and Avondale KG, 1864-1892,
London: W H Allen, 1972.

MARTIN HOWELLS and KEITH SKINNER
The Ripper Legacy
London: Sidgwick and Jackson, 1987.

ELWYN JONES and JOHN LLOYD
The Ripper File
London: Arthur Barker, 1975.

STEPHEN KNIGHT
Jack the Ripper: The Final Solution
London: George G. Harrap, 1976; St Albans: Granada, 1977.

LEONARD MATTERS
Jack the Ripper
London: Pinnacle Books (W H Allen), n.d.

DONALD McCORMICK
The Identity of Jack the Ripper
London: Jarrolds, 1959. (New and Revised Edition published by John Long and Arrow books, 1970 *).

ROBIN ODELL
Jack the Ripper in Fact and Fiction
London: Harrap, 1965.

DONALD RUMBELOW
The Complete Jack the Ripper
London: W H Allen, 1975; London: Star Books, 1976; (Revised 1981 and revised again 1987 *).

COLIN WILSON and ROBIN ODELL
Jack the Ripper: Summing Up and Verdict
London: Bantam Press, 1987.

PETER UNDERWOOD
Jack the Ripper: One Hundred Years of Mystery
London: Blandford Press, 1987.

RICHARD WHITTINGTON-EGAN
A Casebook on Jack the Ripper
London: Wildy and Sons Ltd., 1975.

Other Sources

ROBERT ANDERSON
Criminals and Crime: Some Facts and Suggestions
London: Nisbet, 1907.

ROBERT ANDERSON
The Lighter Side of My Official Life
London: Hodder, 1910.

ROBERT ANDERSON
'The Lighter Side of My Official Life. XI. At Scotland Yard.'
Blackwood's Magazine, Edinburgh, March 1910.

GEOFFREY BELTON COBB
Critical Years at the Yard: The Career of Frederick Williamson of the Detective Department and the C.I.D.
London: Faber, 1956.

ARTHUR GEORGE FREDERICK GRIFFITHS
Mysteries of Police and Crime vol. 1
London: Cassell, 1898.

Records three suspects: a Polish Jew, a Russian doctor and a doctor who was later found drowned (obviously Kosminski, Ostrog and Druitt). The phraseology leaves no doubt in my mind that Griffiths derived his information from Sir Melville Macnaghten. Other near-contemporary writers who name one or more of these men cannot be shown to have derived their information from a source independent of Macnaghten, Griffiths or George R. Sims (who also took his information from Macnaghten.

MELVILLE MACNAGHTEN
Days of My Years
London: Arnold, 1915.

JOHN MOYLAN
Scotland Yard and the Metropolitan Police
London: Putnam, 1929.

MAJOR HENRY SMITH
From Constable to Commissioner: The Story of Sixty Years, Most of Them Misspent
London: Chatto and Windus, 1910.
A highly coloured and rather inaccurate source.

BASIL THOMSON
The Story of Scotland Yard
London: Grayson and Grayson, 1935.

WATKIN WYNN WILLIAMS
The Life of General Sir Charles Warren: By His Grandson
Oxford: Backwell, 1941.

INDEX

252

253